Directory of
CLYDE
Paddle Steamers

ALISTAIR DEAYTON

First published 2013

Amberley Publishing Plc
The Hill, Stroud
Gloucestershire, GL5 4EP

www.amberley-books.com

British Library Cataloguing in Publication Data.
A catalogue record for this book is available from the British Library.

ISBN 978 1 4456 1487 8
E-BOOK ISBN 978 1 4456 1493 9

Typesetting and Origination by Amberley Publishing.
Printed in Great Britain.

Contents

Introduction

The Clyde was the first river to have its waters turn to foam under the paddlewheels of a steamer. That was in 1812. The boat was called The Comet and provided a regular service between Glasgow and Greenock, travelling at a speed of six nautical miles an hour. Since that time, more than a million steamers have travelled up and down the Scottish river and the inhabitants of the large commercial city must be extremely used to the winders of steam travel.

Jules Verne, *The Blockade Runners*, 1865

This volume tells the story of over 400 paddle steamers that have graced the waters of the Clyde and the west of Scotland in the 201 years since the *Comet* made her first journey down the Clyde. It includes not only Clyde steamers, but those that served in the West Highlands, on inland lochs, on the coast south as far as Stranraer and as tenders to larger ships moored at the Tail of the Bank. There are also details of a handful of steamers that were laid down for Clyde service, but were completed to serve elsewhere.

The paddle-steamer fleet grew rapidly in its first twenty years or so but, sadly in an era before photography, little information has survived about many of these steamers. What has been pieced together here really needs further research from contemporary newspaper advertisements. In some cases sources differ and what I have put in this volume appears to be the most likely scenario.

Steamer and engine design progressed rapidly from basic wooden boats with adapted stationary engines and sails, through iron hulls, narrow deck saloons and oscillating engines to the ultimate paddle-steamer design, with a steel hull, triple expansion engines and full-width deck saloons and a promenade deck running the full length of the ship.

If you know anything further about any of the steamers in this book, please contact the author c/o the publishers and any additions or correction will be made in any future printings or editions.

Notes on the Steamer Directory

The list of paddle steamers since 1812 is based on the list at the end of Capt. James Williamson's *The Clyde Passenger Steamer from 1812 to 1901* with additions, deletions, and corrections

ADDITIONS:

• Paddle Steamers built since 1904.

• Campbeltown Steamers.

• West Highland steamers not listed by Williamson.

• The steamers that ran from Glasgow to Stranraer.

• The small steamers that ran a ferry service across Loch Fyne from Inveraray to St Catherines and Strachur.

• Tug/tenders that operated mainly at the Tail of the Bank.

• Inland Loch Steamers: Loch Lomond, Loch Katrine & Loch Eck.

• Forth and Clyde Canal steamers.

• Steamers built for Clyde service, which did not sail on the Clyde: Loch Lomond steamers *Marchioness of Breadalbane* (1847), which was too deep for the Loch.

• Blockade runners *Hattie* and *Eagle*, sold on the stocks but ordered for the Wemyss Bay Steamboat Co. and the Eagle Steamer Company respectively, and the NB's *Fair Maid*, lost in World War One.

• Steamers which only ran for a very short period on the Clyde, e.g. the paddle tug *Sunshine* and P & A Campbell's *Britannia*.

DELETIONS:

7	*Morning Star*	1814	No other sources mention this, and it appears that Williamson confused her with the Forth steamer *Morning Star* of 1815

8	*Inveraray Castle*	1814	No others sources list this steamer, she was never registered, and is not in a contemporary list of steamers built by John Wood, so it appears she is fictitious.
31	*Greenock (1818)*	1818	This is listed as a renamed *Princess Charlotte* of 1814, number 9 in Williamson's list
35	*Port Glasgow (1819)*	1819	This is listed as a renamed *Prince of Orange (1814)*, number 11 in Williamson's list
34	*Talbot*	1819	This steamer ran from Holyhead to Dublin and was not a Clyde steamer
43	*Eclipse*	1826	Built for the Glasgow to Belfast service, never appears to have run on the Clyde
46	*James Watt*	1822	Built for the London & Edinburgh Shipping Co.
61	*Eclipse*	1826	Built for the Glasgow to Belfast route
106	*Earl of Arran*	1836	Was actually *Isle of Arran*, No. 134, which was erroneously listed as built in 1847 in Williamson rather than 1937.
119	*British Queen*	1838	Duplicated entry
120	*Queen*	1838	Built for Tod & McGregor's services at Cork
121	*Maid of Erin*	1839	As 120
124	*Paisley*	1839	Most sources state that this was the renamed *Dumbuck*, ex-*Euphrosyne*, originally *Post Boy* of 1820
130	*Princess*	1841	As 120
133	*Defiance*	1841	This was a paddle tug
162	*Princess Alice*	1847	As 120
172	*Prince Arthur*	1851	As 120
195	*Superb*	1855	No evidence of this steamer apart from Williamson, not in builders' lists, registers, or newspaper advertisements

In certain cases also the year of build has been wrong in Williamson's list. Williamson apparently based much of his information on a series of letters to the *Glasgow Herald* in the 1890s about people's memories of old steamers.

Paddle tugs and cross-channel steamers have been omitted unless they operated for part of their career as passenger-carrying steamers on the Clyde and West Coast of Scotland. Early steamers which operated from Glasgow or Greenock to Belfast or Liverpool and may have made intermediate calls at places on the Clyde Coast have been omitted.

The date in brackets after a steamer's name are used to distinguish between different steamers of the same name, rather than the use of Roman numerals, as some authors have done.

Tonnages for steamers built up to 1840 are Tons Burthen unless states Gross Tons, and from 1850 gross tonnage.

In many cases, particularly with early steamers, data has been impossible to come by. Should you, by your own researches, be able to fill any of the gaps, please let the author know so the information can be amended in a future edition of this volume.

Where no engine type is given for early steamers it is assumed to be a side-lever engine.

Many early steamers owned by companies were registered in the names of the directors or nominees. This has been corrected where the company name is known.

Where routes are mentioned for individual steamers, there were the majority of cases, routes that were operated in the peak summer months. Many steamers were laid up out of service for the winter period.

Acknowledgements

Two CDs have been invaluable with regards to early steamers:

British 19th Century Steamships: Issue 4: 'Steamships to 1840' by F. W. Hawks, published by the World Ship Society, 2012

'Steamships 1835–1875' by P. N. Thomas, published by Wine Research Publications, 2008 (sold with accompanying book).

Both use data from the British Shipping Registers in the National Archives at Kew, which is good as far as it goes. Some early Clyde steamers were not registered, although mentioned by various authors on the subject.

I would like to thank Alan Hunter, David Smith, Andreas vin Mach and David Asprey for information about certain steamers sold outwith the Clyde, especially to Russia.

Glasgow University Archives, Thurso Street, Partick and the Clyde-built ship list at www.clydesite.co.uk have been invaluable.

The publications of the Clyde River Steamer Cub have been an invaluable source of information.

CHAPTER 1
Steamers Built 1812–19

1: *Comet* (1812)

Number in Williamson's list: 1
Built: 1812
28 tons, 30 tons (1820). Length 43.5 feet, 65.5 feet (October 1812), 73 feet 10 inches
  (1818)
Builders: John Wood, Port Glasgow
Engine builders: (1) John Robertson, Glasgow, 1811; (2) Anderson, Caird & Co., Cartsdyke,
  1818. Engine type: single-cylinder upright/half-side-lever; (1) 3 hp, (2) 6 hp (1818)
Hull material: Wood
Owner: Henry Bell
1812: August – commenced operation thrice weekly from Glasgow to Greenock, extended to
  Helensburgh at weekends. Was the first commercially operated steam vessel in Europe.
1812: September – made a trip from Glasgow to Fort William via the Crinan Canal.
1812: October – lengthened by 22 feet.
1813: May – went via the Forth & Clyde Canal to Bo'ness for overhaul, made one passenger
  trip on the Forth.
1816: Operated on the Forth from Grangemouth to Newhaven.
1818: New, more powerful engine fitted.
1819: September – commenced a service from Oban to Crinan via the Crinan Canal.
1820: 15 December – wrecked on Craignish Point near Crinan. The engine was salvaged and
  is now on display in the Science Museum.

2: *Elizabeth*

Number in Williamson's list: 2
Built: 1812
30 tons. Length 57.0 feet
Builders: John Wood, Port Glasgow
Engine builders: John Thomson, Tradeston. 8 hp
Hull material: Wood
Owners: J. Hutchinson and J. Thomson, Greenock and Glasgow
1812/13: Built for the Glasgow–Greenock and Helensburgh service.
1813: 5 March – first sailing.
1813: June – started running to Gourock.
1814: Possibly sailed on the Forth.
1815: June – sold to Lt C. Watson & Syndicate, moved to Liverpool, operating Liverpool–
  Runcorn.

1816: Sold to R. Welburn, Liverpool.

1818: Engines removed, converted to be powered by horses working a treadmill, renamed *Safety*. This was reportedly not successful because the horses became seasick!

c. 1820: Broken up.

3: *Clyde*

Number in Williamson's list: 3
Built: 1813
65 tons. Length 72 feet
Builders: John Wood & J. Barclay, Port Glasgow
Engine builders: John Robertson, Glasgow. 14 hp
Hull material: Wood
Owners: J. Robertson & R. Steven
1813: Started operating from Glasgow to Greenock and Gourock.
1823: Renamed *Gourock*.
1825: Renamed *Lord Byron*, started operating from Glasgow to Helensburgh.
1826: Renamed *George IV*.
1828: Broken up.

4: *Glasgow* (1813)

Number in Williamson's list: 4
Built: 1813
52 tons. Length 73.3 feet, 83.3 (1821)
Builders: John Wood & J. Barclay, Port Glasgow
Engine builders: (1) Anderson & Campbell, Greenock; (2) J. Cook & Co., Glasgow, 1814. (1) 16 hp, (2) 10 hp
Hull material: Wood
Owner: J. Cook
1813: Built for the Glasgow–Largs service.
1821: Owners now J. Cook and J. McIntyre, Glasgow.
1825: No longer on the Largs service.
1827: Sold to J. Scott, Greenock.
1834: Broken up.

5: *Trusty*

Number in Williamson's list: 5
Built: 1814
62 tons. Length 68.3 feet
Builders: Archibald McLachlan, Dumbarton
Engine builders: G. Dobie & Co., Glasgow; D. McArthur & Co., Glasgow. Engine type: side-lever. 10 hp, later 18 hp
Hull material: Wood
Owners: Cochrane and McTaggart, Glasgow
1815: Entered service as a luggage boat from Glasgow to Greenock.

1815: Sold to the Clyde Shipping Co.
1849: Converted to a sailing vessel, sold to D. McGill, Bowling.
1850: October – Sold to R. Kenneth and D. W. Owen, Ballycastle.
1853: April – Sold to P. Quinn, Belfast.
1856: Foundered.

6: *Industry*

Number in Williamson's list: 6
Built: 1814
53 tons, 69 gt. Length 68.4 feet
Builders: Fyfe, Fairlie
Engine builders: (1) G. Dobie & Co.; Glasgow (2) Caird & Co. Engine type: (1) Side Lever
    10 hp; (2) 14 hp
Hull material: Wood
Owners: Cochrane and McTaggart, Glasgow
1814: Built as a passenger steamer for the Glasgow–Greenock service.
1814: Converted to a luggage boat after only two trips.
1815: 9 January – ran ashore in Holyhead Bay, Anglesey, while on passage from Cork to
    Dublin with Government stores. Salvaged and returned to service.
1815: Sold to J. Henderson, W. Croll and D. McPhee .
1815: Transferred to the Clyde Shipping Co.
1828: New engine fitted.
1856: Sold to A. Kidston & Co., Glasgow.
c. 1857: Folding funnel fitted to enable her to sail above Glasgow Bridge.
1859: Sold to James Steel & Sons, Glasgow, then to A. McGeorge, Bowling.
1869: Sold to J. Steel and K. McAskill Jr, Greenock.
1873: Withdrawn from service and laid up at Bowling.
1890: Still at Bowling, gradually deteriorating.
The 1828 engine was removed for preservation at some point and is now in the Riverside
    Museum, Glasgow.

7: *Princess Charlotte*

Number in Williamson's list: 9
Built: 1814
50 tons. Length 65.0 feet
Builders: James Munn, Greenock
Engine builders: Boulton & Watt, Soho, Birmingham. Engine type: two-cylinder; 8 hp
Hull material: Wood
Owners: Clyde Steam Boat Co.
1814: Entered service from Glasgow to Greenock.
1818: Laid up, renamed *Greenock*.
1819: Returned to service as *Princess Charlotte*.
1820: Sold to unknown owners at Cork, operated on the Cork–Queenstown (Cobh) service.
1826: Engines removed, returned to the Clyde, renamed *Greenock*, traded as a sailing vessel.
1850: Broken up.

8: *Duke of Argyle* (also known as *Argyle*)

Number in Williamson's list: 10
Built: 1814
78 tons. Length 72.0 feet
Builders: A. Martin & Co., Port Glasgow
Engine builders: James Cook, Glasgow. Engine type: two-cylinder, 14 hp, advertised as 40 hp in 1828
Hull material: Wood
Owners: J. Dick and others, Glasgow
1814: Built for the Glasgow–Greenock service.
1815: May – Sailed to the Thames via Land's End.
1815: June – Sold to R. Cheesewright & Co., London/London & Margate Steam Packet Co., renamed *Thames*.
1815: 3 July – Entered service from London to Margate.
1816: Now ran from London to Gravesend.
1821: Sold to J. Burden (possibly Brander) and others, Cowes & London. Operated for one season only from Portsmouth to Cowes.
1826: Owner now J. Burden (possibly Brander), London.
1828: Sold to J. Morley and others, Gt Yarmouth. Sailed from London to Yarmouth and Norwich.
1835: Broken up.

9: *Prince of Orange*

Number in Williamson's list: 11
Built: 1814
50 tons. Length 64.0 feet
Builders: James Munn, Greenock
Engine builders: Boulton & Watt, Soho, Birmingham. Engine type: two-cylinder, 8 hp, cylinders placed inside boiler
Hull material: Wood
Owners: Clyde Steam Boat Co., Glasgow
1814: Built for the service from Glasgow to Greenock and Helensburgh.
1819: Renamed *Port Glasgow*.
1828: Broken up.
May have been renamed *Robert Bruce* (No. 34) and not *Port Glasgow*.

10: *Margery* (aka *Marjory*)

Number in Williamson's list: 12
Built: 1814
30 tons, 101 tons (1815). Length 63.0 feet
Builders: Archibald McLachlan, Dumbarton
Engine builders: James Cook, Glasgow. 12 hp
Hull material: Wood
Owners: W. Anderson, J. McCubbin & Co., Glasgow
1814: Entered service from Glasgow to Greenock.

1814: November – Sold to A. Cortis & Co., London.

1815: January – Sailed from Glasgow to London via the Forth & Clyde Canal with her paddles removed. 1815: 23 January – Was the first steamer to operate on the Thames. Started running from London to Gravesend.

1816: Ran from London to Margate.

1816: February – sold to A. Pajol & Cie, Paris, renamed *Elise*.

1816: 17 March – Sailed from Newhaven to Le Havre, the crossing lasting eighteen hours. The first crossing of the English Channel by a steamer.

1816: March 18 – Arrived at Paris, where she was greeted by King Louis XVIII; later ran commercially from Rouen to Elbeouf. Was not a success and was laid up.

1888: It was claimed that her timbers were still to be seen on the banks of the Seine.

11: *Tay*

Number in Williamson's list: 13
Built: 1814
43 tons. Length 75.25 feet
Builders: J. Smart, Dundee
Engine builders: J. Robertson, Glasgow. 12 hp
Hull material: Wood
Owner: G. Robertson, Dundee

1814: Built for G. Roberson, Dundee, as *Tay* for the Dundee–Perth service. Was the first steamer on the Tay.

1815: New engine installed.

1818: Sold to A. Dow, Glasgow. Moved to the Clyde, ran from Glasgow to Lochgoilhead.

1821: Sold to A. D. Writer, Glasgow. Renamed *Oscar*.

1827: Sold to the Lochgoil & Loch Long Steamboat Co.

1828: Moved to the Glasgow–Gourock service.

1831: Wrecked at Rosneath.

1836: Register closed, marked 'broken up'.

12: *Stirling Castle*

Built: 1814
69 tons. Length 68.0 feet
Builders: J. Gray, Kincardine
Engine builders: J. Gray, Kincardine. 12 hp
Hull material: Wood
Owners: Stirling Steamboat Co. (Henry Bell)

1818: Built for the Stirling Steamboat Co. (owned by Henry Bell) for the Stirling–Alloa–Newhaven–Dysart service.

1820: Sold to Robert Napier, placed on the Inverness–Fort Augustus service.

1822: Route extended to Banavie on the opening of the Caledonian Canal.

1824: On the Glasgow–Inverness service. Now owned by Henry Bell and others, Inverness.

1828: 14 January – Wrecked at Inverscadail, near Ardgour, after engine failed. One passenger drowned and another, the Clan Chief McDonnell of Glengarry, died later of a head injury sustained during the evacuation of the wreck.

13: *Britannia* (1815)

Number in Williamson's list: 14
Built: 1815
73 tons. Length 93.3 feet
Builders: A. Martin/John Hunter, Port Glasgow
Engine builders: (1) D. McArthur & Co., Camlachie; (2) J. Cook, Glasgow 18??. Engine type: two-cylinder beam; 24 hp, later 16 hp
Hull material: Wood
Owners: L. MacLellan, Glasgow, A. McTaggart, Campbeltown, and others.
1815: Entered service from Glasgow to Tarbert and Inveraray.
1815: Moved to a fortnightly service Glasgow–Rothesay–Campbeltown, also sailed Glasgow–Helensburgh.
1818: Made some Saturday sailings round Ailsa Craig.
1820: Campbeltown route extended to the Giant's Causeway.
1821: Sold to the Britannia & Waterloo Steam Boat Co., Glasgow, placed on the Glasgow–Londonderry route, also made a few trips from Glasgow to Belfast in that year.
1822: Purchased by the Glasgow & Londonderry Steam Packet Co./A. A. Laird & Co.
1829: Moved to service from Glasgow to Newry, Portrush, Coleraine, etc.
1829: 23 November – Wrecked off Donaghadee.

14: *Dumbarton Castle* (1815)

Number in Williamson's list: 15
Built: 1815
108 tons. Length 87 feet
Builders: Archibald McLachlan, Dumbarton
Engine builders: D. McArthur & Co., Camlachie. Engine type: two-cylinder; 30 hp, later 70 hp
Hull material: Wood
Owners: Glasgow Castle Steam Packet Co.
1815: Entered service from Glasgow to Rothesay.
1815: 1 July – Sailing extended to Inveraray. Inveraray sailing not repeated.
1816: First paddle steamer to be deliberately reversed.
1818: Regular Glasgow–Inveraray sailings.
1819: Sold to the Edinburgh, Glasgow & Leith Shipping Co. Operated from Grangemouth to Leith and Dysart.
1823: Now sailing from Glasgow to Stranraer.
1826: Purchased by J. Wilson, J. Gardner, H. Reid Sr and D. McArthur, Glasgow.
1828: Now sailing Glasgow–Stranraer–Newry.
1829: 13 November – ran aground near Bowling.
1830: Purchased by M. Campbell, Glasgow. Converted to a sailing vessel.
1831: Sold to J. McAlly, Glasgow.
1834: 4 February – Wrecked near Sligo. Later salvaged and sold to J. Shevlin and J. James, Sligo.
1836: October – Sold to J. Adair, Dublin.
1838: Lost off the Irish Coast.

15: *Caledonia* (1815)

Number in Williamson's list: 16
Built: 1815
105 tons. Length 94.0 feet
Builders: John Wood & J. Barclay, Port Glasgow
Engine builders: (1) Greenhead Foundry, Glasgow; (2) Boulton & Watt, Soho (1817). Engine type: (1) two-cylinder, 36 hp; (2) 28 hp
Hull material: Wood
Owners: Unknown, Clyde
1815: Built for the Glasgow–Greenock service. She was claimed to be the first Clyde steamer with a two-cylinder engine, referred to at that time as 'two engines'.
1816: Sold to unknown owners. Moved to the Thames and operated from London to Margate.
1817: April – purchased by M. Robinson and James Watt Jr.
1817: October to January 1818 – Made a voyage from Margate to Rotterdam and up the Rhine as far as Koblenz, returning via Antwerp. Was the first steamer on the Rhine.
1819: Sold to S. A. Bille, Denmark. Started a service from Copenhagen to Kiel, Germany. Also operated excursions from Copenhagen. Was the first steamer in Danish waters.
1822: Sold to L. N. Hvidt, Denmark. Continued on the same service.
1830: From this date only used as a relief steamer.
1839: Withdrawn from service.
1843: Broken up.

16: *Greenock* (1815)

Number in Williamson's list: 17
Built: 1815
98 tons. Length 85 feet 3 inches
Builders: Archibald McLachlan, Dumbarton
Engine builders: D. McArthur & Co., Camlachie. Engine type: two-cylinder; 32 hp
Hull material: Wood
Owner: Unknown, Clyde
1815: Entered service from Glasgow to Greenock.
1816: 19 April – Was the first steamer to sail from Scotland to Ireland.
1816: April to May – Ran from Belfast to Bangor.
1816: June – Sold to the United Company of Proprietors of the Ellesmere & Chester Canal. Re-boilered. Renamed *Countess of Bridgwater*. Commenced operating from Liverpool to Runcorn.
1822: Chartered to H. Williams, operated from Liverpool to Woodside until the new steamer *Royal Mail* was completed.
1844: Scrapped.

17: *Argyle* (1815)

Number in Williamson's list: 19
Built: 1815
72 tons. Length 79 feet; 91 feet 1 inch (1821)
Builders: John Wood & J. Barclay, Port Glasgow
Engine builders: (1) Greenhead Foundry, Glasgow; (2) New engine 1823. (1) 1 engine; 32 hp
Hull material: Wood
Owners: G. Brown, T. Richardson, Glasgow
1815: Entered service from Glasgow to Inveraray.
1821: Lengthened by 14 feet.
1822: Now running from Glasgow to Campbeltown and Stornoway.
1823: Made an excursion from Glasgow to Campbeltown, Dublin and Plymouth.
1823: Also operated an excursion from Glasgow to Staffa and Iona.
1824: Placed on the Glasgow–Londonderry service.
1826: Sold to the Argyle Steam Boat Co., Glasgow.
1828: Sold to J. Ritchie, Glasgow. Placed on the Glasgow–Dublin service.
1829: Sold to J. Mitchell, J. Drysdale and others, Alloa.
1830: Moved to the Glasgow–Stranraer service.
1843: Broken up.

18: *Waterloo* (1816)

Number in Williamson's list: 20
Built: 1815
90 tons, 79 tons (1826). Length 72 feet, 100.4 feet (1826)
Builders: A. Martin/John Hunter, Port Glasgow
Engine builders: James Cook, Glasgow. 20 hp
Hull material: Wood
Owners: L. McLellan and A. MacTaggart, Glasgow
1815: Entered service from Glasgow to Inveraray and from Glasgow to Helensburgh.
1816: Operated on the Glasgow–Campbeltown service, continued sailing to Helensburgh.
1825: Sold to W. F. Campbell, Islay. Renamed *Maid of Islay*. Placed on the West Loch Tarbert–Port Askaig/Portree service.
1826: Lengthened by 28.4 feet.
1827: Placed on the Glasgow–Iona–Portree–Tarbert, Harris route. Renamed *Maid of Islay No 1*.
1830: Moves to the Glasgow–Lochgilphead (Ardrishaig) route.
1834: Sold to J. Stalker, Glasgow.
1835: July – Sold to A. Greig, J. Sword, G. Turner and W. Guthrie, Leith. Placed on a Dundee–Leith service, according to some sources.
1835: 27 October – Wrecked.

19: *Duke of Wellington*

Number in Williamson's list: 27
Built: 1815

54 tons. Length 77.33 feet
Builders: Archibald McLachlan, Dumbarton
Engine builders: D. McArthur & Co., Camlachie. Engine type: Side Lever; 16 hp
Hull material: Wood
Owners: Dumbarton Steamboat Co.
1815: September – Entered service from Glasgow to Dumbarton.
1817: Lengthened by 6 feet 11 inches by William Denny, Dumbarton.
1820: Sold to Robert Napier. Lengthened.
1820: November – Sailed from Glasgow to Isleornsay, Skye.
1820: Operated from Glasgow to Fort William replacing *Comet*, which had been wrecked.
1821: May – Sold to J. Sinclair, T. Affleck, R. Porter and others, Dumfries; operated from
    Dumfries to Liverpool and from Glasgow to Stranraer. Renamed *Highland Chieftain*.
1822: Sold to D. McIntosh, P. Neilson, J. McIntyre and others, Glasgow.
1824: Sold to Glasgow & Caledonian Canal S. P. Co. Operated from Glasgow to Inverness
    via the Caledonian Canal.
1825: Sold to J. McColl & Co., Glasgow.
1826: Now operating from the Clyde to the Isle of Man.
1826: September – Sold to the Highland Chieftain Steamboat Co.
1828: May – Sold to J. Laird, A. McConnell and A. Laird.
1832: May – Sold to G. Smith, W. Young and A. Ferguson.
1834: Sold to unknown owners. Engines removed and converted to a sailing schooner.
1838: May – Register closed, 'broken up'.

20: *Neptune* (1815)

Number in Williamson's list: 21
Built: 1816
71 tons. Length 87 feet 4 inches
Builders: John & Charles Wood, Port Glasgow
Engine builders: D. McArthur & Co., Camlachie. 20 hp
Hull material: Wood
Owners: T. Kirkwood, L. Corbett, J. Miller
1816: Entered service from Glasgow to Helensburgh.
1820: Also operating from Glasgow to Rothesay and Loch Fyne.
1826: Broken up.

21: *Lord Nelson*

Number in Williamson's list: 22
Built: 1816
93 tons, 56 tons (1819). Length 71 feet, 81.5 feet (1819)
Builders: John & Charles Wood & J. Barclay, Port Glasgow
Engine builders: (1) Greenhead Foundry, Glasgow; (2) D. McArthur & Co., Camlachie or
    J. Cook, Glasgow, (1) 20 hp; (2) 32 hp
Hull material: Wood
Owner: J. Wilson, Glasgow
1816: Entered service from Glasgow to Largs.
1818–19: Lengthened and re-engined by J. Cook, Glasgow.

1819: Sold to J. Wilson, J. Colquhoun, R. Scott and others. Renamed *Sir William Wallace*.
1819: June – Commenced operating from Glasgow to Belfast.
1820: Purchased (or perhaps repossessed?) by J. Cook, Glasgow.
1820: July – Sold to Fife and Midlothian Ferry Trustees. Operated from Newhaven to Pettycur and Kirkcaldy.
1825: 18 January – Wrecked at Burntisland.

22: *Albion* (1816)

Number in Williamson's list: 23
Built: 1816
69 tons (1820). Length 72 feet, 84 feet 11 inches (1820)
Builders: John Wood & J. Barclay, Port Glasgow
Engine builders: (1) James Cook, Glasgow, (2) Neilson. Engine type: two-cylinder side-lever; (1)20 hp; (2) 32 hp
Hull material: Wood
Owner: J. Kay
1816: Entered service from Glasgow to Largs, Ardrossan and Irvine. Had two funnels athwartships. The height of paddle wheels could be adjusted depending on the load carried.
1820: Lengthened and re-engined.
1822: Sold to Capt. McCallum, Glasgow.
1824: May – Sold to The New Steamboat Co., Glasgow.
1827: Sold to The Albion Steam Boat Co., Glasgow (Mr Lapslie).
c. 1833: Route extended to Arran.
1836: Broken up.

23: *Rothsay Castle* (1816)

Number in Williamson's list: 24
Built: 1816
75 tons, 98 tons (1821). Length 92 feet 11 inches, 98.3 feet (1821)
Builders: Archibald McLachlan, Dumbarton
Engine builders: (1) D. McArthur & Co., Camlachie; (2) March 1821. (1) 34 hp; (2) 35 hp
Hull material: Wood
Owners: Rothsay Castle Steam Boat Co. (1817)
1816: Entered service from Glasgow to Rothesay. Also made some sailings from Glasgow to Ardrishaig and Inveraray.
1816: Ran aground near Tarbert; first recorded major accident with a Clyde steamer.
1821: Lengthened and re-engined by J. Lang, Dumbarton.
1826: Lengthened by 5.4 feet by J. Lang, Dumbarton.
1829: Ran from Glasgow to Rothesay and Lamlash.
1830: Sold to North Wales Steam Packet Co.
1830: November – Entered service from Liverpool to the Menai Straits.
1831: 18 August – Wrecked near Beaumaris with the loss of over 109 lives.

24: *Marion*

Number in Williamson's list: 25
Built: 1816 (some sources give build date as 1815 or 1817)
57 tons. Length 60.0 feet
Builders: Archibald McLachlan, Dumbarton
Engine builders: David Napier, Camlachie. 20 hp
Hull material: Wood
Owner: David Napier
1816: Entered service from Glasgow to Greenock.
1817: Steamed up the River Clyde to Clyde Iron Works, Dalmarnock, the furthest upriver any steamer has ever sailed.
1818: Moved to Loch Lomond. Commenced operating from Balloch to Luss and Tarbert. Was the first steamer on Loch Lomond.
1827: Moved to Loch Fyne, renamed *Thalia*. Ran from Inveraray to Strachur and St Catherines.
1832: Wrecked.
(Some sources state that she was wrecked while going down the Leven in 1832 and that *Thalia* was a different steamer.)

25: *Margaret*

Number in Williamson's list: 26
Built: 1816
54 tons. Length 55.0 feet
Builders: J. Smart, Dundee
Engine builders: John Robertson, Glasgow. 12 hp
Hull material: Wood
Owner: Unknown, Glasgow (1818)
1818: Entered service from Glasgow to Greenock.
1822: Ceased operating.
There is very little published information about this steamer.

26: *Active*

Built: 1816
59 tons. Length 60.0 feet
Builders: W. Denny & A. McLachlan, Dumbarton
Engine builders: Napier & McArthur, Glasgow. 10 hp
Hull material: Wood
Owner: David Napier
1816: Entered service from Glasgow to Greenock as a luggage boat.
1839: Still in the same service.
No further information is available on this steamer.

27: *Despatch*

Built: 1816
80 tons. Length 60.0 feet
Builders: W. Denny & A. McLachlan, Dumbarton
Engine builders: Napier & McArthur, Glasgow. 10 hp
Hull material: Wood
Owner: David Napier
1816: Entered service from Glasgow to Greenock as a luggage boat.
1839: Still in the same service.
No further information is available on this steamer.

28: *Defiance*

Number in Williamson's list: 28
Built: 1817
46 tons. Length 58 feet, 72.7 feet (1819)
Builders: John & Charles Wood, Port Glasgow
Engine builders: (1) John Robertson, Glasgow; (2) Girdwood & Co. (1819). 12 hp; 20 hp
   (1819)
Hull material: Wood
Owner: J. Robertson, Glasgow
1817: Entered service from Glasgow to Helensburgh and Loch Goil.
1819: Renamed *Highland Lad*. Placed on a service from Glasgow to the West Highlands.
1826: Sold to E. Girdwood & Co., Glasgow.
1826: An experimental system of chain paddle floats was fitted. This was unsuccessful.
1827: The steam engine was replaced with a 20-hp regenerative air engine designed and built
   by James Stirling. This also was unsuccessful.
1827: Broken up.

29: *Woodford*

Number in Williamson's list: 29
Built: 1818
83 tons. Length 71.0 feet
Builders: W. Denny, Dumbarton
Engine builders: David Napier, Camlachie. 30 hp
Hull material: Wood
Owners: R. Dennistoun and R. Campbell, Glasgow
1818: Entered service from Glasgow to Helensburgh.
1819: Sold to Sir R. Woodford, Trinidad.
1819: 20 December – Commenced operating from Port of Spain to San Fernando.
1822: May – Sold to H. Fuller, Trinidad.
1823: April – Sold to G. Fitzwilliam and P. Butler, Trinidad.
1829: Broken up.

30: *Marquis of Bute* (1818)

Number in Williamson's list: 30
Built: 1818
55 tons. Length 55.0 feet
Builders: John & Charles Wood, Port Glasgow
Engine builders: (1) John Robertson, Glasgow; (2) Dr Stevenson (1825). (1) 14 hp, (2) 30 hp
Hull material: Wood
Owner: J. Robertson, Glasgow
1818: Entered service from Glasgow to Rothesay.
1825: April – Sold to J. Stevenson, Glasgow; re-engined, commenced operating from Belfast to Carrickfergus and Bangor and excursions from Belfast to Donaghadee. Renamed *Bangor Castle*.
1828: Moved to the Glasgow–Helensburgh route.
1833: Broken up.

31: *Rob Roy* (1818)

Number in Williamson's list: 32
Built: 1818
82 tons. Length 71.0 feet
Builders: W. Denny, Dumbarton
Engine builders: David Napier, Camlachie. Engine type: side-lever; 32 hp
Hull material: Wood
Owner: David Napier
1818: Commenced operating from Glasgow to Dublin, with some sailings Glasgow–Arrochar. She was the first seagoing steamer in regular service in the world.
1820: Moved to the Dover–Calais route.
1821: May – Owners now David Napier, T. Boyd and J. Craig, Glasgow.
1823: Purchased by the French Government, Post Office Department, renamed *Henri Quatre*. Later renamed *Duc d'Orleans*.
No record appears to have survived of how long she operated or of her final fate.

32: *Robert Burns* (1819)

Number in Williamson's list: 33
Built: 1819
66 tons. Length 76 feet
Builders: John & Charles Wood, Port Glasgow
Engine builders: David Napier, Camlachie. 20 hp
Hull material: Wood
Owner: J. D. Napier
1819: Entered service on the Glasgow–Helensburgh service. She was the first Clyde steamer to have a sharp bow, all previous steamers having had rounded bows.
1826: Moved to the Glasgow–Holy Loch and Arrochar service. Renamed *Robert Bruce*.
c. 1828: Withdrawn from service.
No records survive regarding her fate.

33: *Fingal*

Number in Williamson's list: 36
Built: 1819
202 tons. Length 62 feet
Builders: W. Simons & Co., Greenock
Engine builders: David Napier, Camlachie. Engine type: two-cylinder; 100 hp
Hull material: Wood
Owner: Unknown
1819: Entered service from Glasgow to Lochgoilhead for unknown owners.
1822: Route now Glasgow–Helensburgh. Renamed *Rosneath Castle*.
1826: Sold to J. Martin and G. & J. Burns. Renamed *Fingal*. Started operating from Glasgow to Belfast.
Early 1830s: Laid up.
Mid-1830s: Resumed Glasgow–Belfast service.
1835: Sold to R. Purdon, Newry.
1838: Sold to G. McTear, Belfast.
1850s: Laid up again.
1859: Reported to have rotted away by this date.

34: *Robert Bruce* (1819)

Number in Williamson's list: 37
Built: 1819
155 tons. Length 94 feet
Builders: Scott & Sons, Greenock
Engine builders: David Napier, Camlachie. Engine type: two-cylinder side-lever; 60 hp
Hull material: Wood
Owners: W. Mills, J. Athlone, E. Richardson and others, Glasgow
1819: Commenced operating from Glasgow to Kilmun.
1821: Placed on the Glasgow–Liverpool service. Was the first steamer to sail from Glasgow to Liverpool.
1821: 23 August – Sank off Anglesey after a fire.

35: *Waterloo* (1819)

Number in Williamson's list: 38
Built: 1819
200 tons. Length 100 feet
Builders: Scott & Sons, Greenock
Engine builders: James Cook, Glasgow. Engine type: two-cylinder; 60 hp
Hull material: Wood
Owners: L. McLennan and others, Glasgow
1819: Commenced operation from Glasgow to Helensburgh and Rosneath.
1821: Moved to the Belfast–Liverpool route.
1824: Sold to G. Langtry, Belfast.
1825: Sold to General Steam Navigation Co., London. Operated from London to Gravesend and Margate.

1839: Burnt and withdrawn from service.
1847: Sold.

36: *Samson*

Number in Williamson's list: 39
Built: 1819
53.8 tons. Length 82 feet
Builders: W. Denny, Dumbarton
Engine builders: (1) D. McArthur & Co., Camlachie; (2) Caird & Co., Greenock. Engine type:
   (1) side-lever 40 hp; (2) two-cylinder side-lever 45 hp
Hull material: Wood
Owners: Clyde Shipping Co.
1819: Entered service from Glasgow and Greenock, possibly also to the Gareloch. Also used
   as a tug.
1827: Registered as *Sampson*.
1831: Re-engined by Caird & Co., Greenock.
1855: Sold to T. Wishart, Port Glasgow. Converted to a sailing schooner.
1860: Sold to J. Enwright and G. Winder, Limerick.
1887: Ships registry closed, must have been broken up before then.

CHAPTER 2
Steamers Built 1820–29

37: *Dumbarton* (1820)

Number in Williamson's list: 40
Built: 1820
71 tons. Length 83.5 feet
Builders: W. Denny, Dumbarton
Engine builders: D. McArthur & Co., Camlachie. 42 hp
Hull material: Wood
Owners: Dumbarton Steamboat Co., Dumbarton
1820: Entered service from Glasgow to Dumbarton, Helensburgh and Rosneath.
1833: Sold to T. Greig, Leith. Moved to the Forth, operated from Newhaven to Stirling.
1835: June – Sold to W. Hutton, Dundee.
1836: April – Owned by W. B. McKean, Leith.
1837: Sold to Forth Steam Towing Co. Used as a tug from then onwards.
1852: Broken up.

38: *Post Boy*

Number in Williamson's list: 41
Built: 1820
95 tons. Length 74.0 feet
Builders: W. Denny, Dumbarton
Engine builders: David Napier, Camlachie. Engine type: side-lever single-cylinder; 20 hp
Hull material: Wood
Owner: David Napier
1820: Entered service from Glasgow to Dumbarton and Glasgow to Greenock. Had very shallow draught to enable her to sail from Glasgow at any state of the tide.
1827: Moved to Loch Lomond.
1829: Owners became Napier and McCurrich.
1833: Renamed *Euphrosyne*.
1837: Sold to R. B. Clelland, Paisley. Renamed *Dumbuck*.
1838: Made some sailings from Paisley
1838: Operated from Glasgow to Dumbarton and Glasgow to Greenock.
1839: Renamed *Paisley*.
No record appears to exist of her eventual fate.

39: *Inverary Castle* (1820)

Number in Williamson's list: 42
Built: 1820
79 tons. Length 95.5 feet
Builders: John & Charles Wood, Port Glasgow
Engine builders: David Napier, Lancefield. Engine type: two-cylinder; 40 hp
Hull material: Wood
Owners: Inverary Castle Steamboat Co.
1820: Entered service from Glasgow to Inveraray.
1828: Also made some Glasgow–Brodick sailings.
1829: Also made some Glasgow–Lamlash sailings.
1832: Owners became Castle Steam Packet Co.
1836: Sold to A. Barlas. Moved to the Oban–Staffa and Iona service.
1838: Scrapped.

40: *Caledonia* (1821)

Built: 1821
84 tons. Length 85.0 feet
Builders: John Wood, Port Glasgow
Engine builders: Boulton & Watt, Soho, Birmingham. Engine type: two-cylinder side-lever; 28 hp
Hull material: Wood
Owner: David Napier
Route: Glasgow–Helensburgh
1821: Entered service from Glasgow to Helensburgh. A list of ships built by John Wood notes
   her as having 'sailed for a great many years on the Clyde'.
1822: Reported as being at Helensburgh.
No further information was available.

41: *Highlander*

Built: 1821
51 tons. Length 78.5 feet
Builders: John & Charles Wood, Port Glasgow
Engine builders: D. McArthur & Co., Camlachie. 24 hp
Hull material: Wood
Owners: Henry Bell and others
1821: Entered service.
1822: March – Placed on the Glasgow–Fort William service.
1822: May – On the Glasgow–Tobermory service.
1822: Also operated from Glasgow to Staffa and Iona.
1824: Moved to the Glasgow–Inverness route. Also sailed from Glasgow to Skye and Glasgow
   to Strontian.
1826: July – Sold to the Highlander Steam Boat Co.
1832: Sold to A. McEachern.
1835: Sold to Robert Napier.
1836: 1 July – Wrecked (some sources state 'broken up in 1836').

42: *Comet* (1821)

Number in Williamson's list: 44
Built: 1821
47 tons. Length 81.0 feet
Builders: James Lang, Dumbarton
Engine builders: D. McArthur & Co., Camlachie. 25 hp
Hull material: Wood
Owners: R. Flyter, D. McIntyre, J. McGrigor and others, Fort William
1821: 6 July – Entered service from Glasgow to Fort William.
1822: 25 October – Took part in opening ceremony for the Caledonian Canal from Loch Oich to Banavie.
1822: November – Route extended to Inverness following the opening of the Caledonian Canal throughout.
1823: Was on the Forth for the visit of King George IV to Edinburgh.
1825: 21 October – Was in collision with the steamer *Ayr* (No. 54) off Kempock Point, Gourock, at around 2 a.m. Sank in three minutes; around seventy lives were lost and only thirteen saved. The wreck was later raised. This was the worst peacetime disaster befalling any Clyde steamer at any time from 1812 to the present day.
1828–29: Hull converted to sailing gabbart *Ann*, according to some sources.
1876: Broken up.
The engine that was claimed to have been in *Comet* (1821) and is preserved in the Riverside Museum, Glasgow, has recently been discovered not to have been a marine steam engine at all.

43: *Toward Castle*

Number in Williamson's list: 47
Built: 1822
79.1 tons. Length 101.8, 115.6 feet (1921)
Builders: J. Lang, Dumbarton
Engine builders: (1) D. McArthur & Co., Camlachie; (2) J. & W. Napier 1835, fitted 1838. (1) 45 hp, (2) 150 hp
Hull material: Wood
Owners: Toward Castle Steamboat Co.
1822: Entered service from Glasgow to Rothesay and Inveraray.
1829: Moved to the Glasgow–Arran route.
1831: Sold to J. & A. Gairdner, Belfast. Lengthened by 13.8 feet. Placed on the Glasgow–Belfast service.
1834: Sold to the Clyde Steam Navigation Co. (Thomson and McConnell).
1838: Now operated again from Glasgow to Inveraray. Engine swapped with that of *Brenda*.
1839: Started operating from Oban to Portree.
1842: Operating from Glasgow to Portree, also from Glasgow and West Loch Tarbert to Islay.
1844: Sold to the City of Glasgow Steam Packet Co.
1849: June – Sold to J. Waldie, Leith. Engines removed and converted to a schooner.
1849: July – Sold to J. B. Thomson, Leith.
1850: Sold to R. Bell & Co., Dumbarton.

1850: Sold to T. Fletcher, Goole.
1851: Sold to C. & E. Tayleur, Liverpool.
1854: Broken up.

44: *Largs* (1822)

Number in Williamson's list: 48
Built: 1822
83 tons. Length 93.5 feet, 104.3 feet (1833)
Builders: John & Charles Wood, Port Glasgow
Engine builders: Claude Girdwood, Glasgow. 36 hp
Hull material: Wood
Owners: Largs Steam Boat Co., Glasgow
1822: Entered service from Glasgow to Largs and Millport.
1829: Sold to the Albion Steam Boat Co., Glasgow.
c. 1830: Moved to the route from Ardrossan or Saltcoats to Lamlash.
1833: Lengthened by 10.8 feet.
1835: Now on the route from Glasgow to Rothesay, Lochgilphead and Inveraray.
1840: Sold to G. Castle Jr, London. Converted to a sailing vessel.
1841: Sold to D. Cannon, Liverpool.
1842: Sold to J. B. Poteard, Sheerness.
1844: Broken up.

45: *Duke of Lancaster*

Built: 1822
95 tons. Length 103.5 feet
Builders: Mottenhead & Hayes, Liverpool
Engine builders: W. Fawcett, Liverpool. Engine type: side-lever two-cylinder; 50 hp
Hull material: Wood, flush-decked
Owners: J. Winder, W. Fawcett, J. Cook, F. Fairhurst, G. Littledale and H. Littledale,
    Liverpool
1822: Entered service from Liverpool and Hoylake to Bagillt.
1822: July – Sold to the War Office Steam Packet Co., Bristol.
1822: July – Commenced service from Bristol to Cork, calling at Ilfracombe.
1822: September – Moved to the Bristol–Chepstow route for a month.
1823: March–May: On the Bristol–Ilfracombe and Tenby service.
1823: May: Operated from Bristol to Dublin.
1823: September – On the Bristol–Waterford service for one month only.
1823: October – Laid up.
1825: Sold to the Liverpool & Bagillt Steam Packet Co., operated from Liverpool and
    Hoylake to Bagillt.
1826: Sold to the Campbeltown & Glasgow Steam Packet Joint Stock Ltd. Placed on the
    Glasgow–Campbeltown route.
1836: Made some trips from Glasgow to Larne and Islay.
1845: Broken up.

46: *Leven* (1824)

Number in Williamson's list: 49
Built: 1824
54 tons. Length 88.1 feet
Builders: James Lang, Dumbarton
Engine builders: Robert Napier, Camlachie. Engine type: side-lever; 33 hp
Hull material: Wood
Owners: Dumbarton Steamboat Co.
1824: Entered service from Glasgow to Dumbarton, also made some trips from Dumbarton to Ayr.
1837: Sold to R. Jamieson Sr, R. Douglas, W. Fullerton and T. Graham, Irvine. Placed on the Ardrossan–Arran service.
1841: Broken up. Her engine was fitted in *Queen of Beauty* in 1844.
Leven's engine survived and is now on display in the grounds of the Denny Tank in Dumbarton.

47: *Favourite*

Number in Williamson's list: 50
Built: 1824
40.6 tons. Length 70.4 feet
Builders: James Lang, Dumbarton
Engine builders: W. Denny & A. McLachlan. 25 hp
Hull material: Wood
Owners: J. Mitchell, J. Neill and A. Drysdale
1824: Entered service from Glasgow to Greenock as a luggage boat.
1837: July – Sold to New Clyde Shipping Co., Glasgow. Continued on the same service.
1843: Sold to T. Jackson and W. Bean, Inverness.
1849: Sold to J. Jackson.
1852: Broken up at Inverness.

48: *Ben Nevis* (1824)

Number in Williamson's list: 51
Built: 1824
44.5 tons. Length 82 feet 9 inches
Builders: James Lang, Dumbarton
Engine builders: Robert Napier, Camlachie. hp
Hull material: Wood
Owners: Glasgow & Caledonian Canal Steamship Co.
1824: Commenced service from Glasgow to Inverness.
1829: Sold to D. McInnes, Glasgow.
1829: Sold to R. Nicolson, A. Stewart, D. McInnes and others, Stornoway. Moved to the Glasgow–Stornoway route.
1831: July – Wrecked at Carskey, near Campbeltown.

49: *Commerce*

Number in Williamson's list: 52
Built: 1824
43.7 tons. Length 74 feet 6 inches
Builders: James Lang, Dumbarton
Engine builders: Robert Napier, Camlachie. 25 hp
Hull material: Wood
Owners: J. Mitchell, J. Neill and A. Drysdale
1824: Entered service as a luggage boat from Glasgow to Greenock.
1837: Sold to New Clyde Shipping Co., Glasgow. Continued on the same service.
1844: Sold to W. Middleton and others, Sligo. Moved to operate out of Sligo.
1868: Broken up.

50: *George Canning*

Number in Williamson's list: 53
Built: 1824
80.9 tons. Length 99.6 feet
Builders: James Lang, Dumbarton
Engine builders: J. Henderson & Son, Renfrew. 35 hp
Hull material: Wood
Owners: H. Price, J. Henderson and A. McKellar
1824: Entered service from Glasgow to Rothesay.
1824–1825: Also ran from Glasgow to Belfast.
1826: Moved to the Glasgow–Inveraray route.
1833: Sold to six Jersey merchants. Operated from Jersey to St Malo.
1837: Sold to unknown owners at Archangel, Russia. Was the first steamship at Trondheim
   when she called for repairs en route to Archangel. Operated out of Archangel.
No further records of her have been found.

51: *Sovereign* (1824)

Number in Williamson's list: 54
Built: 1824
69 tons. Length 92.8 feet
Builders: James Lang, Dumbarton
Engine builders: Claude Girdwood, Glasgow. 36 hp
Hull material: Wood
Owners: D. Henderson & A. McKellar, Glasgow
1824: Entered service from Glasgow to Helensburgh and the Gareloch.
1828: Moved to the Glasgow–Arrochar service.
1833: August – Sold to J. Askew, J. Southern and A. Davies, Liverpool. Placed on the
   Liverpool–Egremont route.
1839: Broken up at Liverpool.

52: *Commodore*

Built: 1824
? tons. Length ? feet
Builders: J. Wood, Port Glasgow
Engine builders: Robert Napier, Camlachie. Engine type: two engines; 300 hp
Hull material: Wood
Owners: Glasgow & Caledonian Canal Steamship Co. (J. McLeod)
1824: Operated from Glasgow to Inverness.
1828: Sold to A. McEachern.
1835: Sold to D. Wright & Co., Glasgow.
1836: Withdrawn from service by this date.

53: *Maid of Islay No. 2*

Built: 1824
92 tons. Length 94.2 feet
Builders: John Wood, Port Glasgow
Engine builders: Claude Girdwood, David Napier. 50 hp
Hull material: Wood
Owner: W. F. Campbell, Islay
1827: Commenced service from West Loch Tarbert to Islay, Oban, Tobermory and Portree in the summer months and Greenock to Islay, Oban, Tobermory and Portree in the winter months.
1836: Renamed *Maid of Islay*.
1845: Sold to Glasgow Castle Steam Packet Company.
1846: July – Sold to G. & J. Burns.
1846: October – Sold to W. C. Townley, Liverpool.
1847: December – Sailed from Liverpool to Africa.
1848: 12 May – Vessel stopped by HMS *Alert*, mistaken for a slave trader while off the coast of Sierra Leone. Fired upon, damaged and towed into Freetown by HMS *Alert*.
No further information is available and it assumed she never left Freetown again.

54: *Air* (also known as *Ayr*)

Number in Williamson's list: 45
Built: 1825
76 tons. Length 95.0 feet
Builders: John & Charles Wood, Port Glasgow
Engine builders: Neilson & Co., Glasgow. Engine type: two-cylinder; 60 hp
Hull material: Wood
Owners: The Company of Proprietors of the Steam Packet called the *Air*, *Ayr*
1825: Entered service from Glasgow to Millport, Ayr and Stranraer.
1825: Chartered to G. & J. Burns.
1825: 25 October – Ran down and sank *Comet* (1822, No. 42) off Gourock. Immediately returned to Greenock to avoid sinking.
1831: Sold to W. H. Hutchinson and others, Liverpool. Used on towage and excursions from Cork.
1835: Sold to St George Steam Packet Co., Cork.

Mid-1830s: Operated Cork–Youghal and Cork–Glengariff.

1836: Operated on the River Lee, Cork, but was unsuccessful, as her draught was too much.

1837: Sold to Cork Steam Towing & Coasting Co.

1839: Sold to J. McNamara, Cork.

1840: Sold to G. Bickerton, Passage West.

1840: May – Sold to the Bristol General Steam Navigation Co. Operated on excursions from Bristol to Weston-Super-Mare.

1849: From now on, purely used as a tug.

1853: Sold to Bristol United Steam Towing Co., Bristol.

1855: Sold to A. Drew.

1860: Converted to a sailing ketch for the coal trade.

1862: 3 May – Foundered off Lavenock Point near Penarth.

55: *St Catherine*

Number in Williamson's list: 55
Built: 1825
70 tons. Length 94.0 feet
Builders: John Wood, Port Glasgow
Engine builders: Neilson & Co., Glasgow. 34 hp
Hull material: Wood
Owners: P. Graham and others, Glasgow

1825: Entered service from Glasgow to Lochgoilhead and Arrochar.

1835: Operated solely to Arrochar after the introduction of *Lochgoil* (1835).

1836: Sold to the Derry & Moville Steam Boat Co. Operated on Lough Foyle from Londonderry to Moville.

1838: Broken up.

56: *Helensburgh* (1825)

Number in Williamson's list: 56
Built: 1825
81.6 tons. Length 100 feet 3 inches
Builders: W. Denny, Dumbarton
Engine builders: Robert Napier, Camlachie. Engine type: single-cylinder side-lever; 52 hp
Hull material: Wood
Owners: Glasgow, Helensburgh & Rosneath Steam Boat Co.

1825: Entered service from Glasgow to Helensburgh and Rosneath. She had the first engines with two eccentrics, one for forward and one for reverse.

1835: December – Sold to the Woodside, North Birkenhead & Liverpool Steam Ferry Co., Liverpool. Placed on the Liverpool–Woodside ferry service.

1842: Sold to Birkenhead Improvement Commissioners.

1844: Broken up.

57: *James Ewing*

Number in Williamson's list: 57
Built: 1825
77.6 tons. Length 101.0 feet
Builders: J. Lang, Dumbarton
Engine builders: David Napier, Lancefield. 35 hp
Hull material: Wood
Owners: H. Price, J. Stevenson and J. Alexander, Glasgow
1825: Entered service from Glasgow to Belfast.
1825: Summer – Ran from Glasgow to Londonderry for a few days.
1827: June – Sold to David Napier. Route now Glasgow–Rothesay. Made occasional Glasgow–Lochgilphead (Ardrishaig) sailings.
1835: March – Sold to J. Gemmill, Glasgow. No longer on the Rothesay service.
1837: July – Sold to New Clyde Shipping Co. Operated from Glasgow to Greenock.
1849: June – Sold to R. Hutton, Glasgow.
1849: December – Sold to R. Strapp, Glasgow.
1852: Broken up.

58: *Benlomond*

Number in Williamson's list: 58
Built: 1825
70 tons. Length 90.9 feet
Builders: J. Lang, Dumbarton
Engine builders: Robert Napier, Camlachie. 35 hp
Hull material: Wood
Owners: Dumbarton Steamboat Co.
1825: Entered service from Glasgow to Dumbarton.
1828: Sold to J. Long (Benlomond Steamboat Co.). Operated from Tobermory to Strontian.
1833: Sold to A. Allan Sr, R. Walker, T. Barclay and others, Glasgow.
1833: Sold to T. Barclay, Glasgow. Now operating on the River Forth from Newhaven to Stirling.
1833: 4 June – Caught fire and sank after leaving Newhaven Pier for Stirling; later salvaged.
1836: Sold to P. Hansen and T. Strong, Newcastle.
1837: Sold to P. Hansen and W. Anderson, Newcastle.
1837: Chartered by L. F. Kalkman, Bremen.
1837: July – Operated from Bremen, Wangerooge and Norderney to Helgoland.
1838: Sold to Flensburg Dampsikibs Co., Flensburg, then in Denmark. Renamed *Union*.
1841: Sold to F. J. J. Frahm, Kiel, converted to a sailing schooner.
No information is available about her fate.

59: *Cyclops*

Built: 1825
34 tons. Length 68 feet
Builders: T. Wilson, Tophill, Glasgow
Engine builders: J. Neilson, Hamiltonhill. Engine type: single-cylinder, fitted 1829; 15 hp
Hull material: Iron
Owners: Forth & Clyde Canal Co.
1825: Built as an unpowered, horse-drawn barge for service on the Forth & Clyde Canal.
1827: Laid up at Bantaskine.
1829: Steam engine and centrally located stern wheel fitted.
1829: September – Entered service from Glasgow to Grangemouth and Alloa mainly for
  freight; she carried fifteen passengers.
1837: Withdrawn from service and converted to a lighter.
No record of her final fate survives.

60: *Lady of the Lake*

Built: 1825
62 tons. Length 82.2 feet
Builders: W. Denny, Dumbarton
Engine builders: Robert Napier, Camlachie. Engine type: side-lever jet condenser; 25 hp
Hull material: Wood
Owners: Loch Lomond Steamboat Co.
1825: Entered service on Loch Lomond.
1828: Sold to The Loch Lomond Steam Boat Co.
1829: March – Sold to J. McMurrich.
1829: June – Taken over by Napier & McMurrich.
1829: Removed from the loch.
1835: Broken up.

61: *Countess of Glasgow*

Number in Williamson's list: 59
Built: 1826
89.7 tons. Length 100 feet
Builders: J. Scott & Sons, Greenock
Engine builders: Robert Napier, Glasgow. hp
Hull material: Wood
Owners: C. S. Parker, James Kerr, John Kerr and others
1826: Entered service from Glasgow to Largs, Millport and Irvine.
1828: Sold to J. Woddrop, J. Kerr and others. Service extended to Arran.
1835: July – Sold to T. B. Blackburn and others. Operated out of Liverpool.
1836: Broken up at Liverpool.

62: *Caledonia* (1826)

Number in Williamson's list: 60
Built: 1826
57 tons. Length 84.0 feet
Builders: W. Denny, Dumbarton
Engine builders: D. McArthur & Co., Camlachie. 32 hp
Hull material: Wood
Owners: Unknown, Glasgow
1826: Entered service from Glasgow to Helensburgh and Garelochhead.
1831: Service cut back to Rosneath.
1835: Operated Glasgow–Dunoon for one year only.
No record exists of her fate.

63: *Sir John Moore*

Number in Williamson's list: 62
Built: 1826
92.3 tons. Length 103 feet 7 inches
Builders: James Lang, Dumbarton
Engine builders: Murdoch & Cross. 50 hp
Hull material: Wood
Owners: Dr Stevenson, H. Price and others, Glasgow
1826: Entered service from Glasgow to Lochgoilhead.
1827: March – Sold to the Postmaster General, London. Renamed *Jonathan Hulls*. Used as a
    mail tender at Liverpool.
1834: March – Sold to W. G. Atherton, Liverpool. Regained the name *Sir John Moore*.
    Operated on the Liverpool–New Brighton ferry service.
1838: March – Owners now W. Atherton and G. Atherton, New Brighton.
1845: August – Sold to W. R. Coulborn & Co., Liverpool.
1846: January – Broken up.

64: *Saint George*

Number in Williamson's list: 63
Built: 1826
78 tons. Length 101.0 feet
Builders: John Wood, Port Glasgow
Engine builders: Neilson & Co., Glasgow. 48 hp
Hull material: Wood
Owners: Lochgoil & Lochlong Steamboat Co.
1826: Entered service from Glasgow to Loch Goil and Arrochar.
1832: May: Sold to J. Henderson, A. McKellar and A. Adam, Glasgow.
1837: June – Sold to A. Greig, Leith. Commenced operating from Newhaven to Largo.
1837: July – Registered at Leith by A. Greig, A. Adam, J. Henderson and A. McKellar.
1838: February – Ownership reverted to A. Greig
1842: July – Now registered by A. Greig and P. Greig
1846: Converted to a coal hulk, engines fitted in *Prince* (1846, No. 190).

65: *Dunoon Castle* (1826)

Number in Williamson's list: 64
Built: 1826
100.1 tons. Length 107.3 feet
Builders: W. Denny, Dumbarton
Engine builders: D. McArthur & Co., Camlachie. 60 hp
Hull material: Wood
Owners: Dunoon Castle Steam Boat Co.
1826: Entered service from Glasgow to Rothesay, Lochgilphead and Inveraray.
1832: March – Owners became Castle Steam Packet Co.
1842: July – Owners became Glasgow Castle Steam Packet Co.
1846: June – Owners became Glasgow & Liverpool Steam Shipping Co. (G. & J. Burns).
1847: January – chartered to Glasgow & Stranraer Steam Packet Co. Operated from Glasgow
  to Ayr, Girvan, Stranraer and Campbeltown.
1851: February – Sold to W. Denny & Bros.
1851: Chartered to W. F. Johnston & Co. Operated on the Glasgow–Rothesay service.
1851: September – Sold to the Glasgow & Lochfine Steam Packet Co. for the Glasgow–
  Inveraray cargo service.
1855: Laid up.
1856: Broken up.
1864: Register closed. The crosshead from her engine served for many years in the works of
  Messrs Stewart & Sons, Paper-makers, McNeil Street, Glasgow.

66: *Ardincaple*

Number in Williamson's list: 70
Built: 1826
87.96 tons. Length 97.8 feet
Builders: James Lang, Dumbarton
Engine builders: Robert Napier, Camlachie. 45 hp
Hull material: Wood
Owners: Glasgow, Helensburgh & Rosneath Steam Boat Co.
1826: Entered service from Glasgow to the Gareloch.
1828: April – Sold to R. Hall, G. A. Lambert and J. Grey, Newcastle. Operated from Newhaven
  to Newcastle.
1838: July – Sold to the General Shipping Co., Berwick-on-Tweed. By now on the Newhaven–
  Berwick-on-Tweed service, carrying passengers and cargo.
1846: May – Sold to Tweed Steam Boat Co., Berwick. Advertised to sail from Berwick to Newcastle.
1847: April – Owners now A. Robertson, A. Riddle and J. Black, Tweedmouth.
1847: September – Sold to A. Ray and J. Wright, Sunderland.
1848: November – Converted to a sailing vessel.
1849: September – Sold to T. Robson, Sunderland.
1851: October – Now registered by J. Robson Sunderland.
1852: January – Now registered by J. H. Robson, Sunderland.
1853: November – Sold to T. Iremonger, Littlehampton.
1871: April – Sold to R. Ratclife, Shoreham.
1872: February – Sold to C. Cliff, Falmouth.
1880: Converted to a hulk.

67: *Maid of Morvern*

Built: 1826
52.5 tons. Length 85.3 feet
Builders: John Wood & J. Barclay, Port Glasgow
Engine builders: D. McArthur & Co., Camlachie. 32 hp
Hull material: Wood
Owners: Maid of Morven Steam Boat Co., Glasgow
1826: Commenced service from Glasgow to Tobermory and from Glasgow to Fort William.
1834: Now running from Glasgow via the Caledonian Canal to Inverness, Cromarty, Invergordon and Burghead.
1835: May: Sold to D. Wright & Co.
1835: December – Sold to Robert Napier. Route not known.
1838: Route now Glasgow–Oban, Tobermory and Skye.
1843: February – Sold to A. McKenzie Jr, Kessock Ferry.
1846: October – Sold to W. Ainslie, Fort William. Placed on Glasgow–Oban and Fort William service.
1849: June – Sold to the Glasgow & Liverpool Steam Shipping Co. (G. & J. Burns).
1850: Broken up.

68: *Clarence*

Number in Williamson's list: 65
Built: 1827
70 tons. Length 92.0 feet
Builders: Lang & Denny, Dumbarton
Engine builders: Robert Napier, Camlachie. 45 hp
Hull material: Wood
Owner: Robert Napier
1827: Entered service from Glasgow to Helensburgh and the Gareloch.
1829: Sold to the City of Dublin Steam Packet Co. Operated on the Lower Shannon from Limerick to Clare Castle (near Ennis). Was the first steam vessel on the Shannon Estuary.
1833: Sold back to Robert Napier and returned to the Glasgow–Rosneath service.
1839: Sold to Carlisle Canal Co., Carlisle. Unknown service.
1847: March – Sold to J. Jack, Liverpool. Placed on the Liverpool–Eastham ferry service across the Mersey.
1847: Sold to H. Nicholls, T. Hilliar and H. Hilliar, Liverpool.
1848: September – Sold to R. Singlehurst, Liverpool.
1848: December – Sold to R. Ratclife, Shoreham.
1849: June – Sold to G. S. Sanderson, Liverpool.
1853: Broken up.

69: *Venus* (1827)

Number in Williamson's list: 66
Built: 1827
86.1 tons. Length 111.3 feet
Builders: John Wood & J. Barclay, Port Glasgow
Engine builders: David Napier, Lancefield. 70 hp
Hull material: Wood
Owner: David Napier
1827: Entered service from Glasgow to Kilmun and Rothesay.
1828: Sank, no further details available.

70: *Aglaia*

Built: 1827
30 tons. Length 62.7 feet
Builders: David Napier, Lancefield
Engine builders: David Napier, Lancefield.
Hull material: Iron base to hull, wooden sides
Owner: David Napier
1827: Entered service on Loch Eck, as part of a route from Kilmun to Inveraray, by steam
 carriage (later horse coach) from Kilmun to the foot of the loch, by horse coach from the
 head of the loch to Strachur, and by steamer to Inveraray. Claimed erroneously to be the
 first iron steamship in the world, her hull had an iron base and wooden sides. Some sources
 say she was built in 1820, and some that she was maliciously scuttled in Loch Eck.
It has also been stated that she was transferred to the Clyde at some stage, and renamed *James
 Gallacher*.
No information is available about how long she served on the loch or about her eventual
 fate.

71: *Glasgow*

Built: 1827
181 tons. Length 130.0 feet
Builders: R. Duncan & Co., Port Glasgow
Engine builders: Caird & Co., Greenock.
Hull material: Wood
Owner: Unknown
1829: Started operating from Dublin to Kingstown.
1834 (possibly 1830): Sold to D. Wright & Co. Glasgow. Renamed *Colonsay*. Operated from
 Glasgow to the West Highlands.
No further information is available.

72: *Cupid*

Number in Williamson's list: 67
Built: 1828
18 tons. Length 58.3 feet
Builders: John Wood & J. Horatio Ritchie, Port Glasgow
Engine builders: David Napier, Lancefield. 10 hp
Hull material: Wood
Owner: David Napier
1828: Operated from Paisley to Greenock.
1828: Chartered to the Forth & Clyde Canal Co. for experimental use as a tug.
1829: Commenced operating from Inveraray to Strachur and St Catherines. Later also operated from Dunoon to Kilmun.
1836: April – Sold to T. Parry, Liverpool. Operated on the Mersey.
1839: May – Sold to Sir Peter Hesketh-Fleetwood, Fleetwood. Operating out of Fleetwood.
1843: August – Sold to the Preston & Wyre Railway. Now operating from Knott End to Fleetwood.
c. 1847: Sold to unknown owners in Newry.
1867: Register closed. Probably broken up several years previously.

73: *Sultan* (1828)

Number in Williamson's list: 68
Built: 1828
69 tons. Length 97.5 feet
Builders: James Lang, Dumbarton
Engine builders: Robert Napier, Camlachie. 42 hp
Hull material: Wood
Owners: J. Henderson and A. McKellar
1828: Entered service from Glasgow to Helensburgh.
1831: Route extended to Rosneath.
1836: Replaced and laid up.
1838: Sold to Runcorn Steam Packet Co., Runcorn. Liverpool–Runcorn service.
1847: Broken up.

74: *New Dumbarton*

Number in Williamson's list: 69
Built: 1828
72 tons. Length 94.0 feet, 82.1 feet (1837)
Builders: W. Denny, Dumbarton
Engine builders: Robert Napier, Camlachie. 45 hp
Hull material: Wood
Owners: Dumbarton Steam Boat Co.
1828: Commenced service on the Glasgow–Dumbarton and Greenock route.
1837: Shortened by 12 feet.
1839: By this time also operating from Glasgow to Arrochar.
1847: Broken up.

75: *Waverley* (1828)

Number in Williamson's list: 71
Built: 1828
45.1 tons. Length 89.3 feet
Builders: James Lang, Dumbarton
Engine builders: Murdoch & Cross. 36 hp
Hull material: Wood
Owner: R. Douglas
1828: Commenced operating from Glasgow to Helensburgh, Rosneath and Garelochhead.
1847: June – Sold to J. Freeman, Hull. Commenced operating as a tug out of Hull.
1840: Now owned by the Hull & Selby Steam Co.
1840: June – For sale at auction.
1848: January – Sold to G. Kershaw & Co., Hull.
1853: Broken up.

76: (Name not known)

Built: 1828
? tons. Length ? feet
Builders: David Napier?
Engine builders: David Napier ? hp
Hull material: Iron/wood
Owner: David Napier
Route: Loch Eck
David Napier mentions this steamer in his autobiography, but no other records survive. It
    replaced *Aglaia* on the loch at some point and was out of service long before the screw
    steamer *Fairy Queen* was built in 1878 for the service on the loch.

77: *Loch Eck*

Number in Williamson's list: 72
Built: 1829
37.5 tons. Length 81.75 feet,
Builders: John Wood & J. Horatio Ritchie, Port Glasgow
Engine builders: David Napier, Lancefield. 30 hp
Hull material: Wood
Owner: D. Napier
1829: Entered service from Glasgow to Kilmun, where David Napier had recently bought
    land for a pier.
1830: August – Sold to J. Askew, Liverpool. Moved to the Mersey and placed on the
    Liverpool–Egremont ferry service.
1834: June – Sold to S. Garner, Liverpool. Lengthened by 66.6 feet.
1835: Sold to the Egremont Steam Packet Co.
1842: Broken up.

78: *Foyle*

Built: 1829
136 tons. Length 122.0 feet
Builders: James Lang, Dumbarton
Engine builders: Robert Napier & Sons, Govan. 70 hp
Hull material: Wood
Owners: The Foyle Steam Boat Co., Londonderry
1829: Entered service from Glasgow to Londonderry via Campbeltown and Portrush with an annual cruise at Glasgow Fair from Glasgow and Londonderry to the West Highlands.
1838: Sold to the Glasgow & Londonderry Steam Packet Co.
1842: Spring – Operated from Glasgow to Belfast.
1842: April and May – Chartered to sail from Glasgow to Islay, Mull, Oban and Skye.
1842: Moved to the Glasgow–Liverpool service.
1844: Sold to the Glasgow & Liverpool Steam Shipping Co. (G & J. Burns).
1847: February – Sold to Hull Steam Packet Co. (W. Brownlow, W. Pearson and G. Holmes, Hull). Now operating from Hull to London.
1853: April – Sold to H. C. Cheeswright and W. T. Miskin, London.
1857: December – Sold to C. Joyce, F. G. Westmoreland, London.
1859: June – Converted to a sailing vessel. Sold to Z. C. Pearson, Hull.
1861: January – Sold to T. R. Oswald, Sunderland.
1861: April – Sold to H. Briggs, Hull.
1861: May – Sold to G. C. Pecket, Sunderland.
1862: 30 September – Lost.

CHAPTER 3
Steamers Built 1830–39

79: *Superb* (1830)

Number in Williamson's list: 73
Built: 1830
76.5 tons. Length 103.8 feet
Builders: James Lang, Dumbarton
Engine builders: James Lang, Dumbarton. 50 hp
Hull material: Wood
Owner: W. McKenzie, Glasgow
1830: Entered service on the Glasgow–Rothesay service.
1832: August – Sold to Belfast Local Steam Boat Co., Belfast. Used as a tug.
1840: April – Sold to Belfast Steam Tug Ltd.
1842: August – Sold to Belfast Steam Packet Co.
1848: May – Sold to N. Fitzsimmons and others, Belfast.
1850: Used on passenger charters out of Belfast.
1851: November – Broken up.

80: *Arran Castle* (1830)

Number in Williamson's list: 74
Built: 1830
81.7 tons. Length 103.75 feet
Builders: John Wood & J. Horatio Ritchie, Port Glasgow
Engine builders: Robert Napier, Camlachie. 50 hp
Hull material: Wood
Owners: Arran Castle Steam Packet Co.
1830: Entered service from Glasgow to Rothesay.
1832: Owners became the Castle Steam Packet Co.
1842: Owners became the Glasgow Castle Steam Packet Co.
1843: December – Sold to L. McClellan, Dublin.
1845: Commenced operating from Dublin to Howth, also ran excursions from Dublin to Wicklow for race meetings there.
1848: August – Sold to J. Fagan, Dublin.
1852: Ceased operating on the Howth service. Probably used as a tug from now onwards.
1856: June – Sold to C. Palgrave and M. Murphy.
1858: April – Sold to H. Sheridan, Dublin.
1860: July – Sold to W. D. Seymour, Queenstown. Also used as a tender here at Cork to emigrant ships and transatlantic liners.

1872: Broken up prior to this date.

81: *Greenock* (1830)

Number in Williamson's list: 75
Built: 1830
70.1 tons. Length 102.25 feet
Builders: W. Denny, Dumbarton
Engine builders: Robert Napier, Camlachie. 50 hp
Hull material: Wood
Owners: J. Henderson and A. McKellar
1830: Entered service from Glasgow to Helensburgh and the Gareloch.
1831: Running from Glasgow to Rosneath.
1839: Broken up.

82: *Lochryan*

Built: 1830
94 tons. Length 106.5 feet
Builders: James Lang, Dumbarton
Engine builders: Caird & Co., Greenock. Engine type: two engines; 50 hp
Hull material: Wood
Owners: Lochryan Steam Boat Co., Stranraer/Stranraer Steam Shipping Co., Stranraer
1830: Entered service from Glasgow to Stranraer.
1835: Made some sailings from Stranraer to Belfast.
1837: Also operated from Whitehaven to Belfast.
1839: Lengthened by 18.5 feet.
1843: October – Sold to J. Reid, Glasgow. Resold immediately to J. Reid and A. Reid, Newcastle. Used for coal trading from Newcastle.
1844: Operated from Newcastle to Leith.
1845: On a Newcastle–Belfast service.
1845: December – Sold to G. Cruddas, Newcastle.
1846: Sold to Netherland Steam Navigation Co., London. Operated from London to Rotterdam and Hamburg.
1846: 7 October – Sank with all hands in the North Sea in a gale en route from Rotterdam to London with between 80 and 100 head of cattle on board.

83: *Saint Mun*

Number in Williamson's list: 76
Built: 1831
63.1 tons. Length 114.25 feet
Builders: W. Denny, Dumbarton
Engine builders: David Napier, Lancefield. 60 hp
Hull material: Wood
Owner: David Napier
1831: Entered service from Glasgow to Kilmun, also operated from Glasgow to Rothesay

and Ayr.

1835: Route now Glasgow–Rothesay, Tarbert, Lochgilphead/Ardrishaig and Inveraray.

1836: March – Sold to A. Newlands, N. Currie and J. Clark, Glasgow.

1839: January – Owner now A. Newlands, Glasgow. Operating from Glasgow to Greenock.

1840: June – Sold to D. Lamont and A. McLachlan, Glasgow.

1842 or earlier: Broken up.

84: *Rothsay* (or *Rothesay*)

Number in Williamson's list: 77
Built: 1831
100 tons, 58 tons (1836). Length 96 feet
Builders: J. Lang, Dumbarton
Engine builders: David Napier, Lancefield. 60 hp
Hull material: Wood
Owner: J. McKinnon, Greenock

1831: Entered service from Glasgow to Rothesay, later ran from Glasgow to the West Highlands.

1834: June – Sold to R. Davidson, Glasgow. Ran from Glasgow to Inverness and Leith.

1836: June – Sold to Dundee & Leith Steam Packet Co., Dundee. Operated from Leith to Dundee and Montrose.

1840: June – Sold to G. Cammell Jr, Hull, probably a shipbroker.

1841: Sold to R. M. Sloman, Hamburg. Used from Hamburg to Helgoland and on towing duties. Renamed *Express*.

1845: Deleted from the registers.

85: *Fairy Queen*

Number in Williamson's list: 78
Built: 1831
40 tons, 68 tons (1834). Length 92 feet, 97 feet (1834)
Builders: John Neilson, Hamiltonhill
Engine builders: David Napier, Lancefield. Engine type: oscillating
Hull material: Iron
Owner: John Neilson, Hamiltonhill

1831: Entered service from Glasgow to Largs and Millport. Was the first iron steamer on the Clyde and the first known to have an oscillating engine.

1834: Now operating from Glasgow to Helensburgh. Lengthened by 5 feet and rebuilt.

1842: August – Broken up at Liverpool.

86: *Gleniffer*

Number in Williamson's list: 79
Built: 1831
32 tons. Length ? feet
Builders: Unknown, Clyde
Engine builders: Unknown, Clyde.

Hull material: Wood
Owner: Unknown, Glasgow or Paisley
1831: Entered service from Glasgow to Largs and Millport, also ran from Paisley to Largs.
1833: Operated from Paisley to Kilmun.
1836: Sold to Thomson & McDougall. Used as a tug to tow barges from the coal wharf at the foot of Wellington Street to Tennent's works at Dalmuir (unconfirmed).
1836: 2 May – Wrecked at Lamorna Cove, Cornwall, en route from Greenock to Dartmouth.

87: *Lord Dundas*

Built: 1831
8 tons. Length 68 feet
Builders: Fairbairn & Lillie, Manchester
Engine builders: Fairbairn & Lillie, Manchester. Engine type: two-cylinder horizontal; 10 hp
Hull material: Iron
Owners: Forth & Clyde Canal Co.
1831: Built at Manchester for service on the Forth & Clyde Canal. Fitted with a stern wheel in a narrow trough. Sailed to the Clyde, in doing so became the first iron-hulled vessel to sail on the open sea.
1831: Commenced operating from Port Dundas to Lock 16.
1834: Converted to be pulled by a chain along the bed of the canal.
1836: Withdrawn from service, converted into a barracks boat for banksmen.

88: *Windsor Castle* (1832)

Number in Williamson's list: 80
Built: 1832
80.9 tons. Length 110.1 feet
Builders: John Wood, Port Glasgow
Engine builders: Robert Napier, Camlachie. 55 hp
Hull material: Wood
Owners: Castle Steam Packet Co.
1832: Entered service from Glasgow to Loch Fyne.
1832: October – Owners became the Glasgow Castle Steam Packet Co.
1835: Service became from Glasgow to Rothesay.
1838: April – Sold to H. Frewen, Rye. Operated from Rye to Boulogne.
1840: January – Sold to J. & A. Blyth, London.
1840: June – Sold to R. N. Burton, London.
1841: December – Sold to H. & J. Blyth, London.
1843: March – Registered by H. D. Blyth, J. Blyth and P. P. Blyth.
1844: April – Reportedly sold to the King of Burma.
No information is available after that date.

89: *Apollo*

Number in Williamson's list: 81
Built: 1832
104.3 tons. Length 131.2 feet
Builders: Hunter & Dow, Kelvinhaugh
Engine builders: T. Wingate & Co., Springfield. 100 hp
Hull material: Wood
Owners: T. Wingate, J. Tassie and J. Hunter
1832: Entered service from Glasgow to Largs, Millport and Ayr.
1834: Sold to the Apollo Steam Packet Co., Southampton. Placed in the service from Southampton to Le Havre.
1836: June – Sold to British & Foreign Steam Navigation Co.
1837: April – Sold to the Commercial Steam Navigation Co., London. Placed on the route from Great Yarmouth to London.
1837: 3 September – Collided with *Monarch* off Northfleet, en route from Yarmouth to London, and sank.

90: *Inverness*

Number in Williamson's list: 82
Built: 1832
43.5 tons. Length 82.5 feet
Builders: Robert Barclay, Stobcross
Engine builders: Robert Napier, Camlachie. 36 hp
Hull material: Wood
Owners: G. Smith, J. Melvin, P. Turner and W. Young
1832: Entered service from Glasgow to Inverness via the Crinan and Caledonian canals.
1834: Route briefly extended to Invergordon.
1835: May – Sold to W. Young and G. Burns. Operated from Glasgow to Mull, Ulva and Strontian.
1835: September – G. Burns now sole owner.
1844: August – Owners now Glasgow & Liverpool Steam Shipping Co. (J. & G. Burns).
1846: Sold to S. Bromhead and S. Hemming, Londonderry.
1848: Broken up.

91: *Hero* (1832)

Number in Williamson's list: 83
Built: 1832
68.7 tons. Length 98.4 feet
Builders: W. Denny, Dumbarton
Engine builders: Robert Napier, Camlachie. 35 hp
Hull material: Wood
Owner: D. McKellar
1832: Entered service from Glasgow to Largs and Millport.
1835: Moved to the Ardrossan–Arran route.
1837: June – Owners now D. McKellar, W. Allan and J. Fleming, Glasgow. Final year on the

Arran run.

1838: December – Sold to the Glasgow & Dumbarton Steam Packet Co., Dumbarton. Now in the Glasgow–Dumbarton service.

1846: February – Sold to S. Howes, Liverpool. Used as a tug.

1849: February – Sold to E. & W. Forster, Liverpool.

1861: Broken up.

92: *Robert Napier*

Number in Williamson's list: 84
Built: 1832
19 tons. Length 99.6 feet
Builders: John Wood, Port Glasgow
Engine builders: Robert Napier, Camlachie. 28 hp
Hull material: Wood
Owner: Unknown

1832: Entered service on Clyde routes.

1835: Sold to Napier & McCurrich, Loch Lomond. Renamed *Balloch*.

1835: July – Entered service on Loch Lomond.

1836: Moved back to the Clyde, renamed *Dumbuck*. Operated from Glasgow to Dumbarton.

1842: October – Purchased by J. B. MacBrayne and J. McIndoe. Operated from Oban to Strontian, Tobermory, Skye and Uist for four months only.

1844: December – Purchased by D. Cameron, Greenock. Returned to the Glasgow–Dumbarton service.

1847: February – Sold to the Dumbarton Steamboat Co.

1852: Broken up.

A. Brown's *Loch Lomond Passenger Steamers* gives the original name as *Robert Napier* and year of build as 1835 but that is not backed up by builders' lists.

93: *Earl Grey*

Number in Williamson's list: 85
Built: 1832
104.7 tons. Length 120.3 feet
Builders: R. Duncan & Co., Greenock
Engine builders: R. Duncan & Co., Greenock. hp
Hull material: Wood
Owner: David Napier

1832: Entered service from Glasgow to Rothesay and Brodick.

1832: Caught fire and sank in Brodick Bay. Raised and returned to service.

1835: 24 July – Boiler exploded while the steamer was lying at Greenock; six killed, fifteen seriously injured, also twelve with minor injuries. Most passengers standing on deck were blown into the sea. Repaired and returned to service.

1836: February – Sold to A. Tennant, G. Ord and H. Price, Glasgow.

1837: June – Owners now A. Tennant and G. Ord, Glasgow.

1838: July – Sold to the Glasgow and Kilmun Steam Packet Co. Operated from Glasgow to Dunoon and Kilmun.

1843: Broken up.

94: *Edinburgh*

Built: 1832
? tons. Length 68 feet
Builders: T. Wilson, Tophill
Engine builders: T. Wilson, Tophill. Engine type: two-cylinder horizontal direct-acting; 14 hp
Hull material: Iron
Owners: London, Leith, Edinburgh & Glasgow Shipping Co.
1832: October – Entered service on the Forth and Clyde and Union Canals from Port Dundas, Glasgow, to Port Hopetoun, Edinburgh. Was fitted with two stern wheels, one on each side.
1833: January – Service ceased after she hit a bridge on the Union Canal in the hours of darkness.
1833: Spring – Sold to the Forth & Clyde Canal Co. Operated from Port Dundas to Lock 16.
1833: December – Converted to side-wheel propulsion. Now used as a tug at Grangemouth.
No record seems to have survived of her eventual fate.

95: *Manchester*

Built: 1832
17 tons. Length 68 feet
Builders: Fairbairn & Lillie, Manchester
Engine builders: Fairbairn & Lillie, Manchester. Engine type: two-cylinder locomotive type; 24 hp
Hull material: Iron
Owners: Forth & Clyde Canal Co.
1832: Intended to be operated on the Forth & Clyde and Union canals from Port Dundas, Glasgow, to Port Hopetoun, Edinburgh. Was fitted with two stern wheels, one on each side.
1832: April – Entered service as a cargo steamer from Port Dundas to Grangemouth and Stirling.
Late 1830s: Service withdrawn.
1839: Broken up.

96: *Staffa*

Built: 1832
46.7 tons. Length 81.7 feet
Builders: Robert Barclay, Stobcross
Engine builders: David Napier, Lancefield. 40 hp
Hull material: Wood
Owners: Staffa Steam Boat Co., Glasgow
1832: Entered service from Glasgow to Inverness.
1834: Route extended to Cromarty and Invergordon.
1835: December – Sold to Robert Napier. Extension beyond Inverness abandoned.
1839: Now operating from Oban to Fort William and Inverness, Oban to Tobermory and Oban to Staffa and Iona.

1844: April – Sold to City of Glasgow Steam Packet Co.
1851: November – Broken up.

97: *Gazelle*

Built: 1832
187 tons, later 269. Length 135.8 feet, 168.5 feet (1844)
Builders: Murries & Clark, Greenock
Engine builders: Caird & Co., Greenock. 250 hp
Hull material: Wood
Owners: Glasgow & Liverpool Steam Packet Co. (G. & J. Burns)
1832: Commenced operating from Glasgow to Liverpool.
1833: Chartered for use from Hull to Rotterdam.
1834: June – Sold to Hull Steam Packet Co. Operated from Hull to London.
1838: Chartered to J. Fleming. Operated from Glasgow to Inverness until 1841.
1842: Commenced operating from Berwick-upon-Tweed to London.
1844: Lengthened by Humphrey & Son by 32.7 feet
1852: Moved to the Hull–Antwerp service.
1861: On a twice-weekly Hull–Dunkirk service.
1863: Sold to J. D. Schultz, Hamburg.
1865: Engines removed and converted to a barge.

98: *Alert*

Number in Williamson's list: 86
Built: 1833
44.17 tons. Length 61.5 feet
Builders: James Lang & William Denny, Dumbarton
Engine builders: James Lang, Dumbarton. 15 hp
Hull material: Wood
Owners: J. Mitchell, J. Neill and A. Drysdale
1833: Entered service from Glasgow to the Gareloch, later ran to Loch Goil.
1837: July – Sold to the New Clyde Shipping Co.
1839: Used as a luggage boat from Glasgow to Greenock by this time.
1845: April – Sold to the Glasgow Castle Steam Packet Co.
1845: December – Sold to D. Ritchie, Glasgow. By now in cargo service on the Firth of Clyde
  as a luggage boat.
1856: Broken up.

99: *Antelope*

Built: 1833
162 tons. Length 137.1 feet
Builders: J. Barclay, Stobcross
Engine builders: Robert Napier, Camlachie. Engine type: geared; 230 hp
Hull material: Wood
Owners: Belfast & Glasgow Steam Boat Co., Belfast

1833: 25 March – Launched.

1833: June – Entered service from Glasgow to Belfast.

1838: Commenced operating from Glasgow to the West Highlands.

1838: September – Owners became the Belfast & Glasgow Steam Shipping Co., Belfast.

1840: August – Sold to J. Burns and G. Burns.

1840: Operated from Glasgow to Newry for one year only.

1844: June – Owners became Glasgow & Liverpool Steam Shipping Co. (G. & J. Burns).

1845: December – Sold to W. B. Brownlow, Hull. Commenced operating from London to Hull.

1848: April – Owners now W. B. Brownlow, J. MacKay and others, Hull.

1856: Broken up.

100: *Vulcan* (1833)

Built: 1833

214 tons. Length 141.75 feet

Builders: John Wood, Port Glasgow

Engine builders: Robert Napier, Camlachie. Engine type: two engines; 200 hp

Hull material: Wood

Owners: Clyde Steam Navigation Co.

1833: Commenced operating from Glasgow to Liverpool, with occasional sailings from Glasgow to Belfast.

1838: Started trips in the summer from Glasgow to the Giant's Causeway, Islay, Iona, Staffa and St Kilda.

1838: 28 July – Was the second steamer ever to call at St Kilda.

1840: Sold to unknown foreign owners.

No further information is available on this steamer.

101: *Kilmun* (1834)

Number in Williamson's list: 87

Built: 1834

102.4 tons. Length 120.5 feet

Builders: John Wood, Port Glasgow

Engine builders: David Napier, Lancefield. 20 hp

Hull material: Wood

Owner: David Napier

1832: Entered service from Glasgow to Kilmun and Dunoon.

1835: September – Sold to J. Stevenson, Glasgow.

1836: February – Sold to A. Tennant, H. Price and G. Ord, Glasgow.

1837: January – Owners now A. Tennant and G. Ord, Glasgow.

1838: January – Owners now Glasgow, Dunoon & Kilmun Steam Packet Co.

1841: March – Sold to E. Mostyn and J. Dawson, Chester, possibly shipbreakers.

1842: Broken up.

102: *Nimrod*

Number in Williamson's list: 88
Built: 1834
96.3 tons. Length 109.33 feet
Builders: John Wood, Port Glasgow
Engine builders: Caird & Co., Greenock. 70 hp
Hull material: Wood
Owners: N. Currie and J. Clark, Glasgow
1834: Entered service from Glasgow to Largs, Millport and Ayr.
1835: Route now from Glasgow to Ayr and Stranraer.
1837: September – Sold to A. Newlands, Glasgow.
1841: March – Sold to J. Young, Glasgow, later the same month sold to G. Miller, London.
1845: Broken up at Bristol.

103: *Rob Roy* (1834)

Number in Williamson's list: 89
Built: 1834
42.1 tons. Length 83.25 feet
Builders: R. Duncan & Co., Greenock (some sources state Tod & McGregor)
Engine builders: R. Duncan & Co., Greenock; New engines 1835. 40 hp
Hull material: Wood
Owner: W. Young
1834: Entered service from Glasgow to Inverness via the Crinan and Caledonian canals.
1835: April – Owners now W. Young and G. Burns. Started running from Glasgow to Mull.
1835: September – G. Burns now sole owner.
1844: August – Owners became the Glasgow & Liverpool Steam Shipping Co. (G. & J. Burns).
1846: Moved back to the Glasgow–Fort William and Corpach service.
1850: Broken up.

104: *James Oswald*

Number in Williamson's list: 90
Built: 1834
68 tons. Length 101.66 feet
Builders: J. Scott & Sons, Greenock
Engine builders: Scott Sinclair & Co., Greenock.
Hull material: Wood
Owner: J. Stevenson
1834: Commenced service from Glasgow to Helensburgh and Garelochhead.
1841: February – Sold to Robert Napier, then to W. McNiven, G. F. Roberts and F. Kayser, Glasgow, in the same month.
1843: March – Sold to J. Anderson Jr and H. T. Patten, Glasgow.
1843: June – Sold to R. Wallace, Glasgow.
1845: June – Broken up.

105: *Albion* (1834)

Number in Williamson's list: 91
Built: 1834
86 tons. Length 111.67 feet
Builders: Hunter & Dow, Kelvinhaugh
Engine builders: Robert Napier, Camlachie. Engine type: two-cylinder; 60 hp
Hull material: Wood
Owner: Unknown, Glasgow
1834: Entered service from Greenock to Largs and Arran. Probably also used as a tug.
1849: May – Sold to J. A Sothern, J. Taylor and E. L. Cross, Liverpool. Used as a tug.
1850: October – Owners now J. A Sothern, E. L. Cross, H. Brown and J. Morgan, Liverpool.
1851: June – Sold to W. Whelon, Settle, Lancashire.
1856: July – Sold to R. Lloyd, Liverpool.
1857: January – Sold to J. L. Lloyd, Liverpool.
1876: Broken up.

106: *Dolphin* (1834)

Number in Williamson's list: 92
Built: 1834
117 gross tons. Length 96.75 feet
Builders: James Lang, Dumbarton
Engine builders: Caird & Co., Greenock. 42 hp
Hull material: Iron
Owners: R. Cochrane and A. McNab, Glasgow
1834: Entered service from Glasgow to Rothesay, Lochgilphead and Inveraray.
1836: May – Sold to M. McLeod, Glasgow. Operated from Glasgow to Tobermory, Barra, North and South Uist and Skye.
1840: January – Sold to the Monks Ferry Co., Liverpool. Re-engined by Johnsons & Co. Placed on the Liverpool–Monks Ferry service.
1841: Sold to the Birkenhead & Chester Railway
1842: July – Sold to A. Jones, Liverpool.
1843: Sold to R. Jones, Porthdinllaen.
1848: November – Sold to J. Delaney, Sligo and Liverpool.
1852: March – Sold to W. C. Tate, Sligo.
1853: September – Owners now W. C. Tate, M. Mound and J. Harper, Sligo.
1855: Sank.

107: *Benledi*

Number in Williamson's list: 93
Built: 1834
115.77 tons. Length 112 feet
Builders: Robert Barclay, Stobcross
Engine builders: Caird & Co., Greenock. Engine type: two-cylinder; 90 hp
Hull material: Wood
Owners: T. & R. Barclay (1837)
1834: Entered service from Glasgow to Largs, Millport and Ayr.
1835: June – Sold to Bristol Channel Navigation Co. Operates from Bristol to Milford.
1836: On the Bristol–Ilfracombe, Swansea and Tenby service.
1837: On the Bristol–Tenby service.
1837: July – Escorted Brunel's new *Great Western* from Bristol to London where her engines were to be fitted.
1839: February – Sold to John Tarleton, Rhyl. Operated from Liverpool to Rhyl.
1840: Sold to the North Wales Steam Packet Co., Rhyl. Continued on the same service.
1856: Sank.

108: *Glen Albyn, (Glenalbyn)*

Built: 1834
131 tons. Length 121.33 feet
Builders: J. Scott & Co., Greenock
Engine builders: J. Scott & Co., Greenock. 165 hp
Hull material: Wood
Owners: Glen Albyn Steamboat Co., Glasgow
1834: Commenced operation from Glasgow to Tobermory, Spar Cave, Skye, Loch Bracadale and, on one occasion, St Kilda. Was the first steamer to call at St Kilda.
1835: Sold to West of Scotland Insurance Co., Glasgow. Ran from Glasgow to Campbeltown.
1837: June – Sold to North British Steam Navigation Co. (G. & J. Burns). Continued operating to Campbeltown.
1838: June – Sold to General Shipping Co., Berwick-upon-Tweed. Operated from Newhaven to Berwick-upon-Tweed.
1841: Sold to Hull & Leith Steam Packet Co. Now operating from Leith to Hull.
1844: Chartered to the Leith & Dundee Steam Packet Co. Route now Leith to Dundee.
1847: Returned to the Leith–Hull service.
1852: On the Hull–Rotterdam service
1854: December – Sold to T., C. L. and J. N. Ringrose, Hull.
1856: 2 March – Wrecked at the mouth of River Maas.

109: *St Columb*

Built: 1834
153 tons. Length 126 feet
Builders: John Wood, Port Glasgow
Engine builders: Robert Napier, Camlachie. Engine type: beam; 130 hp

Hull material: Wood
Owners: The Saint Columb Steam Boat Co., Londonderry
1834: August – Entered service from Glasgow to Londonderry via Campbeltown and Portrush.
1835: Made her first annual cruise at Glasgow Fair from Glasgow to Londonderry, the West Highlands and Skye.
1838: May – Sold to the Glasgow & Londonderry Steam Packet Co.
1841: September – Placed on the Glasgow–Sligo service.
1844: Owners now Glasgow & Liverpool Steam Shipping Co. (G. & J. Burns)
1844: 5 April – Ran aground in Sound of Sanda 5 April 1844; all passengers and crew rescued by *St Kiaran*, which also towed her off at high tide.
1847: Now also operating from Troon to Londonderry.
1849: Now operating from Liverpool to Portrush.
1851: April – Sold to R. P. Stephens, Newry. Placed on the Glasgow–Newry service.
1864: Register closed, 'had been broken up several years ago'.

110: *Northern Yacht*

Number in Williamson's list: 94
Built: 1835
99.1 tons. Length 116.6 feet
Builders: Robert Barclay, Stobcross
Engine builders: Robert Napier, Camlachie. 0 hp
Hull material: Wood
Owners: T. & R. Barclay
1835: Entered service from Glasgow to Millport, Ayr and Stranraer.
1835: Used for annual inspection of lighthouses.
1836: March – Owner now T. Barclay.
1838: May: Sold to Metcalfe & Co., Newcastle. Operated from Leith to Newcastle.
1838: 30 October – Lost en route from Newcastle to Leith.

111: *James Dennistoun*

Number in Williamson's list: 95
Built: 1835
87.2 tons. Length 107.7 feet
Builders: Hunter & Dow, Kelvinhaugh
Engine builders: Robert Napier, Camlachie. Engine type: 70 hp
Hull material: Wood
Owners: J. Stevenson, H. Price, A. Tennant and J. Hunter, Glasgow
1835: Entered service from Glasgow to Largs and Millport. Also claimed to have run from Paisley to Kilmun in 1833.
1840: May – Sold to Sir Peter Hesketh-Fleetwood, Fleetwood. Operated from Fleetwood to Barrow.
1843: January – Sold to F. Kemp, Fleetwood.
1847: May: Sold to T. H. Higgin, Fleetwood.
1847: June – Sold to the Preston & Wyre Railway Co.
Between 1847 and 1854: Sold to the Birkenhead & Chester Railway Company. Moved to the

Liverpool–Monks Ferry route.

1852: April – Sold to the London & North Western Railway and Lancashire & Yorkshire Railways.

1854: Sold to Sampson Moore, Liverpool.

1856: March – Sold to E. Forster, Birkenhead.

1863: Broken up.

112: *Lochgoil* (1835)

Number in Williamson's list: 96
Built: 1835
108 tons. Length 93 feet
Builders: Tod & McGregor, Mavisbank
Engine builders: Claude Girdwood, Glasgow. 48 hp
Hull material: Wood
Owners: Loch Goil & Loch Long Steamboat Company
1835: Entered service from Glasgow to Lochgoilhead.
1841: Ceased operating when *Lochgoil* (1841) was built.
The existence of this steamer is not supported by builders' lists or registration information.

113: *Saint Mungo*

Number in Williamson's list: 98
Built: 1835
108 tons. Length 116.7 feet
Builders: R. Duncan & Co., Greenock
Engine builders: Murdoch, Aitken & Co. Engine type: steeple; 75 hp
Hull material: Iron
Owner: W. Young, Glasgow
1836: Operated from Glasgow to the West Highlands for one month only, then was placed on the Glasgow–Ardrossan route. Was the first inshore steamer in the world to have a steeple engine.
1837: November – Sold to O. Edwards and D. Maddock, Liverpool. Operated on the Mersey.
1838: April – Sold to the Clwyd & Liverpool Steam Packet Co.
1839: October – Sold to R. McDowall and R. Boyd, Belfast.
1841: Commenced to be used on charters out of Belfast.
1848: December – Lost.

114: *Isle of Bute* (1835)

Number in Williamson's list: 99
Built: 1835
94 tons. Length 108.9 feet
Builders: John Wood, Port Glasgow
Engine builders: Robert Napier, Camlachie. Engine type: 63 hp
Hull material: Wood

Owners: Bute Steam Packet Co., Greenock

1835: Entered service from Glasgow to Rothesay.

1841: Chartered to the Glasgow, Paisley & Greenock Railway. Route now from Greenock to Dunoon and Rothesay. Also operated summer excursions on the Firth of Clyde in this year.

1842: January – Sold to the Railway Steam Packet Co. Continued operating out of Greenock.

1846: August – Sold to J. Fagan, Dublin. Placed on the Dublin–Howth service. Also operated excursions to places south of Dublin, including to race meetings at Wicklow.

1856: June – Sold to C. Palgrave, M. Murphy and others, Dublin.

1860: June – Sold to J. Greenough, St Helens, Lancashire.

1861: August – Sold to E. Lealting, Ramsey (Isle of Man).

1862: Broken up.

115: *Maid of Bute*

Number in Williamson's list: 100
Built: 1835
91 tons. Length 110.3 feet
Builders: John Wood, Port Glasgow
Engine builders: Robert Napier, Camlachie. 70 hp
Hull material: Wood
Owners: Bute Steam Packet Co.

1835: Entered service from Glasgow to Rothesay.

1841: Chartered to the Glasgow, Paisley & Greenock Railway: Route now Greenock–Dunoon and Rothesay.

1842: January – Sold to the Railway Steam Packet Co.

1847: June – Sold to D. Bannatyne, Limerick, probably for breaking up.

1848: January – Broken up at Limerick by this date.

116: *Helen McGregor*

Number in Williamson's list: 101
Built: 1835
49.7 tons. Length 82 feet
Builders: R. Duncan & Co., Greenock
Engine builders: Murdoch, Aitken & Co. Engine type: single-cylinder, steeple; 35 hp
Hull material: Wood
Owners: G. Burns, W. Young

1835: Entered service from Glasgow to Inverness.

1835: September – Owner now solely G. Burns.

1839: Route now Crinan–Oban and Oban–Staffa and Iona.

1844: June – Owners became Glasgow & Liverpool Steam Shipping Co.

1848: Broken up, engines placed in *Lapwing* (No. 205).

117: *Edinburgh Castle* (1835)

Built: 1835
104 tons. Length 117.5 feet
Builders: Hunter & Dow, Kelvinhaugh
Engine builders: Hunter & Dow, Kelvinhaugh. 80 hp
Hull material: Wood
Owners: Castle Steam Packet Co.
1835: Entered service from Glasgow to Rothesay.
1838: June – Sold to C. H. Frewin, Rye. Operated from Rye to Boulogne for one season only
1840: Sold to the Commercial Steam Navigation Co., London
1843: March – Registered by W. J. Chaplin, and A. Humphreys, London and J. W. Drew, Southampton
1843: April – Owners now South Western Steam Packet Co., Southampton. Operated from Southampton to Le Havre and the Channel Islands
1845: April – Sold to W. Greenwood, London
1847: February – Sold to J. Spinks and S. Harden, Liverpool. Used as a tug at Liverpool from this date onwards
1847: November – Owners now the Liverpool Steam Tug Co.
1853: 12 February – Sank.

118: *Falcon*

Built: 1835
230 tons. Length 155.6 feet
Builders: Hunter & Dow, Kelvinhaugh
Engine builders: Hunter & Dow, Kelvinhaugh. 200 hp
Hull material: Wood
Owners: G. & R. Langtry and William Herdman, Belfast.
1835: Entered service from Liverpool to Belfast.
1845: October – Sold to James Matheson, Stornoway, and others. Commenced operating from Ardrossan to Stornoway.
1846: May – Ceased operating to Stornoway after a fire on board. Sold to Earl of Eglinton and Winton, Irvine.
1847: June – Sold to Hardy Hislop, London.
1847: September – Sold to Jose Perry, Oporto.
1854: Sold to J. Marques da Costa Jr, Oporto. Renamed *Dom Pedro V*.
1858: Sold to unknown Brazilian owners.
No record of her fate is available.

119: *Saint Kiaran*

Built: 1835
120 tons. Length 115.8 feet
Builders: R. Duncan & Co., Greenock
Engine builders: J. & W. Napier, Govan. 120 hp
Hull material: Wood

Owners: Campbeltown & Glasgow Steam Packet Joint Stock Ltd
1835: Entered service from Glasgow to Campbeltown.
1848: May – Sold to J. & E. Davidson, Leith.
1848: October – Sold to J. Waldie, Leith.
1848: November – Sold to J. McIndoe, Leith.
1850: Commenced operating from Leith to Copenhagen.
1851: April – Sold to R. P. Stephens, Glasgow.
1853: June – Sold to J. Ibbotson, Goole.
1854: June – Sold to unknown foreign owners.
No record of her eventual fate has survived.

120: *Vale of Leven*

Number in Williamson's list: 102
Built: 1836
112 gross tons. Length 93.1 feet
Builders: Tod & McGregor, Mavisbank
Engine builders: Robert Napier, Camlachie. 50 hp
Hull material: Iron
Owner: Unknown
1836: Entered service from Glasgow to Dumbarton.
1840: December – Registered by the Dumbarton Steam Boat Co.
1841: Placed on the Glasgow–Gareloch service.
1845: Sold to the Glasgow Castle Steam Packet Co.
1846: Commenced operating cargo sailings on the Firth.
1847: Sold back to the Dumbarton Steamboat Co.
1852: Lost.

121: *Brenda*

Number in Williamson's list: 103
Built: 1836
107.96 tons. Length 123.6 feet
Builders: A. McFarlane Jr & Co., Dumbarton
Engine builders: J. & W. Napier, Govan. 100 hp
Owner: Robert Napier
1836: Operated on the Glasgow–Gareloch service, but drew too much water. Moved to a route from Corpach to Tobermory.
1838: Engine swapped with that of the *Toward Castle*.
1839: Moved to the Glasgow–Ardrishaig service.
1840: Now running from Crinan to Oban and Oban to Staffa and Iona.
1841: Also operated from Crinan to Oban and Corpach.
1842: Also operated from Glasgow to Inverness.
1844: April – Sold to the City of Glasgow Steam Packet Co.
1844: August – Final sailing out of Oban.
1846: February – Broken up.

122: *Royal Tar*

Number in Williamson's list: 104
Built: 1836
79 tons. Length 125.7 feet
Builders: Tod & McGregor, Mavisbank
Engine builders: Tod & McGregor, Mavisbank. 75 hp
Hull material: Iron
Owners: J. Henderson and A. McKellar
1836: Entered service from Glasgow to Helensburgh and Rosneath.
1843: Sold to A. Greig, Leith. Operated from Newhaven to Largo.
1845: Sold to the Edinburgh & Dundee Steam Packet Co. Continued on the same route.
1846: May – Sold to H. J. Nicholls, Eastham. On the Liverpool–Eastham service on the Mersey.
1847: March – Owners became H. J. Nicholls and W. & T. Hilliar, Liverpool.
1850: July – Sold to the Rock Ferry Company (J. Crippen and W. R. Forster), Liverpool. Operated from Liverpool to Rock Ferry.
1852: Broken up.

123: *Express* (1836)

Number in Williamson's list: 105
Built: 1836
89.9 tons. Length 130.4 feet
Builders: Robert Barclay, Stobcross, or Tod & McGregor
Engine builders: Robert Barclay, Stobcross. 70 hp
Hull material: Wood
Owners: H. Price, C. McGregor, R. Watson and others
1836: 3 December – Launched.
1836: Entered service from Glasgow to Helensburgh.
1840: May – Sold to Sir Peter Hesketh-Fleetwood, Fleetwood. Commenced operating excursions out of Fleetwood.
1843: September – Sold to Preston & Wyre Railway, Harbour & Dock Co.
1847: May: Sold to T. H. Higgin, Fleetwood, probably for breaking up.
1847: Broken up.

124: *Tarbert Castle* (1836)

Number in Williamson's list: 107
Built: 1836
100.8 tons. Length 122.2 feet
Builders: Wood & Mills, Little Miln, Dumbuck
Engine builders: Wood & Mills, Little Miln, Dumbuck. Engine type: steeple; 100 hp
Hull material: Wood
Owners: Glasgow Castle Steam Packet Co.
1836: Entered service from Glasgow to Inveraray.
1838: March – Sold to the Montrose & Forth Steam Navigation Co., Montrose. Operated from Montrose to Leith.

1844: April – Owners now Montrose & Forth New Steam Co., Montrose.
1847: March – Sold to J. Brown, Montrose. Converted to a schooner.
1853: July – Sold to J. Russell, Kincardine.
1853: 15 November – Arrived at Port Philip, Australia, after a voyage from the UK.
1853: December – Sold to J. Dobson, Melbourne.
1854: October – Sold to C. Griffith, Melbourne, and F. A. Downing, Hobart.
1862: Sold to R. G. Gibbons, Dunedin, and converted to a hulk at Dunedin.
1877: Broken up.

125: *Victor*

Number in Williamson's list: 108
Built: 1836
70.16 tons. Length 109.8 feet
Builders: Hunter & Dow, Kelvinhaugh
Engine builders: Hunter & Dow, Kelvinhaugh.
Hull material: Wood
Owner: D. McKellar
1836: Entered service from Glasgow to Largs and Millport.
1845: Broken up.

126: *Lochlomond* (1836)

Number in Williamson's list: 114
Built: 1836
54 tons. Length 95 feet
Builders: David Napier, Lancefield
Engine builders: David Napier, Lancefield. 39 hp
Hull material: Iron
Owners: D. Napier and J. McMurrich
1836: Entered service on Loch Lomond.
1845: May – Owners now Loch Lomond Steamboat Co.
1846: Sold to W. Ainslie, Fort William. Renamed *Glencoe*. Moved out of the loch. Commenced operating on the Caledonian Canal from Gairlochy to Dochgarroch.
1849: August – Taken over by the Glasgow & Liverpool Steam Shipping Co. (G. & J. Burns). Service was now from Inverness to Banavie. Renamed *Curlew*.
1851: Moved to a service from Inverness to Cromarty and Little Ferry.
1851: July – Taken over by D. Hutcheson & Co.
1853: Laid up.
1855: April – Sold to W. Willoughby & Son/W. Hughes, C. Lancaster and W. Iley, Liverpool. Operated on the Mersey from Liverpool to Tranmere and/or Birkenhead.
1865: November – Broken up.

127: *Maid of Galloway*

Built: 1836
127 tons. Length 116.6 feet
Builders: J. Barclay, Stobcross
Engine builders: Tod & McGregor, Mavisbank. 100 hp
Hull material: Wood
Owners: Joint Stock Company to own the Steam Boat *Maid of Galloway* (Stranraer Steam Shipping Co.), Stranraer
1836: August – Entered service from Glasgow to Stranraer and from Belfast to Stranraer.
1837: Operated from from Belfast to Whitehaven via the Isle of Man and Belfast to Port Carlisle added.
1843: Isle of Man calls ceased.
1844: Sold to Stranraer Steam Packet Co.
1845: February – Sold to H. Smith, Preston.
1845: March–April – Sold to Galloway, Liverpool & Lancashire Shipping Co. Operated from Wigtown to Kirkcudbright, Fleetwood, Liverpool and Garlieston.
1845: August – Route changed to Ardrossan to Campbeltown, Port Ellen, Oban, Tobermory, Portree and Stornoway.
1850: 31 March – Wrecked at Balbriggan, north of Dublin, after a boiler explosion off Holyhead en route from Liverpool to Goole in ballast.

128: *Modern Athens*

Built: 1836
133 tons. Length 119.6 feet
Builders: T. Adamson, Broughty Ferry
Engine builders: P. Borrie, Dundee. Engine type: two-cylinder side-lever; 120 hp
Hull material: Wood
Owners: Dundee & Leith Steam Packet Co.
1836: Entered service from Leith to Dundee.
1840: May – Registered by J. Small and others, Dundee.
1844: August – Sold to Dundee & Edinburgh Steam Packet Co.
1846: March – Owners now Edinburgh & Dundee Steam Packet Co.
1846: June – Sold to J. Ramsay and others, Islay. Operated from Glasgow to Port Ellen and from West Loch Tarbert to Port Ellen.
1849: October – Sold to Tod & McGregor in part exchange for *Islay* (No. 208). Laid up.
1852: January – Sold to J. Bremner, Liverpool, and A. Bremner, Glasgow.
1854: July – Sold to F. McMahon, J. Craggs and others, Liverpool. May have been used as a tug.
1857: Sold to T. Walker and others, Liverpool.
1864: Reduced to a coal hulk.
No information is available about her final fate.

129: *Tartar*

Built: 1836
218 tons. Length 148 feet
Builders: Wood & Mills, Little Miln, Dumbuck
Engine builders: Robert Napier, Camlachie. Engine type: two-cylinder; 340 hp
Hull material: Wood
Owners: Clyde Steam Navigation Co.
1836: Entered service from Greenock to Belfast.
1844: February – Owners became City of Glasgow Steam Packet Co.
1846: Placed on the service from Glasgow to Oban, Tobermory and Portree.
1851: April – Sold to W. Denny & Bros, Dumbarton.
1852: May: Broken up.

130: *Tobermory*

Built: 1836
55 tons. Length 80.1 feet
Builders: Scott & Co., Greenock
Engine builders: Scott Sinclair & Co., Greenock. 40 hp
Hull material: Wood
Owners: Tobermory Steam Boat Co.
1836: Entered service from Glasgow to the West Highlands.
1838: February – Sold to Thomson and McConnell.
1839: June – Sold to J. Tomkinson, Liverpool. Placed on the Liverpool–Woodside ferry
    service.
1840: June – Owners now J. Tomkinson, Liverpool, and J. Turner, Fleetwood.
1846: July – Sold to the Commissioners for the Improvement of the Township of
    Birkenhead.
1849: Broken up.

131: *Luna*

Number in Williamson's list: 109
Built: 1837
49.55 tons. Length 108.6 feet
Builders: J. & W. Napier, Govan
Engine builders: J. & W. Napier, Govan. Engine type: steeple; 45 hp
Hull material: Wood
Owners: J. & W. Napier
1837: Entered service from Greenock to Kilmun. Was the first Clyde steamer with a tubular
    boiler.
1839: By now operating from Glasgow to Helensburgh.
1843: May – Sold to J. B. MacBrayne and John McIndoe.
1843: December – Sold to A. McGeorge, Janet McIndoe and others, Glasgow.
1844: November – Sold to J. Kibble, Glasgow.
1846: May – Sold to J. R. Mullens, London.
1846: October – Sold to J. Mason, Memel. Operated out of Memel, now Klaipeda in Lithuania.

1867: Sold to Stantier and Becker, Memel.
1869: No record after this date, probably broken up by then.

132: *Grand Turk*

Number in Williamson's list: 110
Built: 1837
369 gross tons. Length 135.3 feet
Builders: R. Duncan & Co., Greenock
Engine builders: Murdoch, Aitken & Co. Engine type: 160 hp
Hull material: Wood
Owner: W. Young, Glasgow
1837: June – Entered service from Glasgow to Rothesay and Millport.
1837: November – Sold to Commercial Steam Packet Co., London.
1838: Operated from London to Boulogne.
1838: Commenced operation from Weymouth to Cherbourg and the Channel Islands and from Guernsey to Morlaix weekly.
1841: September – Made an excursion from Southampton round the Isle of Wight.
1843: Sold to South Western Steam Packet Co., Southampton.
1847: Summer and autumn – Operated from Southampton to Plymouth and Penzance.
1847: October – Owners became New South Western Steam Navigation Co., Southampton.
1849: Chartered in connection with P&O. Operated from Alexandria to Beirut and Tripoli.
1851: Charter ended: Operated from Southampton to Le Havre and Morlaix.
1854: Service finished.
1856: Broken up.

133: *Rothsay Castle* (1837)

Number in Williamson's list: 111
Built: 1837
96.18 tons. Length 133.8 feet
Builders: Tod & McGregor, Mavisbank
Engine builders: Tod & McGregor, Mavisbank. Engine type: single-cylinder; 100 hp
Hull material: Iron
Owners: Castle Steam Packet Co.
1837: Entered service from Glasgow to Rothesay.
1842: April – Owners became Glasgow Castle S. P. Co.
1846: Sold to Glasgow & Liverpool Steam Shipping Co. (G. & J. Burns).
1847: Moved to the Glasgow–Ardrishaig service for one year only, extended to Inveraray on Saturdays.
1849: Operated from Inverness to Little Ferry and Inverness to Banavie.
1851: August – Sold to H. P. Maples and W. Denny & Bros. Placed on the Newhaven–Dieppe service.
1851: November – Owners now W. Denny & Bros.
1855: Back on the Ardrishaig service.
1856: Back on the Rothesay service.
1857: Sailed for Australia under sail.
1857: 13 February – Reported wrecked at St Thomas.

1857: April – Reported for sale at St Thomas. Another source states broken down at Georgetown, Demerara, at this time.

No further information is available.

134: *Isle Of Arran* (1837)

Number in Williamson's list: 164
Built: 1837
79 tons, 77 tons (1846), 153 gross tons (1860). Length 98.4 feet, 110.6 feet (1846), 125.9 feet (1860)
Builders: John Wood & Co., Port Glasgow
Engine builders: Robert Napier, Lancefield. Engine type: single-steeple; 60 hp
Hull material: Wood, flush-decked
Owners: Arran Steam Vessel Co., Irvine
1837: Entered service from Ardrossan to Lamlash. Claimed erroneously to be the final Clyde steamer to be built with a wooden hull. Some sources state built 1847.
1846: Owners became Isle of Arran Shipping Co., Lamlash. Rebuilt and lengthened by 12.2 feet.
1850: 6 February – Seriously damaged by fire at Ardrossan.
1850: 10 August – Returned to service after repairs.
1860: January – Sold to J. MacMillican, Invergordon. Rebuilt and lengthened by 15.3 feet.
1860: May – Sold to J. Johnston, Leith. Operated in the Firth of Forth.
1861: December – Sold to R. Reeve and J. B. Clarke, Norwich. Service not known.
1863: June – Sold to W. Adamson, Willington Quay (River Tyne). Service not known.
1864: Converted to screw propulsion.
1867: January – Sold to C. M. Butt, London.
1867: July – Sold to J. Martin, Dublin.
1868: 25 April – Lost off Holyhead.

135: *British Queen*

Number in Williamson's list: 112
Built: 1838
81 tons. Length 125.4 feet
Builders: T. Wingate & Co., Springfield, Glasgow
Engine builders: T. Wingate & Co., Springfield, Glasgow. 90 hp
Hull material: Wood
Owners: J. Henderson and A. McKellar
1838: Entered service from Glasgow to Helensburgh and the Gareloch.
1851: Broken up.

136: *Argyle* (1838)

Number in Williamson's list: 113
Built: 1838
106.98 tons. Length 118.7 feet
Builders: R. Duncan & Co., Greenock
Engine builders: Smith & Rodger. 85 hp

Hull material: Unknown
Owners: J. McDonald , J. Fleming and B. R. Ronald
1838: Commenced operation from Glasgow to Inveraray.
1838: November – Owners now J. McCall & Co., J. Fleming and B. R. Ronald.
1839: Boiler exploded at Renfrew.
1840: 4 December – Wrecked at Vera Cruz in the Gulf of Mexico.

137: *Royal Victoria*

Number in Williamson's list: 115
Built: 1838
58.4 tons. Length 106.8 feet
Builders: Barr & McNab, Paisley
Engine builders: Barr & McNab, Paisley. 53 hp
Hull material: Iron
Owner: W. Barr, Paisley
1838: Unknown service.
1840: May: Sold to A. McConnell and D. Chapmen, Glasgow. Operated from Glasgow to Belfast.
1841: January – Operated from Glasgow to Garelochhead.
1841: March – Sold to Robert Napier.
1841: December – Commenced operating from Greenock to Helensburgh and the Gareloch in connection with the Glasgow, Paisley & Greenock Railway.
1842: June – Purchased by the Railway Steam Packet Co.
1843: Ceased operation.
1845: April – Taken by Barr & McNab in part exchange for *Petrel* (No. 183).
c. 1846: Sold to W. Willoughby & Son, Liverpool. Operated from Liverpool to Tranmere.
1846: March – Sold to the Dundee & Perth S. P. Co. Operated from Dundee to Perth and on excursions.
1850: Chartered to the Alloa, Stirling & Kincardine S. S. Co. Operated from Granton to Stirling.
1853: Chartered to Hall & Stoker. Operated from Leith to Kirkcaldy.
1854: September – Sold to J. Tarleton, Rhyl.
1855: Sold to Chester Steam Packet Co. From now on operated as a tug and also as a ferry.
1856: December – Sold to J. Johnson, Liverpool.
c. 1875: Scrapped, although she was not removed from the registers until 1885.

138: *Robert Burns* (1838)

Number in Williamson's list: 116
Built: 1838
110.3 tons. Length 132.1 feet
Builders: R. Duncan & Co., Greenock
Engine builders: David Napier, Lancefield. 80 hp
Hull material: Iron
Owner: W. Young
1838: Entered service from Glasgow to Largs, Millport and Ayr, possibly extended to Stranraer.

1841: July – Sold to J. Robinson, London.

1841: August – Commenced operating from Southampton to Le Havre, Granville and Jersey.

1841: November – Sold to the Commercial Steam Navigation Co. (W. J. Chaplin, W. Humphreys and J. W. Drew).

1843: June – Sold to the South Western Steam Packet Co.

1847: October – Now owned by the New South Western Steam Packet Co.

1853: Scrapped.

139: *Windsor Castle* (1838)

Number in Williamson's list: 118
Built: 1838
1541 gross tons. Length 128.7 feet
Builders: Tod & McGregor, Mavisbank
Engine builders: Tod & McGregor, Mavisbank. Engine type: steeple; 80 hp
Hull material: Iron
Owners: Castle Steam Packet Co.
1838: Entered service from Glasgow to Inverness.
1839: Now operating from Glasgow to Rothesay.
1842: April – Owners became the Glasgow Castle Steam Packet Co.
1844: August – Sold to A. and P. Greig and T. Barclay, Edinburgh. Entered service from Granton to Newcastle and Granton to Dundee.
1844: 1 October – Made a special cruise from Granton to cruise round Queen Victoria's new steam yacht, moored off Dundee. On the return journey, sailing close inshore, she hit the Carr Rock beacon and was run ashore 2 miles east of Crail. All the crew and passengers were saved, most by fishing boats. When the tide came in, the steamer rolled on her side and broke up.

140: *Tarbert Castle* (1838)

Built: 1838
121 gt. Length feet
Builders: Hedderwick & Rankin, Lancefield
Engine builders: Tod & McGregor, Springfield. Engine type: steeple; 90 hp
Hull material: Iron, flush-decked
Owners: Castle Steam Packet Co.
1838: April – Launched.
1838: Entered service from Glasgow to Inveraray.
1839: 17 January – Wrecked in Kilfinan Bay, Loch Fyne.
The hull was salvaged and later scrapped. The engines were salvaged and installed in *Inverary Castle* (No. 146).

141: *Queen Of Scots*

Built: 1838
114 gross tons. Length 118.5 feet
Builders: Smith & Rodger, Govan

Engine builders: Smith & Rodger, Govan. 60 hp
Hull material: Wood
Owners: L. McLellan and T. Barclay
1838: Entered service from Glasgow to Arrochar, including some Communion Sunday sailings.
1838: Moved to Loch Lomond. Operated on the loch.
1841: Moved off the loch.
1843: Operated from Ayr to Girvan and Campbeltown.
Late 1840s: Made some excursions to Arrochar.
1849: Owner now solely T. Barclay.
1852: Broken up.

142: *Glow-Worm*

Built: 1838
161 tons. Length 153 feet
Builders: Laird, Birkenhead
Engine builders: Robert Napier, Govan. Engine type: two-cylinder; 100 hp
Hull material: Iron
Owners: T. Assheton Smith II (Yacht)
1838: Built as a paddle yacht.
1844: Sold to the Ardrossan Steam Navigation Co. Operated from Ardrossan to Belfast.
1850: Route changed to Ardrossan–Portrush and Londonderry.
1851: Chartered by J. Ramsey and others. Operated from Glasgow to Islay and Stornoway in 1851, 1853 and 1855.
1855: July – Returned to the Ardrossan–Belfast service.
1856: Sold to Stephens & Co., Drogheda. Operated out of Drogheda.
1858: Taken over by the Glasgow Underwriters Association.
1859: Wrecked.

143: *Sir William Wallace* (1839)

Number in Williamson's list: 117
Built: 1839
195 gross tons. Length 129.9 feet
Builders: R. Duncan & Co., Greenock
Engine builders: R. Duncan & Co., Greenock. 120 hp
Hull material: Wood
Owner: W. Young
1839: Entered service from Glasgow to Largs, Millport and Ayr, possibly extended to Stranraer.
1841: July – Sold to J. Robinson, London.
1841: November – Owners now C. Bleaden, J. Harman and J. Whisson, London.
1843: February – Owners now W. Coates, J. Brothers and J. Robinson, London.
1843: Chartered to the New Commercial Steam Packet Co. London. Operated from Dover to Boulogne.
1847: February – Purchased by the Commercial Steam Packet Co. London. Registered by J. Hopkinson and E. Morris, London.

1855: Broken up.

Some sources have confused this steamer with the screw steamer *Ayrshire Lass* (1848).

144: *Ayrshire Lassie*

Number in Williamson's list: 122
Built: 1839
84.19 tons. Length 123.8 feet
Builders: R. Duncan & Co., Greenock
Engine builders: T. Wingate & Co., Springfield. Engine type: side-lever; 95 hp
Hull material: Wood
Owners: W. Young, H. Price and J. Hunter
1839: Entered service from Glasgow to Largs, Millport and Ayr.
1841: September – Owners now J. Hunter and H. Price. Operated from Ayr to Stranraer and from Ayr to Belfast.
1841: October – Sold to J. Southern and others, Liverpool.
1845: Now used as a tug at Liverpool, and from Liverpool to North Wales.
1848: January – Sold to J. Spinks and S. Harden, Liverpool.
1850: October – Sold to J. H. Bryant, Brighton. Operated from Brighton and Newhaven to Dieppe.
1851: June – Sold to Maples and Morris.
1851: November – Sold to W. Denny & Bros, Dumbarton.
1851: December – Sold to J. Crabb and others, Liverpool. Used as a tug.
1858: June – Broken up.

145: *Shandon* (1839)

Number in Williamson's list: 123
Built: 1839
105 tons. Length 134.9 feet
Builders: Wood & Reid, Port Glasgow
Engine builders: Robert Napier, Lancefield. Engine type: side-lever; 90 hp
Hull material: Wood
Owners: R. Napier and R. G. Clelland
1839: Entered service from Glasgow to Helensburgh and Garelochhead.
1841: May – Sold to Thomson & McConnell. Moved to the Glasgow–Ardrishaig service.
1842: According to some sources, ran from Glasgow to Dunoon and Kilmun.
1844: March – Sold to City of Glasgow Steam Packet Co.
1846: Call at Tarbert introduced.
1846: Moved to the Crinan–Oban route on the Ardishaig service.
1851: May – Taken over by D. Hutcheson & Co.
1853: June – Sold to J. Anderson, Glasgow/Melbourne.
1854: Sailed to Melbourne under sail (with paddles removed). Arrived at Melbourne 24 April 1854.
1854: August – Sold to Wharton Caird & Co., Melbourne. Operated from Melbourne to Geelong thrice weekly.
1854: November – Sold to Crawford Maine, Melbourne.
1858: Commenced operating from Melbourne to Port Albert.

1861: February – Sold to W. W. Law, Hong Kong. Moved to Singapore and later to northern China, where she operated to Ningpo.
1865: Broken up.

146: *Inverary Castle* (1839)

Number in Williamson's list: 125
Built: 1839
120 tons, 209 gross tons (1862), 230 gross tons (1873). Length 136.1 feet, 140 feet (1857), 158.5 feet (1862), 172.9 feet (1873)
Builders: Tod & McGregor, Mavisbank
Engine builders: Tod & McGregor, Mavisbank. Engine type: two-cylinder steeple (1838); 100 hp
Hull material: Iron
Owners: Castle Steam Packet Co.
1839: Entered service on the Glasgow–Inveraray cargo service. Fitted with the engine of *Tarbert Castle* (1838) (No. 140)
1842: April – Owners became Glasgow Castle Steam Packet Co.
1846: June – Now owned by Glasgow & Liverpool Shipping Co. (G. & J. Burns).
1852: February – Sold to W. Denny & Bros., Dumbarton.
1851: Sold to the Glasgow & Lochfine Steam Packet Co.
1857: February – Sold to D. Hutcheson & Co. Laid up. Lengthened by 3.9 feet.
1859: Operated from Glasgow to Oban and Inverness via Mull of Kintyre for this year only.
1860: Returned to the Glasgow–Inveraray cargo run.
1862: Lengthened by 18.5 feet. Renamed *Inveraray Castle*.
1873: Lengthened by 14.4 feet.
1879: May – Owner now David MacBrayne.
1892: Withdrawn and broken up.

147: *Superb* (1839)

Number in Williamson's list: 126
Built: 1839
76 tons. Length 136.4 feet
Builders: J. Reid & Co., Port Glasgow
Engine builders: Robert Napier, Lancefield. 65 hp
Hull material: Iron
Owners: Alloa, Stirling & Kincardine Steamboat Co.
1839: Built for the Alloa, Stirling & Kincardine Steamboat Co., but was rejected because she drew too much water. Purchased by the Shandon & Glasgow Steam Packet Co. (Robert Napier). Entered service from Glasgow to Garelochhead.
1848: Sold to Henderson and McKellar.
1850: March – Sold to T. Rose, Jersey (Jersey Steam Navigation Co.). Entered service from Jersey to St Malo and Granville.
1850: 24 September – Wrecked on the Minquiere Rocks, about 9 miles south of Jersey.

148: *Warrior*

Number in Williamson's list: 127
Built: 1839
162 gross tons. Length 128.3 feet
Builders: R. Duncan & Co., Greenock
Engine builders: T. Wingate & Co., Springfield. Engine type: steeple; 110 hp
Hull material: Wood
Owners: D. McKellar, J. Fleming and W. Allan
1839: Entered service from Glasgow to Ayr and from Glasgow to Greenock, Largs, Millport, Ardrossan and Arran.
1841: Chartered to the Board of Excise, Dublin. Used for Survey and Excise work around the coast of Ireland.
1844: Purchased by the Board of Excise, Dublin.
1851: September – Sold to J. Dickie, Glasgow.
1851: October – Sold to J. McKissock, Plymouth.
1853: February – Sold to W. T. Chafe, Devonport.
1853: Converted to a sailing ship.
1854: August – Sold to unknown owners in Portugal.
No record of her eventual fate is available.

149: *Maid of Leven*

Built: 1839
140 gross tons. Length 103.5 feet, 124.3 feet (1844)
Builders: Barr & McNab, Paisley
Engine builders: Barr & McNab, Paisley. 60 hp
Hull material: Iron
Owners: Dumbarton & Glasgow Steam Packet Co., Dumbarton
1839: Entered service from Glasgow to Dumbarton.
1841: Moved to the Glasgow–Garelochhead service.
1844: June – Sold to J. Gladstone, Montrose. Lengthened by 20.8 feet.
1847: January – Chartered to the Edinburgh & Northern Railway and Edinburgh, Perth & Dundee Railway. Operated from Granton to Burntisland. Also operated in the Tay in this year.
1853: July – Sold to C. Watson, Middlesbrough.
1854: March – Sold to W. J. Anderson, Leith. Operated from Leith to Largo.
1857: October – Sold to Paris owners.
No further information is available.

150: *Sultan*

Built: 1839
57 tons. Length 104.8 feet
Builders: J. McAuslan, Dumbarton
Engine builders: Robert Napier, Lancefield. 50 hp
Hull material: Wood
Owners: J. Henderson, A. McKellar
1839: Entered service from Glasgow to Helensburgh.
1845: October – Sold to A. Frazer, Newcastle.

1847: September – Sold to Dampskibet Lolland, Nakskov, Denmark. Renamed *Lolland*. Route unknown.

1856: Sold to C. P. A. Koch, Copenhagen.

1857: Broken up.

The Broomielaw was the departure point for Clyde steamer trips prior to the opening of the railways to the coast railheads. Here can be seen the basic paddle housings that were used before the landing platforms on top of them were introduced. Captain McLean's *Marquis of Bute* is lying of the berth with the bow of the Dunoon & Rothesay Carriers' *Dunoon Castle* in the right foreground; *Petrel*, then owned by H. Dore and on a service to Largs, Millport and Arran, is inboard of her; and Peter Denny's *Loch Lomond* on the Dumbarton service is to the right of *Marquis of Bute*'s funnel. This picture must have been taken in 1868, as *Loch Lomond* was laid up after that season.

The Broomielaw saw large crowds waiting to embark on the steamers, as seen in this view with the Loch Goil steamer *Carrick Castle* having just departed and Captain Bob Campbell's *Benmore* with the familiar Campbell white funnel at the berth. This was taken between the introduction of *Benmore* in 1876 and the sale of *Carrick Castle* to Leith owners in 1881.

The crowds are evident on the decks of the steamers and on land in this view from 1885 with Bob Campbell's *Benmore* awaiting loading, his *Meg Merrilies*, still with two funnels prior to her reboiling in 1888, in mid-stream, and the bow of the Arrochar steamer *Chancellor* of 1880, Buchanan's 1864 *Eagle* and his recently-purchased *Vivid*, all with heavy passenger loads already and still moored at the quay.

The Broomielaw between 1912 and 1914 with Buchanan's *Isle of Arran* berthing and the Firth of Clyde Steam Packet Co.'s *Ivanhoe* having just departed for Rothesay.

The promenade deck extended to the bow with the sides open below enabled passengers to go right to the bow while ropes were handled from the deck below, as seen here on *Eagle III* heading down river on her daily sailing to Rothesay in the 1930s.

An image of the 1852 *Eagle*, showing the haystack boiler apparently exhausting directly up the funnel.

Craigendoran Pier, built in 1882, showing the two arms, with three North British paddlers berthed.

Greenock Princes Pier, showing the Italianate pier buildings dating from 1894 and *Neptune* berthing.

Gourock Pier, dating from the opening of the railway extension from Greenock in 1889, with *Marchioness of Breadalbane* berthed, showing the magnificent half-timbered pier building which has now been almost completely demolished, with only two or three bays remaining, now finished in grey.

Looking towards the Cloch lighthouse from Kirn, with the Caledonian Steam Packet *Galatea* and a GSWR paddler in view, *c.* 1895.

The present *Waverley* under construction at A. & J. Inglis at Pointhouse, at the location of the present Riverside Museum, in 1946, showing the paddle wheel housing and fore deck.

Waverley being fitted out at A. & J. Inglis' yard at Pointhouse in 1947, still to receive her funnels, with DEPV *Talisman* on the slipway for overhaul in the background.

The launch of *Isle of Arran* on 14 May 1892 at T. B. Seath's yard at Rutherglen.

Columba and the 1891 *Lord of the Isles* racing in 1910 in Loch Fyne.

Sultan in Williamson colours prior to her sale to the GSWR in 1890 and *Chancellor* of 1880 in Lochgoil colours after 1885 racing, both burning copious amounts of coal, off Greenock.

A three-steamer race with three GSWR steamers. *Marquis of Bute* is about to be passed by *Neptune* and *Chancellor* is drawing ahead in the background, racing off Greenock in the evening commuter rush to the coast.

Above: The race has finished as the victorious steamer approaches the pier, Craigmore in this instance, with a North British steamer arriving and another from the same fleet not far behind her.

Right: The Rothesay steamer *Neptune* of 1861, which had been sold for running the blockade after only two seasons on the Clyde, captured by the Union Navy and put into service in September 1863 as the patrol steamer USS *Clyde*.

Rothesay Castle of 1861, which had been sold for running the blockade, survived the Civil War and was sold to Canadian owners and rebuilt as *Southern Belle* to run from Toronto to Hamilton on Lake Ontario.

The *Rothesay Castle* of 1865 went to Bordeaux, and is seen to the left here as *Gironde-Garonne No. 1ère* at Royan on the Atlantic coast with the similar *Gironde-Garonne No 2*, which was built by H. McIntyre of Paisley in 1880, to the right and a good crowd on the pier.

MacBrayne's *Chevalier* of 1866 aground on Barmore Island, near Tarbert, after her starboard paddle wheel fractured during a gale and she ran aground on 25 March 1927.

Mountaineer of 1852 doing what it says on the tin! Aground on Lady Rock off the south end of Lismore on 27 September 1889 after the tide had gone down.

Redgauntlet ashore on the Iron Rocks in southern Arran on 14 August 1893.

Lord of the Isles of 1877 when in service on the Thames, at St Paul's Wharf on the Thames above London Bridge, between 1891 and 1898. She had been fitted with telescopic funnels to pass under London Bridge, and the fore funnel is partially collapsed in this view.

Rolls-Royce *Lucy*, as used for experimental jet propulsion trials in 1950 and 1951.

An unusual visitor berthed at Craigendoran during the Second World War, *Fair Maid* from the Forth; previously Buchanan's *Isle of Skye* and built in 1886 for Captain Bob Campbell of Kilmun as *Madge Wildfire*, she had served in the CSP fleet under that name from 1888 until 1911. She was used as a decontamination vessel during the war years but had a week replacing *Lucy Ashton* in spring 1944, and is seen here dressed for VE Day in 1945.

Dunoon Pier with the *Isle of Arran* just departing. The pier is little altered today.

Lord of the Isles (1891) with a full complement of passengers after her promenade deck had been extended to the bow..

Arrochar, unusually with four steamers berthed, from an album of photographs taken by the contractors building the West Highland Line. From the left can be seen *Chancellor* in GSWR colours, the NB's *Lady Rowena*, the GSWR's *Neptune* and the CSP's *Marchioness of Lorne*.

The 1899 *Waverley* with an assortment of smaller pleasure craft, *c.* 1920.

Waverley berthed on the outside of Millport Pier in CalMac colours in 1973.

Rothesay Pier in an image from a lantern slide, probably from the 1870s, with what is probably *Athole* (1866) lying across the end of the pier.

Rothesay in a pre-1910 postcard view with *Kenilworth* departing, *Marchioness of Breadalbane* across the west end of the pier and *Columba* arriving.

Rothesay pier in pre-1923 days with *Jupiter* departing and the 1899 *Waverley* berthed along the pier.

The western end of Rothesay Pier with *Ivanhoe* berthed across the end, *Columba* arriving and *Eagle III* and *Duchess of Rothesay* along the front of the pier.

Marmion as a minesweeper 1915–19, showing the sweeping equipment on the stern and the built up bow as well as her gun.

The unfortunate *Fair Maid* of 1915, built as a Clyde paddle steamer but which never saw service as such, being called up for war service while fitting out and sunk after less than a year's service as a minesweeper.

HMS Eagle III in war service as a minesweeper in April 1916.

Grenadier as the minesweeper HMS *Grenade* between 1916 and 1919.

The design of the 1934 twins *Mercury* and *Caledonia* enabled cars to be carried at certain states of the tide, as seen in this 1930s view of a car being loaded onto *Mercury* at Millport.

CHAPTER 4
Steamers Built 1840–49

151: *Flambeau*

Number in Williamson's list: 128
Built: 1840
180 gross tons. Length 139.2 feet
Builders: R. Duncan & Co., Greenock
Engine builders: R. Duncan & Co., Greenock. 80 hp
Hull material: Wood
Owners: J. Thomson, J. Miller & Co.
1840: 13 March – Launched.
1840: Entered service from Glasgow to Arran.
1841: Operated for this year only from Greenock to Rothesay.
1842: March – Sold to Caird & Co., Greenock.
1847: March – Sold to S. Howes Jr, Liverpool. Used as a tug and excursion steamer at Liverpool.
1847: April – Sold to J. Crippin and others, Liverpool.
1847: 19 December – Sank after a collision in the Mersey with the ferry *Wirral*.

152: *Dumbarton Castle* (1840)

Number in Williamson's list: 129
Built: 1840
83 tons. Length 114.7 feet
Builders: G. Mills, Bowling
Engine builders: G. Mills, Bowling. 65 hp
Hull material: wood
Owners: Dumbarton & Glasgow Steam Packet Co.
1840: Entered service from Glasgow to Dumbarton.
1847: Sold to the Dumbarton Steamboat Co.
1850: February – Sold to A. Rigby and T. Prestopino, Liverpool. Used as a tug and excursion steamer at Liverpool. Renamed *Prince Albert*.
1851: 4 August – Sank off Southport while on an excursion from Preston to the Menai Straits.

153: *Prince Albert* (1840)

Built: 1840
73 tons. Length 107.6 feet
Builders: T. Wingate & Co., Whiteinch
Engine builders: T. Wingate & Co., Whiteinch. 65 hp
Hull material: Iron
Owners: Dumbarton Steamboat Co.
1840: Entered service from Glasgow to Dumbarton
1848: Sold to J. Sothern and others, Liverpool. Operated from Liverpool-Egremont.
1849: Sold to G. P. Sanderson, Liverpool.
1850: 9 August – Lost.

154: *Telegraph*

Number in Williamson's list: 131
Built: 1841
100 tons. Length 118 feet 7 inches
Builders: Hedderwick & Rankine, Lancefield
Engine builders: J. M. Rowan, Greenock. Engine type: locomotive type; 50 hp
Hull material: Wood
Owner: J. McIndoe
1841: Entered service from Glasgow to Helensburgh. Fitted with experimental high-pressure
    engine.
1842: 21 March – Destroyed by a boiler explosion at Helensburgh, twenty-five killed, hull
    blown apart.

155: *Loch Goil* (1841)

Number in Williamson's list: 132
Built: 1841
tons. Length feet
Builders: Unknown, Clyde
Engine builders: Unknown, Clyde. Engine type: steeple; ? hp
Hull material: Wood
Owners: Loch Goil & Loch Long Steamboat Company
1841: Entered service from Glasgow to Lochgoilhead.
1846: Renamed *Powerful*. Moved away from the Lochgoilhead service.
1850: Operated from Ardrossan to Arran.
No further information is available about this steamer.

156: *Glasgow* (1841)

Built: 1841
63 tons. Length 80.5 feet
Builders: Caird & Co., Greenock
Engine builders: Caird & Co., Greenock. Engine type: side-lever; 35 hp

Hull material: Iron
Owners: Clyde Shipping Co.
1841: Entered service as a luggage boat from Glasgow to Greenock.
1859: January – Sold to John Steel and others, Greenock.
1859: February – Sold to Alexander McGeorge, Bowling.
1861: January – Sold to Glasgow & Greenock Shipping Co. (James Steel & Sons).
1861: August – Sold to J. Cowie and others, Manchester, registered at Liverpool.
1863: Sold to M. Wells, Lurgan, Co. Armagh, continued to be registered at Liverpool.
1864: Scrapped.

157: *Greenock* (1841)

Built: 1841
74 tons. Length 80.7 feet
Builders: Caird & Co., Greenock
Engine builders: Caird & Co., Greenock. Engine type: side-lever; 35 hp
Hull material: Iron
Owners: Clyde Shipping Co.
1841: Entered service as a luggage boat from Glasgow to Greenock.
1859: January – Sold to John Steel and others, Greenock.
1859: February – Sold to Alexander McGeorge, Bowling.
1861: January – Sold to Glasgow & Greenock Shipping Co. (James Steel & Sons).
1861: August – Sold to J. Cowie and others, Manchester, registered at Liverpool.
1863: Sold to M. Wells, Lurgan, registered at Liverpool.
1864: April – Engines removed and converted to a barge.
1865: October – Sold to A. Cansh, Liverpool.
1867: November – Sold to W. Barrel, Liverpool.
1870: Sold to P. & H. Bagot, Liverpool.
1876: Sold to J. T. Bragg, Liverpool.
1876: Scrapped.

158: *Lady Brisbane*

Number in Williamson's list: 134
Built: 1842
81.7 tons. Length 133 feet
Builders: Barr & McNab, Paisley
Engine builders: Barr & McNab, Paisley. Engine type: steeple; 70 hp
Hull material: Iron
Owners: W. Young and M. Preston
1842: Entered service from Millport and Largs to Glasgow. Started in some years from Ardossan.
1844: Operated from Ayr to Stranraer for two years.
1846: 9 August – Made an excursion from Stranraer to Rothesay.
1845: 16 August – Made an excursion from Stranraer to Campbeltown.
1846: Back on the Millport–Glasgow service.
1849: Sold to the Glasgow, Largs & Millport Union Steam Boat Co.
1862: Placed on the Glasgow–Arrochar service.

1864: Back on the Millport–Glasgow service.

1868: Sank after collision with tug *Flying Cloud* off Bowling 18 April 1868, raised and repaired.

1869: Sold to Keith and Campbell. Placed on the Glasgow–Dumbarton service. Renamed *Balmoral*.

1875: Moved to the Glasgow–Gareloch service.

1884: Sold to W. Buchanan. Operated from Greenock to Helensburgh with one daily trip to Lochgoilhead.

1891: Machinery collapsed between Helensburgh and Greenock after a race down the Gareloch, and was unable to be repaired. Her Clyde career of forty-nine years was a record for a steamer of this era. Sold to unknown owners at Newry and converted for use there as a coal hulk.

No information is available about her final fate.

159: *Duntroon Castle*

Number in Williamson's list: 136
Built: 1842
258 gross tons. Length 140.1 feet
Builders: Anderson & Gilmour, Glasgow
Engine builders: Anderson & Gilmour, Glasgow. Engine type: steeple; 130 hp
Hull material: Iron
Owners: Glasgow Castle Steam Packet Co.
1842 Entered service from Glasgow to Inveraray.

1846: Taken over by G. & J. Burns, managed by Thomson and McConnell.

1849: Moved to the Glasgow–Oban and Portree route.

1850: 26 October – Collided off the Cloch lighthouse with *Duke of Cornwall* (No. 160), which sank.

1851: Taken over by D. Hutcheson & Co.

1851: Sold to Maples and Morris, London. Used as a reserve steamer from Newhaven to Dieppe.

1859: Sold to T. Chiltern Jr and M. M. Miller.

1863: Sold to E. Drouke, Cork.

1863: Lost.

160: *Duke of Cornwall*

Built: 1842
189 gross tons. Length 122.9 feet
Builders: Caird & Co., Greenock
Engine builders: J. & W. Napier, Govan. Engine type: single-cylinder; 90 hp
Hull material: Iron, flush-decked
Owners: Campbeltown & Glasgow Steam Packet Joint Stock Co. Ltd
1842: Entered service from Glasgow to Campbeltown.

1847: Chartered to Portuguese Government during blockade of Porto.

1847: Re-boilered.

1850: 26 October – Sank after colliding off the Cloch lighthouse with *Duntroon Castle* (No. 159). Raised and returned to service.

1858: Laid up.
1866: 20 October – Scrapped.

161: *Loch Long* (1842)

Built: 1842
153 gross tons. Length 131.1 feet
Builders: W. Craig & Co., Glasgow
Engine builders: W. Craig & Co., Glasgow. 75 hp
Hull material: Flush-decked; iron
Owners: Lochgoil & Lochlong Steamboat Co.
1842: Entered service from Glasgow to Lochgoilhead.
1847: Chartered to the Furness Railway Co. Operated from Piel Pier, Barrow-in-Furness, to Fleetwood.
1848: December – Purchased by the Furness Railway Co. Renamed *Helvellyn*.
1867: September – Withdrawn.
1868: Sold to L. M. Le Blanch.
1870: Final year in British register.
No further information is available.

162: *Engineer*

Number in Williamson's list: 137
Built: 1843
202 gross tons. Length 168 feet
Builders: W. Napier & Son
Engine builders: J. & W. Napier, Govan. Engine type: steeple; 104 hp
Hull material: Iron
Owners: Holy Loch Steam Packet Co. (G. Lyon, W. Paterson, W. Chalmers).
1843: Entered service from Glasgow to Millport.
1845: Sold to Thomas Pearson, Liverpool. Route not known, may have been used as a tug.
1849: Sold to F. Greenstreet and T. Paton, Liverpool.
1850: Sold to G. S. Sanderson, Liverpool.
1851: Sold to T. Fletcher, Goole.
1852: Sold to T. Purnell, Scarborough.
1852: Sold to J. Ibbotson, Goole.
1853: Sold to owners in Belgium.
No record of her final fate can be found.

163: *Lady Kelburne*

Number in Williamson's list: 138
Built: 1843
158 gross tons. Length 149.2 feet
Builders: Barr & McNab, Paisley
Engine builders: Barr & McNab, Paisley. Engine type: steeple; 87 hp
Hull material: Iron

Owners: W. Young

1843: Entered service from Glasgow to Millport, on occasion extended to Arran.

1845: March – Operated from Ayr to Stranraer, relieving *Lady Brisbane*.

1846: Sold to Glasgow, Largs & Millport Union Steam Boat Co.

1867: Laid up.

1869: Sold to W. Wright. Did not sail again.

1877: Scrapped.

164: *Emperor*

Number in Williamson's list: 139

Built: 1843

62 tons. Length 121.7 feet

Builders: Tod & McGregor, Mavisbank

Engine builders: Tod & McGregor, Mavisbank. Engine type: steeple; 50 hp

Hull material: Iron

Owners: Henderson and McKellar

1843: Entered service from Glasgow to Garelochhead.

1853: Owner now J. Henderson. Operated excursions on the Firth of Clyde, including from Glasgow to the Holy Loch and the Gareloch. Made the first Sunday sailings on the Clyde, thus becoming the first 'Sunday Breaker'.

1853: Sold to J. Anderson.

1862: Laid up.

1863: Sold to P. L. Henderson. Operated from Greenock to Helensburgh in this and the following year. Renamed *Acquilla*.

1867: 6 June – Sank en route from Liverpool to Jersey.

165: *Gipsy*

Built: 1843

tons. Length feet

Builders: Unknown, Stirling

Engine builders: Unknown.

Hull material: Wood

Owner: Unknown, Stirling

1843: Built as an experimental craft for use on the Forth & Clyde Canal.

1843: Moved to Loch Katrine.

1843: Disappeared one night after only a week in service: it is believed she was maliciously scuttled by the owners of the large rowing boat, *Water Witch*, which she had replaced.

166: *Waterwitch*

Built: 1843
tons. Length 130 feet
Builders: Caird & Co., Greenock
Engine builders: Caird & Co., Greenock. Engine type: single diagonal; 50 hp
Hull material: Iron
Owners: Glasgow & Kilmun Steam Packet Co. (MacBrayne and McIndoe)
1843: 2 August – Launched.
1843: Entered service from Glasgow to Kilmun.
1844: 30 April – Following the bankruptcy of her owners, sold to the New Loch Lomond
　　Steamboat Co. Moved to Loch Lomond, operating from Balloch to Inverarnan.
1845: April – Sold to the Loch Lomond Steamboat Co.
1849: 3 August – Carried Prince Albert from Tarbert to Balloch.
1852: Withdrawn from service. Engines removed and installed in *Queen Victoria* (No. 228).

167: *Invincible*

Number in Williamson's list: 140
Built: 1844
131 gross tons. Length 130.1 feet
Builders: Tod & McGregor, Mavisbank
Engine builders: Tod & McGregor, Mavisbank. Engine type: steeple; 80 hp
Hull material: Iron
Owners: W. Allan and D. McKellar (Glasgow, Largs & Millport Union Steam Boat Co.)
1844: Entered service from Glasgow to Largs and Millport.
1853: Sold to Tod & McGregor.
1856: Final year on the Millport service.
1857: Sold to J. Barr
1858: Sold to J. Moss Jr.
1859: Sold to Z. C. Pearson, Hull.
1868: Last year in UK registry.

168: *Cardiff Castle*

Number in Williamson's list: 141
Built: 1844
207 gross tons. Length 170.3 feet
Builders: Caird & Co., Greenock
Engine builders: Caird & Co., Greenock. Engine type: double diagonal; 84 hp
Hull material: Iron
Owners: Glasgow Castle Steam Packet Co.
1844: Entered service from Glasgow to Rothesay. Also operated from Glasgow to Kilmun and
　　Glasgow to Inveraray at times during her early career.
1846: Sold to G. & J. Burns
1847: August – Moved to the Glasgow–Ardrishaig route.
1851: Sold to W. Johnston, N. McGill and D. Kerr. Continued on the same route.
c. 1853: Sold to the Eagle Steamer Co.

1855: Laid up.
1857: Returned to the Glasgow–Ardrishaig service.
1861: Sold to A. Watson.
1864: Started to be used as a Sunday Breaker.
1866: Sold to Henry Sharp.
1867: Sold to J. Dore and laid up.
Late 1860s: Broken up.

169: *Craignish Castle*

Number in Williamson's list: 142
Built: 1844
206 gross tons. Length 170.3 feet
Builders: Caird & Co., Greenock
Engine builders: Caird & Co., Greenock. Engine type: double diagonal; 84 hp
Hull material: Iron
Owners: Glasgow Castle Steam Packet Co. (W. Campbell, J. Watson, A. S. Finlay)
1844: Entered service on the Glasgow–Rothesay and Glasgow–Kilmun routes.
1849: Sold to G. & J. Burns.
1851: Sold to Glasgow & Lochfine S. P. Co. (W. Johnston, N. McGill and D. Kerr).
1862: Sold to W. J. Grazebrook, Liverpool, and supposedly renamed *Adler*, supposedly for
    blockade running, but there is no record of a steamer of that name ever being used as a
    blockade runner.
There is no further record of this steamer.

170: *Countess of Eglinton* (May have been named *Countess of Eglington*)

Number in Williamson's list: 143
Built: 1844
68.6 tons. Length 139.6 feet
Builders: Barr & McNab, Paisley
Engine builders: Barr & McNab, Paisley. Engine type: steeple; 70 hp
Hull material: Iron
Owner: W. Young
1844: Entered service from Glasgow to Largs and Millport.
1845: 27 March – Wrecked at Millport, when she blown from her moorings and drifted onto
    the Eileans; her engine was fitted in *Monarch* (No. 193) in 1846.

171: *Caledonia* (1844)

Number in Williamson's list: 144
Built: 1844
67 tons. Length 132 feet
Builders: Smith & Rodger, Govan
Engine builders: Smith & Rodger, Govan. 40 hp

Hull material: Iron
Owner: Unknown, Glasgow
1844: Entered service from Glasgow to Kilmun
No further information is available.
www.clydesite.co.uk erroneously describes this steamer as having been built for Cunard.

172: *Edinburgh Castle* (1844)

Number in Williamson's list: 145
Built: 1844
114 gross tons, 124 gross tons (1875). Length 138.1, 148.5 feet (1875)
Builders: Smith & Rodger, Govan
Engine builders: Smith & Rodger, Govan. Engine type: steeple; 45 hp
Hull material: Iron
Owners: Glasgow Castle Steam Packet Co.
1844: Entered service from Glasgow to Kilmun.
Early 1846: Moved to the Inverness–Banavie route and the Loch Ness mail run.
1846: June – Sold to Glasgow & Liverpool Steamship Company (G. & J. Burns).
1851: February – Sold to D. Hutcheson & Co.
1860: 18 March – Sold to R. Curle and J. Hamilton, Glasgow, and resold to unidentified foreign owners.
1860: 28 March – Sold back to D. Hutcheson & Co. after her previous owners did not take delivery.
1863: Re-boilered.
1875: June – Lengthened by 10.4 feet and fore and aft deck saloons added. Renamed *Glengarry*.
1879: Taken over by David MacBrayne.
1905: Owners became David MacBrayne Ltd.
1927: December – Withdrawn from service and scrapped at Inverness after a career of eighty-three years, by which time she was thought to be the oldest steamer in the world.

173: *Pioneer* (1844)

Number in Williamson's list: 146
Built: 1844
196 gt, 144 gt (1857), 209 gross tons (1875). Length 159.8 feet, 186.6 feet (1874)
Builders: Barr & McNab, Paisley or West Renfrew.
Engine builders: Barr & McNab, Paisley. Engine type: steeple; 95 hp
Hull material: Iron
Owners: Railway Steam Packet Co.
1844: Entered service on a rail-connected service from Greenock to Rothesay.
1847: Sold to G. & J. Burns. Moved to the Glasgow–Ardrishaig service.
1850: Back on the Greenock–Rothesay service.
1851: Sold to D. Hutcheson & Co. Returned to the Glasgow–Ardrishaig service.
1852: August – Started operating from Oban to Crinan, Mull and Fort William.
1862: Ran aground at Silvercraigs, east of Ardrishaig. Re-boilered. Clipper bow added. Moved to the Oban–Staffa and Iona and Oban–Corpach services.
1863: Added a weekly Oban–Gairloch trip.

1874/5 winter: Lengthened by 26.8 feet.
1879: Taken over by David MacBrayne.
1881: Moved to the Oban–Sound of Mull route.
1884: Re-boilered again.
1888: Stranded in Loch Sunart. Salvaged and returned to service.
1893: Laid up.
1895: Scrapped.

174: *Pilot*

Number in Williamson's list: 147
Built: 1844
192 gross tons. Length 137.4 feet
Builders: Barr & McNab, Paisley
Engine builders: Barr & McNab, Paisley. Engine type: steeple; 60 hp
Hull material: Iron
Owners: Railway Steam Packet Co.
1844: Entered service from Greenock to Kilmun on rail-connected services.
1847: Sold to G. & J. Burns.
1849: August – Moved to the Oban–Ballachulish and Fort William service for three months only.
1850: Sold to the Lochlomond Steamboat Co. Moved to Loch Lomond. Started operating excursions from Balloch.
1850: 17 July – Sank on Loch Lomond after striking an uncharted rock, raised and returned to service a month later. The rock she struck is known as the Pilot Rock to this day.
1853: Sold to R. Henderson and others, Belfast. Moved out of Loch Lomond and operated from Belfast to Bangor.
1862: Scrapped.

175: *Queen of Beauty*

Number in Williamson's list: 148
Built: 1844
140 gross tons. Length 137.8 feet
Builders: T. Wingate & Co., Springfield, Glasgow
Engine builders: (1) Robert Napier, Lancefield, engine built 1824, from *Leven* No. 46. (2) D. Napier 1850. Engine type: (1) side lever, 33hp; (2) side-lever; 30 hp
Hull material: Iron
Owners: J. Smith, J. Gourlay, J. Kibble
1844: Entered service from Glasgow to Kilmun. Fitted with engine from *Leven* (No. 46). Fitted with 'Kibble's patented chain floats', with a chain and two paddle shafts.
1845: December – Sold to W. Ainslie, Fort William. Moved to the Fort William to Oban, Staffa and Iona route. Normal paddles replaced the experimental ones.
1849: June – Sold to Glasgow & Liverpool Steam Shipping Co., Glasgow (G. & J. Burns).
1850: Renamed *Merlin*. New engine fitted. The original engine has been preserved in the open air at Dumbarton ever since, and is now in the grounds of the Denny Tank Museum. Placed on the Glasgow–Ardrishaig service.
1852: Sold to W. F. Johnstone. Operated from Glasgow to Rothesay.

1853: 18 October – Was in a collision at the Broomielaw, and was sunk for a while at Napier's Wharf.
1856: Damaged in a severe storm at Rothesay. Did not sail again.
Some sources state:
1859: Ran from Glasgow to Helensburgh. Regained the name *Queen of Beauty*.

176: *Albion* (1844)

Built: 1844
259 tons. Length 151 feet
Builders: Tod & McGregor, Meadowside
Engine builders: Tod & McGregor, Mavisbank. Engine type: two-cylinder; 150 hp
Hull material: Iron
Owners: Stranraer Steam Packet Co., Stranraer
1844: Entered service from Glasgow to Stranraer.
1849: Sold to the Glasgow & Stranraer Steam Packet Co., Stranraer.
1847: Calls at Campbeltown added.
1853: Also sailed to Belfast, Brodick and off Ballantrae.
1860: Reportedly operated from Copenhagen to Lübeck under the British flag.
1861: Reportedly operated from Flensburg to Aalborg, Denmark, under the British flag.
No further information is available.

177: *Dolphin* (1844)

Built: 1844
248 gross tons. Length 161 feet
Builders: Robert Napier & Sons, Govan
Engine builders: Robert Napier & Sons, Govan. Engine type: steeple; 100 hp
Hull material: Iron
Owners: G. & J. Burns
1844: August – Entered service from Crinan to Oban and Corpach.
1846: Moved to the Oban–Staffa and Iona routes.
1847: Now on a daily service from Oban to Staffa and Iona.
1851: Taken over by D. Hutcheson & Co. Returned to the Oban–Ballachulish and Fort William service as well as running to Staffa and Iona.
1853: Operated Oban–Loch Coruisk day trips in this year.
1855: Moved to a route from Glasgow to Portree, Gairloch, Ullapool and Lochinver alternating with Stornoway.
1857: Moved to the Glasgow–Inveraray cargo service.
1862: Sold to W. R. Grazebrook, Liverpool, for use as a blockade runner.
1863: 25 March – Captured Puerto Rico and St Thomas, en route to Nassau for blockade running, by USS *Wachusett*.
1864: July – Taken to New York and auctioned to unknown buyer. Renamed *Annie* (erroneously stated to be *Ruby* by some UK sources).
1865: 22 October – Wrecked on the south side of Fig Island in the Savannah River after hitting a snag. Raised by the Coast Wrecking Co. of New York after two hours of pumping.
1867: Sold to unknown owners in Memphis, Tennessee.
1874: Wrecked.

178: *Ondine*

Built: 1844
160 gross tons. Length 140 feet
Builders: Miller, Ravenhill & Co., Blackwall
Engine builders: Miller, Ravenhill & Co., Blackwall. Engine type: oscillating; 106 hp
Hull material: Iron, flush-decked
Owners: Dover Royal Mail Steam Packet Co.
1844: Entered service from Folkestone to Boulogne and from Dover to Calais and Ostend.
1847: Taken over by the Admiralty. Continued on the same service.
1854: Sold to Jenkins and Churchward, Dover.
1854: Sold or chartered for the *Morning Herald* newspaper. Used from Dover to Calais to carry urgent news dispatches to the newspaper.
1857: Renamed *Undine*.
1863: Sold to H. S. Forbes.
1864: Used for excursions from Dover. Regained the name *Ondine*.
1868: Sold to H. J. Sharpe.
1871: Sold to H. R. Price, London.
1871: Sold to Donald Munro, Stornoway. Operated from Stornoway to Ullapool.
1873: Taken over by Sir James Matheson, Stornoway.
1878: Sold to unknown owners in Glasgow. No longer sailing to Stornoway.
1883: Sold to C. Daniel, Portishead. Commenced operating on the Bristol Channel.
1886: Sold to unknown owners in London.
1889: Broken up.

179: *Mars* (1845)

Number in Williamson's list: 149
Built: 1845
94 tons. Length 135.8 feet
Builders: T. Wingate & Co., Springfield, Glasgow
Engine builders: T. Wingate & Co., Springfield. Engine type: steeple; 70 hp
Hull material: Iron
Owners: J. Fleming, W. Allan and D. A. McKellar
1844: Entered service from Glasgow to Largs and Millport.
1846: Now owned by the Glasgow, Largs & Millport Union Steam Boat Co.
1855: 10 April – Wrecked at Largs at mouth of the Gogo Burn after her paddle shaft broke in a storm.

180: *Culloden*

Number in Williamson's list: 150
Built: 1845
143 gross tons. Length 141 feet
Builders: Caird & Co., Greenock
Engine builders: Caird & Co., Greenock. Engine type: steeple; 60 hp
Hull material: Iron
Owners: J. Burns, W. Smellie, C. McKenzie (G. & J. Burns)

1845: Entered service from Glasgow to Kilmun.

1846: Operated from Inverness to Banavie for G. & J. Burns.

1847: June – Started operating from Oban to Loch Etive and Oban to Corpach via Ballachulish.

1848: April – Operated from Glasgow to Ardrishaig.

1850: Operated from Oban to Ballachulish.

1851: Sold to William Denny, Dumbarton.

1851: April – Sold to Maples and Morris. Operated from Newhaven to Dieppe.

1852: Sold to R. Henderson, Belfast. Operated from Belfast to Bangor.

1852: December – Sold again to William Denny, Dumbarton.

1853: Sold to the Derwent & Huon S. N. Co., Hobart, Tasmania, Australia. Sailed to Australia under sail, engine refitted when she got there. Operated out of Hobart.

1864: Ceased operating at Hobart.

1866: Sold to E. T. Beith, Sydney. Used as a tug at Sydney, with occasional passenger sailings.

1866: Sold to R. Whitaker and J. Broomfield.

1871: Sold to M. Johnston.

1871: 28 April – Wrecked in the Richmond River.

181: *Lochlomond* (1845)

Number in Williamson's list: 151
Built: 1845
106 gross tons. Length 124.1 feet
Builders: Denny Bros, Dumbarton
Engine builders: Smith & Rodger, Govan. 70 hp
Hull material: Iron
Owners: Dumbarton Steamboat Co.

1845: Entered service from Glasgow to Dumbarton.

1852: Sold to the Railway Steam Packet Co. Operated from Greenock to the Holy Loch, etc.

1854: Sold to H. Nicholls, Eastham. Operated on the ferry service from Liverpool to Eastham.

1862: Sold to J. Whitehead, Preston. Operated out of Preston.

1864: Sold to W. Allsup, Preston.

1864: Sold to J. McLeod Campbell, Preston.

1864: Broken up.

182: *Fire Queen*

Number in Williamson's list: 152
Built: 1845
114, later 149, gross tons. Length 132.6 feet
Builders: Robert Napier & Sons, Govan
Engine builders: Robert Napier & Sons, Govan. Engine type: 40 hp
Hull material: Wood?
Owners: Built as a yacht, James and John Napier
This may have been a screw steamer, but is included as it was the only screw steamer

ever to have operated on the Firth of Clyde services, apart from those that served Campbeltown prior to the advent of the turbine steamer. There has been a lot of confusion with three steam yachts of that name built for Thomas Assheton Smith around that time.

1845: Entered service from Glasgow to Garelochhead.

1851: Sold to W. Ward, Hull.

1857: Sold to foreign owners.

1883: Scrapped.

183: *Petrel*

Number in Williamson's list: 153

Built: 1845

192 gross tons, 162 gross tons (1859). Length 165.5 feet

Builders: Barr & McNab, Paisley

Engine builders: Barr & McNab, Paisley. Engine type: steeple; 90 hp

Hull material: Iron

Owners: Railway Steamboat Co.

1845: Entered service from Greenock to Largs and Millport on rail-connected services.

1847: Sold to G. & J. Burns.

Early 1850s: Sold to William Denny.

1853: Sold to the Eagle Steamer Co.

1856: Operated from Glasgow to Lochgoilhead.

1858: Sold to H. Sharp and A. Watson. Used as a Sunday Breaker.

1860: Chartered to Brown and McFall, Belfast. Operated from Belfast to Bangor.

1864: Charter ended.

1865: Returned to use as a Sunday breaker.

1866: June – Sold to H. Dore. Re-boilered. Two funnels reduced to one. Operated from Glasgow to Largs, Millport and Arran and continued to make Sunday trips.

1874: Sold to Henry Sharp.

1885: Broken up.

184: *Sovereign* (1845)

Number in Williamson's list: 154

Built: 1845

70.3 tons. Length 138.8 feet

Builders: Tod & McGregor, Mavisbank

Engine builders: Tod & McGregor, Mavisbank. Engine type: steeple; 50 hp

Hull material: Iron

Owners: Henderson and McKellar

1845: Entered service from Glasgow to Helensburgh and Rosneath.

1853: Laid up.

1856: Sold to J. Henderson.

1857: June – Sold to J. O. Lever, Manchester. Service unknown.

1864: Probably sold to foreign owners.

185: *Scotia* (1845)

Number in Williamson's list: 155
Built: 1845
81.7 tons. Length 141.3 feet
Builders: Tod & McGregor, Mavisbank
Engine builders: Tod & McGregor, Mavisbank. Engine type: single-cylinder; 80 hp
Hull material: Iron
Owners: James Reid, John Reid, D. Tod
1845: Entered service from Ayr to Stranraer.
1849: Owners became Glasgow & Stranraer Steam Packet Co.
1861: Operated from Stranraer to Belfast in this year only.
1863: Sold to O. H. Kaselack for blockade running.
1863: November – Made the first of three return trips from Nassau to Wilmington, over the following three months.
1864: 1 March – Captured by USS *Connecticut* off Cape Fear.
1864: July – Reported running from Portland, Maine, to Augusta, Maine.
No further informnation is available on this steamer.

186: *Prince Of Wales* (1845)

Number in Williamson's list: 155
Built: 1845
154 gross tons. Length 130.3 feet
Builders: J. Reid & Co., Port Glasgow
Engine builders: Robert Napier & Sons, Govan. 80 hp
Hull material: Iron
Owners: Alloa, Stirling & Kincardine Steamboat Co.
1845: Entered service from Granton to Alloa and Stirling.
1853: Route curtailed to Alloa in this and the following year.
1874: Sold to Stirling Steamboat Co. (W. Beveridge), Alloa.
1876: Sold to W. Chalmers and D. McIntyre, Glasgow. Lay at D. & W. Henderson's yard for sale.
1877: Sold to D. Dewar, Glasgow. Operated from Glasgow to Garelochhead.
1878: Commenced operation as a Sunday Breaker from Glasgow to Greenock and Gourock.
1879: April – Registry closed.

187: *Rob Roy* (Loch Katrine)

Built: 1845
30 tons. Length 70 feet
Builders: W. Denny & Bros., Dumbarton
Engine builders: T. Wingate & Co., Springfield. 15 hp
Hull material: Iron
Owners: New Loch Lomond Steamboat Co.
1847: Sold to the Loch Katrine Steam Boat Co. Entered service on Loch Katrine.
1855: Withdrawn from service, being replaced by a screw steamer of the same name. Sold to Glasgow Water Works contractor and used as a workboat.

c. 1859: Scuttled in the loch.

188: *Windsor Castle* (1845)

Built: 1845
120 tons. Length feet
Builders: Tod & McGregor, Mavisbank
Engine builders: Tod & McGregor, Mavisbank. Engine type: steeple; 120 hp
Hull material: Iron
Owners: Glasgow Castle Steam Packet Co.
Route: Glasgow–Rothesay 1845–46
Scrapped 1846
1845: Entered service from Glasgow to Rothesay.
1846: Scrapped. Engine fitted in *Dunrobin Castle* (No. 189).

189: *Dunrobin Castle*

Number in Williamson's list: 156
Built: 1846
207 gross tons. Length 162.6 feet
Builders: Tod & McGregor, Mavisbank
Engine builders: Tod & McGregor, Mavisbank (1845). Engine type: steeple; 120 hp
Hull material: Iron
Owners: Glasgow Castle Steam Packet Co.
1846: Entered service from Glasgow to Rothesay, Ardrishaig and Inveraray. Fitted with the
  engines from *Windsor Castle* (No. 188).
1846: Sold to G. & J. Burns.
1851: Sold to William Denny.
1852: Renamed *Telegraf*.
1853: Sold to F. Baird, Kronstadt, Russia. Operated from St Petersburg to Kronstadt.
1859: Used from now on shipyard service at St Petersburg.
1863: Sold to Peterburgo-Volzhskoe parokhstva. Used at Kronstadt.
1878: Sold to Antonov. Used as a tug.
1881: Sold to I. S. Volkox. Used as a tug based at Astrakhan. Renamed *Aleksandr Volkov*.
1891; Sold to D. Artemen, Baku.
1892: Sold to A. A. N. Magmetov, A. K. K. R. K. Ogly and A. K. U. Mekhmed, Baku.
1892: Lost.

190: *Prince*

Number in Williamson's list: 157
Built: 1846
107 gross tons. Length 120.6 feet
Builders: Denny & Rankin, Dumbarton
Engine builders: Neilson & Co., Glasgow 1826. 48 hp
Hull material: Wood
Owners: J. Henderson and A. McKellar

1846: Entered service from Glasgow to Garelochhead. Fitted with engine from *Saint George* (No. 64).

1853: Laid up.

1855: Sold to D. Campbell, Glasgow.

1857: Sold to D. McIntosh, Glasgow. Engines removed and converted to a schooner.

1859: 16 January – Wrecked at Melfort.

191: *Mary Jane*

Number in Williamson's list: 158

Built: 1846

211 gross tons, 193 gross tons (1865), 226 gross tons (1875). Length 149.5 feet, 153 feet (1865), 165.4 feet (1875)

Builders: Tod & McGregor, Mavisbank

Engine builders: Tod & McGregor, Mavisbank. Engine type: steeple; 120 hp

Hull material: Iron

Owner: Sir James Matheson, Stornoway

1846: June – Entered service from Glasgow to Portree and Stornoway, calling at Lochinver fortnightly.

1851: April – Sold to the Glasgow & Lochfine Steam Packet Co. Operated from Glasgow to Rothesay and Inveraray.

1857: Sold to D. Hutcheson & Co. Continued to operate on the same service.

1858: March – Operated from Glasgow to Ardrishaig for three weeks.

1865: Lengthened by 3.5 feet.

1875: Renamed *Glencoe*. Lengthened by 12.4 feet. Deck saloons added. Operated from Oban to Gairloch, continued doing so until 1884 and from 1886 to 1889.

1879: Taken over by David MacBrayne.

1880: Surface condenser replaced the original jet type.

1883: Re-boilered.

1885: Operated from Strome Ferry to Portree for one season only.

1890: Moved to the West Loch Tarbert–Islay route.

1901: Boiler fitted which had previously been in *Fusilier*.

1905: Moved to the Mallaig–Kyle of Lochalsh and Portree mail service.

1917: November – Chartered to the Glasgow & South Western Railway for two months. Operated from Ardrossan to Arran.

1918: April – Chartered to the Caledonian Steam Packet Co. Ltd until July. Operated on services out of Wemyss Bay.

1918: July – Operated excursions out of Oban.

1918: December – Chartered to Clyde Cargo Steamers Ltd for three months. Operated on the cargo service from Glasgow to Loch Fyne.

1920: Returned to the Portree mail service after a few months laid up.

1928: Owners became David MacBrayne (1928) Ltd.

1928: Boiler fitted which was previously in *Grenadier*.

1931: 4 June – On display at Glasgow alongside the new diesel-electric vessel *Lochfyne*.

1931: Withdrawn from service and broken up at Ardrossan after a career, unsurpassed in Clyde and West Highland waters, of eighty-five years. Her engine was purchased for preservation by Glasgow Corporation and was stored in the basement of Kelvingrove Art Gallery, but was destroyed during the Second World War.

192: *Premier*

Number in Williamson's list: 159
Built: 1846
98 tons, 115.2 gross tons (1878). Length 140 feet 2 inches, 148.5 feet (1878)
Builders: Denny Bros, Dumbarton
Engine builders: (1) Smith & Rodger; (2) J. Penn, Blackheath (1878). Engine type: (1) steeple,
    55 hp (2) two-cylinder oscillating, 50 hp
Hull material: Iron
Owners: Dumbarton Steamboat Co.
1846: Entered service from Glasgow to Dumbarton.
1859: Sold to J. Tizard, Weymouth. Used on excursions from Weymouth.
1860: Sold to Cosens & Co., Weymouth. Continued to be used on excursions from
    Weymouth.
1878: Lengthened by 8.63 feet and re-engined.
1885: Re-boilered.
1910: Re-boilered.
1938: Broken up after a career of ninety-two years, by which time she was the oldest vessel
    listed in Lloyds Register.

193: *Monarch*

Number in Williamson's list: 160
Built: 1846
118 gross tons. Length 126.8 feet
Builders: J. Barr, Renfrew
Engine builders: Barr & McNab, Paisley (1844). Engine type: steeple; 60 hp
Hull material: Iron
Owners: Henderson and McKellar
1846: Entered service from Glasgow to Rosneath. Fitted with the engine from the *Countess
    of Eglinton* (No. 170).
1854: Sold to D. Brown and T. Thompson, Hobart, Tasmania. Sailed out to Hobart under sail
    in 100 days.
1854: October – Commenced operating from Hobart to New Norfolk, a service she
    maintained for the next forty years.
1855: December – Sold to E. Luttrell and F. H. Wise.
1857: September – Owner now F. H. Wise.
1897: Engines removed to power a sawmill. Hull abandoned.
1950s: Hull still visible in New Town Bay, Hobart, at this date.

194: *Vesta* (1846)

Number in Williamson's list: 161
Built: 1846
112 gross tons. Length 160.8 feet
Builders: Barr & McNab, Paisley
Engine builders: Barr & McNab, Paisley. Engine type: steeple; 70 hp
Hull material: Iron

Owners: M. Paton, A. A. Laird, M. Langlands
1846: Operated from Glasgow to Largs and Millport.
1846: Sold to the Delphin Co., St Petersburg. Operated from St Petersburg to Kronstadt.
1880: Moved to River Service.
c. 1890: Withdrawn from service.
No record of her ultimate fate has survived.

195: *Breadalbane*

Number in Williamson's list: 163
Built: 1847
144 gross tons, 161 gross tons (1856). Length 140 feet, 146.4 feet (1856)
Builders: Smith & Rodger, Govan
Engine builders: Smith & Rodger, Govan. Engine type: steeple; 70 hp
Hull material: Iron
Owner: D. McMurrich
1847: Entered service from Glasgow to Loch Goil.
1856: Sold to W. Towns and others, Sydney. Lengthened by 6.4 feet. Went to Australia under sail, the engine being reinstalled after she arrived there. Operated under charter from Melbourne to Williamstown and was also used as a tug/tender, later operated at Brisbane, mainly to Ipswich.
1862: Moved to Sydney. Operated to Manly at weekends, and as a tug-cum-cargo steamer during the week.
1868: Owned now by the Brighton and Manly Steam Ferry Co. (T. Heselton and T. J. Parker).
1871: Purely used as a cargo steamer from this date.
1877: 23 January – Owners became the Port Jackson Steamboat Co.
1883: Scrapped.

196: *Jenny Lind*

Built: 1847
85 tons. Length 133.5 feet, 150.9 by 1854
Builders: Denny Bros, Dumbarton
Engine builders: Robert Napier & Sons, Govan. Engine type: steeple; 60 hp
Hull material: Iron
Owner: Built as yacht for Thomas Assheton Smith
1847: Laid down as the yacht *Sprite*, launched as *Jenny Lind*. Operated from Paisley to Largs.
1848: Renamed *Duchess of Argyle*.
1849: April – Sold to Robert Napier. Operated from Glasgow to Garelochhead.
1854: Sold to J. and A. Campbell, the uncles of Captain Bob Campbell of Kilmun.
1857: Sold to the Midland Great Western Railway Co., Ireland. Sailed to Limerick, cut in half and transported to Athlone, where she was joined together again. Operated on the River Shannon from Athlone to Killaloe.
1857: Was holed after hitting a rock in fog.
1860: Owners taken over by the Great Southern & Western Railway.
1863: Withdrawn from service. No information is available about her ultimate fate.

197: *Briton* (1847)

Built: 1847
215 gross tons. Length 144.8 feet
Builders: Tod & McGregor, Meadowside
Engine builders: Tod & McGregor, Meadowside. Engine type: 100 hp
Hull material: Iron
Owners: Glasgow & Stranraer Steam Packet Co., Stranraer
1847: Entered service from Glasgow to Stranraer.
1849: July – Operated excursions from Ayr and Stranraer to Douglas, Isle of Man. Later operated from Stranraer to Belfast and Liverpool.
1855: 31 January – Hit a rock and was lost off Ballantrae.

198: *Countess Of Galloway* (1847)

Built: 1847
492 gross tons, 452 gross tons (1860). Length 165.5 feet
Builders: Tod & McGregor, Mavisbank
Engine builders: Tod & McGregor, Mavisbank. 200 hp
Hull material: Iron, flush-decked
Owners: Galloway Steam Navigation Co., Wigtown
1847: Entered service from Wigtown to Garlieston, Isle of Whithorn, Kirkcudbright and Liverpool.
1876: Sold to J. Langlands, Glasgow. Operated from Glasgow to Stranraer and Liverpool.
1880: Scrapped.

199: *Marchioness of Breadalbane* (1847)

Built: 1847
135 gross tons. Length 140.1 feet
Builders: Denny Bros., Dumbarton
Engine builders: Caird & Co., Greenock. Engine type: two-cylinder oscillating; 64 hp
Hull material: Iron
Owners: Loch Lomond Steam Boat Co. (not accepted)
1847: Built for service on Loch Lomond, but did not operate there because her draught was too deep for the loch.
1848: Taken back by William Denny. Chartered to the Peninsular & Oriental Steam Navigation Co. Operated from Alexandria to Cairo through the Nile Delta in connection with P&O steamers.
1857: Gifted to the Pasha of Egypt.
No further information is available.

200: *Vesper* (1848)

Number in Williamson's list: 165
Built: 1848
122 gross tons. Length 148.3 feet
Builders: J. Henderson & Son, Renfrew
Engine builders: Barr & McNab, West Renfrew. Engine type: steeple; 90 hp
Hull material: Flush-decked
Owner: J. Henderson
1848: Entered service from Glasgow to Kilcreggan and Kilmun.
1857: The final year for which records exist for this steamer. One source states sold to unidentified owners in London.

201: *Plover* (1848)

Number in Williamson's list: 166
Built: 1848
141 gross tons. Length 150.9 feet
Builders: T. Wingate & Co., Whiteinch
Engine builders: T. Wingate & Co., Whiteinch. Engine type: steeple; 50 hp
Hull material: Iron
Owners: Glasgow & Liverpool Steam Shipping Co. (J. & G. Burns), C. McKenzie.
1848: Commenced operating from Glasgow to Bowling, connecting with trains to Balloch.
1851: Sold to D. Thompson.
1851: 5 February – Boiler exploded while lying at the Broomielaw. Repaired by William Denny. Did not operate on the Clyde again.
1852: Sold to the Lancashire & Furness Railway Co. Operated from Fleetwood to Barrow.
1861: Lost at sea.

202: *Argyle* (1848), (registered as *Argyll*)

Built: 1848
39 tons. Length 76 feet
Builders: T. Wingate & Co., Springfield
Engine builders: T. Wingate & Co., Springfield. 25 hp
Hull material:
Owners: Loch Goil & Loch Long Steamboat Co.
1848: Entered service from Inveraray to St Catherines.
1852: Sold to Preston & Co.
1865: Operated from Inveraray to Strachur until around 1867.
No information is available about her fate.

203: *Celt*

Built: 1848
271 tons. Length 155.9 feet
Builders: Denny Bros, Dumbarton
Engine builders: T. Wingate & Co., Whiteinch. Engine type: single-cylinder; 140 hp
Hull material: Iron, flush-decked
Owners: Campbeltown & Glasgow Steam Packet Joint Stock Co. Ltd
1848: Entered service from Glasgow to Campbeltown.
1867: Laid up.
1869–79: Sailed to India. Became a tug on the River Hooghly.
1879: Sold to P. Dixon.
1871: Sold to D. McCrae.
No information is available about her eventual fate.

204: *Cygnet* (Launched as *Ben Nevis*)

Built: 1848
107 gross tons. Length 77.5 feet
Builders: Wood & Reid, Port Glasgow
Engine builders: (1) J. & G. Thomson, Finnieston; (2) Barclay Curle & Co. at an unknown
    date. Engine type: single-cylinder; (1) 50 hp, (2) 50 hp
Hull material: Iron
Owners: Glasgow & Liverpool Steam Shipping Co. (G. & J. Burns)
1848: Built and launched as *Ben Nevis*. Entered service as *Cygnet* from Glasgow to Inverness
    via the Crinan Canal.
1850: Moved to the routes from Glasgow to Tobermory and Glasgow to Fort William
1851: Taken over by D. Hutcheson & Co.
1873: Re-boilered.
1879: Taken over by David MacBrayne
1882: Wrecked at Loch Ailort, where she had been sent for a cargo of wood.

205: *Lapwing*

Built: 1848
110 gross tons. Length 82.7 feet
Builders: J. Reid & Co., Port Glasgow
Engine builders: Murdoch, Aitken & Co. 1835. Engine type: steeple; 44 hp
Hull material: Iron
Owners: Glasgow & Liverpool Steam Shipping Co. (G. & J. Burns)
1848: Entered service from Glasgow to Inverness via the Crinan Canal. Fitted with the engine
    from the *Helen McGregor* (No. 116).
1851: Taken over by D. Hutcheson & Co.
1859: 22 February – Sank off Kintyre after a collision with the screw steamer *Islesman* of
    Martin Orme, with the loss of two lives.

206: *Marquis of Stafford*

Built: 1848
365 gross tons. Length 173 feet
Builders: J. Reid & Co., Port Glasgow
Engine builders: J. & G. Thomson, Govan. 154 hp
Hull material: Iron
Owners: Sir J. Matheson and the Duke of Sutherland
1849: Entered service from Stornoway to Poolewe.
1851: Route now from Stornoway to Ullapool and Lochinver.
1851: Service ceased.
1852: Sold to R. Rubattino, Genoa. Operated out of Genoa. Renamed *Piemonte*.
1860: May – Commandeered by Garibaldi to sail from Genoa to Marsala as part of an invasion fleet.
1860: 11 May – Captured by troops of the Kingdom of the Two Sicilies at Marsala after landing Garibaldi's forces.
1866: Demolished.

207: *STAR*

Number in Williamson's list: 168
Built: 1849
186 gross tons. Length 156 feet
Builders: Tod & McGregor, Meadowside
Engine builders: Tod & McGregor, Meadowside. Engine type: steeple; 100 hp
Hull material: Iron
Owners: Glasgow, Largs & Millport Union Steamboat Co.
1849: Entered service from Glasgow to Largs, Millport, Brodick and Lamlash.
1860: Chartered to J. D. Luke. Operated excursions on the Forth and from Dundee to Leith.
1863: September – Sold to D. McNutt for blockade running.
1863: December to January 1864: Ran the blockade from Nassau to Wilmington, making one return trip.
1864: Sold to Herman Decker, Nassau. Used as an inter-island ferry in the Bahamas.
1864: December – Boiler explosion at Nassau. Repaired and returned to service.
1928: Deleted from Lloyds Register.

208: *Islay* (1849)

Built: 1849
320 gross tons. Length 167 feet
Builders: Tod & McGregor, Meadowside
Engine builders: Tod & McGregor, Meadowside. Engine type: two-cylinder; 160 hp
Hull material: Iron
Owners: Morrison, Buchanan and Ramsay, Islay
1849: Entered service from Glasgow to Islay and West Loch Tarbert to Islay.
1851: 19 May – Route extended to Skye and Stornoway.
1856: Operated from Crinan to Islay.
1857: December – Ran aground near Port Ellen, salvaged and returned to service.

1868: February – Sold to David Hutcheson & Co. Renamed *Dolphin*.

1868: July – Sold to the Donagahadee & Portpatrick Short Sea Steam Packet Co. Operated from Donaghadee to Portpatrick until October of that year.

1870: Sold to T. Honeychurch, London.

1872: Sold to Robinson Ridley, Plymouth.

No further information is available.

209: *Maid of Lorn*

Built: 1849

110 gross tons, 120 gross tons (1854). Length 82.5 feet

Builders: T. Wingate & Co., Whiteinch

Engine builders: (1) Robert Napier & Sons, Govan. Engine type: (1) steeple; 59 hp, (2) unknown, (3) unknown.

Hull material: Iron

Owners: Glasgow & Highland Steam Packet Co.

1849: Entered service from Glasgow to Inverness via the Crinan Canal and from Glasgow to Inveraray. Operated on alternate weeks to Salen (Loch Sunart).

1850: 15 May – Struck rocks at Salen Mull, and filled with water. The watertight bulkheads held and she sailed for Glasgow for repairs.

1852: Operated in conjunction with D. Hutcheson & Co.

1858: December – Sold to Barclay Curle & Co.

1859: 1 January – Sold back to D. Hutcheson & Co. Renamed *Plover*.

1869: Re-engined

Unknown date: Was the last paddle steamer to sail through the Crinan Canal.

Unknown date: Operated from Oban to Loch Sunart.

1878: Re-engined.

1883: 1 February – Sold to W. C. Williamson. Engines and paddles removed and converted to a hulk, moored in the Gareloch.

1891: Sold to Jamieson & Co. and scrapped.

CHAPTER 5
Steamers Built 1850–59

210: *Queen*

Number in Williamson's list: 169
Built: 1850
132 tons. Length 141 feet 7 inches
Builders: W. Denny & Bros., Dumbarton
Engine builders: Smith & Rodger, Govan. Engine type: steeple; 70 hp
Hull material: Iron
Owner: P. L. Henderson
1850: Entered service from Glasgow to Dumbarton, Lochgoilhead and Arrochar.
1852: Ceased operating on the above route.
1859: Sold to the Silloth Bay Steam Navigation Co. (J. Carruthers) Carlisle. Used as a tender at Silloth.
1864: January – Sold to the North British Railway.
1864: Sold to J. P. Henderson, Glasgow, and scrapped.

211: *Koh-I-Noor*

Number in Williamson's list: 170
Built: 1850
73 tons. Length 146.4 feet
Builders: T. Wingate & Co., Whiteinch
Engine builders: T. Wingate & Co., Whiteinch. 52 hp
Hull material: Iron
Owner: R. Young
1850: Entered service from Glasgow to Dunoon and Kilmun.
1852: Chartered to W. Dargan, Limerick. Operated on the Shannon estuary from Limerick to Kilrush.
1855: Sold at Admiralty auction to W. Orell, Liverpool.
1855: 16 May – Sank under tow off Inishboffin Island, Ireland, on the way from Limerick to Galway on her way back to the Clyde.

212: *Eclipse* (1850)

Number in Williamson's list: 171
Built: 1850
200 tons. Length 165 feet

Builders: T. Wingate & Co., Whiteinch
Engine builders: T. Wingate & Co., Whiteinch. Engine type: steeple; 62 hp
Hull material: Iron
Owners: A. McKellar, Glasgow
1851: Entered service from Glasgow to Dunoon and Kilmun.
1854: 2 September – Wrecked on the Gantocks. Engine salvaged and fitted in *Nelson* (No. 248).

213: *Prince Albert* (1850)

Built: 1850
109 tons. Length 142.2 feet
Builders: W. Denny & Bros., Dumbarton
Engine builders: Caird & Co., Greenock. Engine type: two-cylinder diagonal; 60 hp
Hull material: Iron; flush-decked
Owners: Loch Lomond Steamboat Co.
1850: Entered service on Loch Lomond from Balloch to Inverarnan.
1862: Sold to the Dumbarton Steamboat Co. Moved out of the loch and operated from Glasgow to Dumbarton.
1863: Sold to Henry Gough, Liverpool. Operated as a ferry from Liverpool to Eastham. Renamed *Richmond*.
1864: June – Became a blockade runner. Regained the name *Prince Albert*. Made one return trip from Nassau to Charleston.
1864: 9 August – Ran onto the wreck of *Minho* on her second trip entering Charleston Harbour and was destroyed by fire by the Union shore batteries.
1873: Wreck removed and broken up.
Alternative sources state:
1871: Purchased by Thompson and Gough, Liverpool, after the death of Henry Gough.

214: *Victoria* (1851)

Number in Williamson's list: 174
Built: 1851
69.2 tons. Length 123.6 feet
Builders: Robert Napier & Sons, Govan
Engine builders: Robert Napier & Sons, Govan. Engine type: oscillating; 80 hp
Hull material: Iron
Owners: J. Napier and J. McLean
1851: Built. Fitted with the first oscillating engine made by Robert Napier, and was the first Clyde steamer with feathering paddle wheels.
1852: Sold to J. Napier and J. Campbell. Entered service from Glasgow to Garelochhead.
1854: Purchased by J. & A. Campbell.
1859: Sold to unidentified Russian owners.
1859: September – Lost near Anholt in the Kattegat on her delivery voyage to Russia.

215: *Ardentinny*

Number in Williamson's list: 175
Built: 1851
108.9 tons. Length 163.4 feet
Builders: T. Wingate & Co., Whiteinch
Engine builders: T. Wingate & Co., Whiteinch. Engine type: steeple; 72 hp
Hull material: Iron
Owners: J. Ballardie and J. Reid
1851: Entered service from Glasgow to Loch Goil.
1854: Ended Loch Goil service.
1857: Sold to Haslett & McLelland, Glasgow.
1858: Sold to Foyle Steam Boat Co., Londonderry. Operated from Londonderry to Moville.
1859: Sold to Captain W. Coppin, Londonderry.
1860: June – Made en excursion to welcome the *North Briton*, the first transatlantic liner to
    call at Londonderry.
1864: Sold to M. G. Klingender, Liverpool, for blockade running. Renamed *Golden Pledge*.
1864: 17 July – Lost in a collision prior to running the blockade.

216: *Severn*

Built: 1851
106 gross tons. Length 137 feet
Builders: D. Napier, Millwall
Engine builders: Lang & Sons, Gloucester. Engine type: two-cylinder; 16 hp
Hull material: Iron
Owners: David Napier, Worcester
1851: Built as an experimental craft with two paddle wheels at the stern. Some sources state
    built 1859.
1859: Renamed *Kilmun*. Operated from Cardiff to Portishead and Bristol.
1860: Operated on the River Severn, possibly at Worcester.
1863: Operated from Glasgow to Kilmun for one week only.
Information about this steamer is sparse.

217: *Stork*

Built: 1851
396 tons. Length 190.7 feet
Builders: W. Denny & Bros., Dumbarton
Engine builders: Caird & Co., Greenock. Engine type: side-lever; 200 hp
Hull material: Iron, flush-decked
Owners: G. & J. Burns
1851: Entered service from Glasgow to Liverpool.
1857: Sold to D. Hutcheson & Co.
1857: July–August – Operated from Oban to Portrush.
1858: Operated from Glasgow to Stornoway.
1861: Sold to the Italian Government. Renamed *Plebiscito*.
1875: March – Scrapped.

218: *Reindeer*

Number in Williamson's list: 176
Built: 1852
84.1 tons. Length 166 feet
Builders: Blackwood & Gordon, Paisley
Engine builders: Blackwood & Gordon, Paisley. 70 hp
Hull material: Iron
Owners: P. Ralston, J. Donnelly, J. McLaren (Glasgow & Gourock Steam Packet Co.)
1852: Entered service from Glasgow to the Kyles of Bute.
1856: Sold to J. Mason, Memel, Lithuania.
1856: Reported lost.

219: *Glasgow Citizen*

Number in Williamson's list: 177
Built: 1852
162 tons. Length 156.9 feet
Builders: J. Barr, Kelvinhaugh
Engine builders: J. Barr, Kelvinhaugh. Engine type: steeple; 75 hp
Hull material: Iron
Owner: J. Barr
1852: Entered service from Glasgow to Helensburgh. Also ran from Glasgow to Rothesay.
1853: Call at Innellan introduced.
1854: Sold to R. Little & Co. Sailed to Australia. Entered service from Melbourne to Geelong.
1857: Sold to the Geelong Steam Navigation Co., Australia.
1861: October – Sold to T. Woodhouse.
1861: November – Sold to T. Norton, Melbourne, for use in the New Zealand Gold Rush.
1862: 11 October – Sank en route to New Zealand.

220: *Venus* (1852)

Number in Williamson's list: 178
Built: 1852
176 tons. Length 159.2 feet
Builders: J. & G. Thomson, Govan
Engine builders: J. & G. Thomson, Govan. Engine type: steeple; 90 hp
Hull material: Flush-decked
Owners: Largs & Millport United Steam Boat Co.
1852: Entered service on day excursions from Glasgow to Largs, Millport and Arran.
1859: Sold to Largs & Millport Union Steam Boat Co.
1864: Sold to Duncan McKellar.
1867: Sold to Gillies & Campbell.
1871: Now operated from Wemyss Bay to Arran.
1875: Scrapped.

221: *Mountaineer* (1852)

Number in Williamson's list: 180
Built: 1852
173 tons. Length 174.3 feet, 184.1 feet (1869), 195.6 feet (1871)
Builders: J. & G. Thomson, Govan
Engine builders: J. & G. Thomson, Govan. Engine type: steeple; 120 hp
Hull material: Flush-decked
Owners: D. Hutcheson & Co.
1852: Entered service from Glasgow to Ardrishaig year round. Was the first steamer with repeating engine room telegraphs.
1855: Moved in summer to the Oban–Fort William and Oban to Staffa and Iona routes, also from Oban to Loch Coruisk in this year only. Continued to run to Ardrishaig in the winter months.
1861: Re-boilered.
Early 1860s: Operated from Oban to Crinan.
1869: Lengthened by 9.8 feet.
1871: Lengthened again, this time by 11.5 feet.
1876: Fore and aft deck saloon added.
1879: Owners taken over by David MacBrayne.
1889: Moved to the Oban–Gairloch service.
1882: Re-boilered.
1889: 27 September – Ran aground on the Lady Rock, near Duart Castle, while inward bound for Oban. When the tide fell, she was left perched on the rock, emulating her namesakes.
1889: 7 October – Broke in two with the after half sinking in deep water.

222: *Gourock*

Number in Williamson's list: 181
Built: 1852
75 tons. Length 113.7 feet
Builders: Scott & Co., Greenock
Engine builders: (1) A. Campbell & Son, Anderston, (2) Verman, Riga (1864). 50 hp
Hull material: Iron
Owners: Railway Steamboat Co.
1852: 5 April – Entered service from Glasgow to Greenock and Gourock.
1852: August – Registered by T. Seath and others (Caledonian Railway nominees).
1853: April – Sold to unknown foreign owners.
1854: Renamed *Stella*.
c. 1860: Sold to J. Mason, Memel. Started operating out of Memel.
1861: Sold to J. Jacobs, Riga. Started operating out of Riga. Renamed *Phönix*.
1864: New engine fitted at Riga. Renamed *Adler*.
1869: Sold to Veydner, Riga.
1871: Sold to G. G. Weidner (or Weirdner), Riga.
1880: Sold to Lange and Skuje, Riga.
1891: Sold to K. Skue, Riga.
1897: Sold to D. Skue, Riga.
1906: Sold to T-vo A. Augsburg, Riga. Renamed *Adler No. 3*.
No record of her final fate is available.

223: *Eagle* (1852)

Number in Williamson's list: 182
Built: 1852
176 tons. Length 169.9 feet
Builders: Alex Denny, Dumbarton
Engine builders: McNab & Clark, Greenock. Engine type: oscillating; 70 hp
Hull material: Flush-decked
Owners: W. Denny, A. Denny & Bros and others, Dumbarton.
1852: Entered service from Glasgow to Rothesay, the Kyles of Bute, and Arran.
1853: Sold to the Eagle Steamer Company (Williamson, Cook and Buchanan).
1856: Route now Glasgow–Arran.
1862: Sold to G. Wigg for the Navigation Company for blockade running.
1863: February – Made one round trip as a blockade runner from Nassau to Wilmington.
1863: March – Started running the blockade from Nassau to Galveston. Made three trips.
1863: 18 May – Captured by US Navy 18 May 1863, sold at prize court and returned to blockade running under the name *Jeanette*, sometime referred to as *Jeannette*.
1865: January – Made a trip from Havana to Galveston.
1865: July – Operating from Tampico to Havana.
No further information is available about this steamer, and her fate.

224: *Osprey*

Number in Williamson's list: 183
Built: 1852
193 tons. Length 169.6 feet
Builders: R. Barclay & Curle, Stobcross
Engine builders: Caird & Co., Greenock. Engine type: two-cylinder; 101 hp
Hull material: Iron
Owners: F. Johnstone, N. McGill and D. Weir
1852: Entered service from Glasgow to Rothesay.
1854: January – Sold to the Pacific Steam Navigation Co., Liverpool. Her intended service was on the Peruvian coast from Callao to Pisco and Huacho.
1854: Went missing after leaving Bermuda en route for Peru on her delivery voyage.

225: *Duke of Argyll*

Built: 1852
101 tons. Length 166.7 feet, 209.4 feet (1855)
Builders: Scott, Sinclair & Co., Greenock
Engine builders: Scott, Sinclair & Co., Greenock. Engine type: single-cylinder; 176 hp
Hull material: Iron
Owners: Glasgow & Lochfine Steam Packet Co.
1852: Entered service on the Glasgow–Inveraray cargo service.
1855: June – Lengthened by 42.7 feet.
1857: Sold to D. Hutcheson & Co. Operated from Glasgow to Oban, Portree, Gairloch, Dunvegan and Stornoway.
1858: 12 January – Sank in Sound of Mull en route to Stornoway.
1858: 15 March – Raised.
1858: December – Broken-up by this date.

226: *Dunoon*

Built: 1852
114.9 tons. Length 135 feet
Builders: Laurence Hill & Co., Port Glasgow
Engine builders: Scott Sinclair & Co., Greenock. 43 hp
Hull material: Iron
Owners: Railway Steamboat Co.
1852: Entered service from Greenock to Dunoon and the Holy Loch on rail-connected services.
1852: November – Sold to the Geelong Steam Navigation Co. (D. Hoyle). Renamed *Geelong*.
1852: 18 November – Sank in the Bay of Biscay on her delivery voyage to Australia.

227: *Helensburgh* (1852)

Built: 1852
115 tons. Length 135 feet
Builders: Laurence Hill & Co., Port Glasgow
Engine builders: Scott Sinclair & Co., Greenock. 43 hp
Hull material: Iron
Owners: Railway Steamboat Co.
1852: 1 June – Entered service on rail-connected service from Greenock to Helensburgh and Garelochhead.
1852: November – Sold to the Geelong Steam Navigation Co. (D. Hoyle). Renamed *Melbourne*. Sailed out to Australia under sail. Operated from Melbourne to Geelong.
1854: August – Sold to F. Cadell. Operated from Melbourne to the Murray River to the Beechworth and Ovens goldfields. One of very few steamers that navigated from the sea into the River Murray.
1856: Sold to Thorne, Sparks & Co., Port Adelaide. Operated from Port Adelaide to Goolwa.
1859: 16 November – Wrecked at the Murray Mouth.

228: *Queen Victoria*

Built: 1852
93 tons. Length 131.7 feet
Builders: Alex Denny, Dumbarton
Engine builders: Caird & Co., Greenock. Engine type: two-cylinder diagonal; 30 hp
Hull material: Iron; flush-decked
Owners: Loch Lomond Steamboat Co.
1852: Entered service from Balloch to Ardlui. Fitted with the engine from *Waterwitch*.
1868: Sold to unidentified foreign owners.
1868: Sold to J. Swallow, Whitby. Renamed *Swallow*. Operated excursions in the Wash.
1871: May have operated at Scarborough.
1872: Sold to the Wallasey Local Board. Operated from Liverpool to Wallasey and Liverpool
    to New Brighton.
1876: Moved to the route from Liverpool to Egremont.
1882: July – Sold to T. Seed.
1883: Scrapped.

229 *Rotary/Rotatory Steamer*

Number in Williamson's list: 179
Built: 1853
66 tons. Length 146.2 feet
Builders: J. Henderson & Son, Renfrew
Engine builders: T. Wingate & Co., Whiteinch. Engine type: (1) Rotary, (2) Diagonal 1855;
    50 hp in 1860
Hull material: Iron
Owner: David Napier
1853: Initially advertised to sail from Glasgow to Paisley. Had an experimental rotary engine,
    which was unsuccessful. Only ran for a few weeks.
1855: Re-engined. Renamed *Dumbarton*.
1857: Operated from Glasgow to Dumbarton.
1860: Sold to W. R. Coulborn. Operated from Greenock to Garelochhead. Renamed
    Gareloch.
1861: Sold to P. L. Henderson.
1863: April – Sold to E. Latham, Cowes. Operated from Stokes Bay to Ryde.
1865: February – Service ceased.
1865: Sold to the Isle of Wight Ferry Co.
1868: Sold to T. Crowder, Cowes.
1869: Sold to W. Coppin, Londonderry (Foyle Steam Towing Co.), operated from Londonderry
    to Moville.
1870: June – Chartered to the Hollywood Steam Packet Co. Operated from Belfast to Bangor.
1880: Scrapped.

230: *Baron*

Number in Williamson's list: 184
Built: 1853
121.84 tons. Length 189.1 feet
Builders: J. Henderson & Son, Renfrew
Engine builders: (1) J. W. Hoby & Co., Renfrew; (2) Blackwood & Gordon (1854). Engine
    type: (2) oscillating steeple (1854); 110 hp
Hull material: Iron
Owner: J. Ward Hoby
1854: Entered service from Glasgow to the Gareloch re-engined.
1857: July – Moved to the Glasgow–Rothesay service.
1857: August – Sold to unknown owners at Le Havre. Renamed *Normandie*.
Unknown date: Sold to owners in Italy. Renamed *Giulia*.
No further information is available.

231: *Wellington*

Number in Williamson's list: 185
Built: 1853
97.53 tons. Length 163.6 feet
Builders: J. Barr, Kelvinhaugh
Engine builders: J. Barr, Kelvinhaugh. Engine type: steeple; 60 hp
Hull material: Flush-decked
Owner: A. McKellar
1853: Entered service from Glasgow to Kilmun and Dunoon.
1860: Scrapped. Engine fitted in *Sultan* (No. 273).

232: *Eva*

Number in Williamson's list: 186
Built: 1853
83 tons. Length 141.6 feet
Builders: Alex Denny, Dumbarton
Engine builders: M. Paul, Dumbarton. 0 hp
Hull material: Iron
Owners: Morton, Little, etc., (Railway Steamboat Company)
1853: Entered service on rail-connected sailings from Greenock to the Gareloch.
1853: December – Sold to Australian owners.
1853: 27 December – Sank off Lambey Island en route for Australia under sail.

233: *Chancellor* (1853)

Number in Williamson's list: 187
Built: 1853
161 tons. Length 167.4 feet
Builders: W. Denny & Bros., Dumbarton

Engine builders: W. Denny & Bros Ltd., Dumbarton. Engine type: diagonal; 80 hp
Hull material: Iron
Owners: Dumbarton Steamboat Co.
1853: Entered service from Glasgow to Arrochar.
1862: May – Sold to the Isle of Wight Ferry Co. Entered service from Stokes Bay to Ryde.
1863: 1 July – Wrecked at Ventnor.

234: *Vesta* (1853)

Number in Williamson's list: 188
Built: 1853
124 tons. Length 162 feet 3 inches
Builders: J. Barr, Kelvinhaugh
Engine builders: J. Barr, Kelvinhaugh. Engine type: steeple; 75 hp
Hull material: Iron
Owners: Largs & Millport Union Steamboat Co.
1853: Entered service from Glasgow to Largs and Millport.
1863: Sold to J. and P. L. Henderson. Moved to the Glasgow–Rothesay service.
1866: Sold to J. & R. Campbell, Kilmun. Moved to the Glasgow–Kilmun service.
1871: Owners became Keith and Campbell.
1871–1872 – winter – Chartered to the North British Steam Packet Co. Ltd. Operated from Helensburgh to Garelochhead.
1872: Route extended to Lochgoilhead on certain days.
1875: Re-boilered.
1876: May–July – Operated from Glasgow to Millport, also did so in 1877.
1878: Moved to the Glasgow–Rothesay service.
1884: December – Sold to Capt. W. Buchanan. Used on the Glasgow–Holy Loch service.
1886: 2 March – Destroyed by fire while at Ardnadam overnight. Sank in the Holy Loch and broken up.

235: *Lochgoil* (1853)

Number in Williamson's list: 189
Built: 1853
124.1 tons. Length 163.9 feet
Builders: J. Barr, Kelvinhaugh
Engine builders: J. Barr, Kelvinhaugh. Engine type: steeple; 80 hp
Hull material: Iron
Owners: Loch Goil & Loch Long Steamboat Company
1854: Entered service from Glasgow to Lochgoilhead.
1875: Sold to Steel and McAskill, Londonderry. Used as a tender and also from Londonderry to Moville. Renamed *Lough Foyle*.
1877: Company name changed to Steel & Bennie.
1877: Sold to G. Iron, Clynder. Operated from Glasgow to the Gareloch.
1880: Sold to Henry Sharp.
1881: Used as a Sunday Breaker and for excursions.
1886: Sold to David MacBrayne. Renamed *Loch Ness*. Used on the Loch Ness mail service from Inverness to Fort Augustus.
1912: Scrapped.

236: *Chevalier* (1853)

Built: 1853
329 tons. Length 174.3 feet
Builders: J. & G. Thomson, Govan
Engine builders: J. & G. Thomson, Govan. Engine type: two-cylinder simple oscillating; 120 hp
Hull material: Iron, raised quarterdeck
Owners: D. Hutcheson & Co.
1853: Entered service from Glasgow to Oban and Portree via the Mull of Kintyre, with occasional trips to Stornoway and Scrabster.
1854: 24 November – Wrecked in the Sound of Jura.

237: *Diamond*

Built: 1853
187 tons. Length 182.1 feet
Builders: J. W. Hoby, Renfrew
Engine builders: J. W. Hoby, Renfrew. 110 hp
Hull material: Iron
Owner: J. Henderson
1857: Operated from Glasgow to Lamlash.
1858: Taken by her owner to St Petersburg, and offered for sale to the Russian Navy (Marine Ministry) but the price her owner asked was too high.
1863: 1 July – Returned to the Clyde for a proposed Clyde service.
1863: 3 July – Sold to an unknown owner and sent to run the blockade.
1863: 19 September – Arrived at Nassau.
1863: 23 September – Captured by USS *Stettin* on her first run from Nassau. Taken over by the US Navy Quartermaster's department.
1872: Abandoned.

238: *Flamingo* (1853)

Built: 1853
92 tons. Length 170.4 feet
Builders: J. W. Hoby, Renfrew
Engine builders: J. W. Hoby, Renfrew. Engine type: oscillating; 60 hp
Hull material: Iron
Owners: Railway Steam Packet Co.
1853: Entered service on rail-connected service from Greenock to Dunoon, the Holy Loch and the Gareloch.
1853: November – Sold to R. Little & Co., Greenock, for a proposed service in Australia. Renamed *Bell Bird*.
1853: 22 December – Sank in mid-Atlantic on her delivery voyage to Port Philip.

239: *GEM*

Number in Williamson's list: 190
Built: 1854
146 tons. Length 161 feet
Builders: J. Henderson & Son, Renfrew
Engine builders: J. Henderson & Son, Renfrew. Engine type: steeple; 75 hp
Hull material: Iron
Owner: J. Henderson
1854: Entered service from Glasgow to Garelochhead.
1862: Operated from Helensburgh to Rothesay.
1863: Sold to O. H. Kaselack for blockade running
1863: November – Chartered to the Cobia Co., Charleston. Ran the blockade from Nassau
    to Charleston, making one return trip.
Survived the US Civil War but no further information is available. There is a record of a
    steamer named *Gem* running on the Delaware River from Philadelphia to Bordentown in
    the 1870s, but this may well be another vessel.

240: *Rothesay Castle* (1854)

Number in Williamson's list: 191
Built: 1854
171 tons. Length 181.8 feet
Builders: Caird & Co., Greenock
Engine builders: Caird & Co., Greenock. Engine type: diagonal; 100 hp
Hull material: Iron
Owners: W. F. Johnstone and N. McGill
1854: Entered service from Glasgow to Rothesay.
1855: Operated for one year only from Glasgow to Ardrishaig.
1860: Sold to unknown owners at Calcutta. Renamed *Goyra*.
1861: Attempted to sail to India, but returned after nine months and was sent to Calcutta in
    sections. Operated on the rivers Hooghly and Ganges.
1864: Sold to the Oriental Indian Steam Navigation Co., India. Moved to the River
    Indus.
1869: Sold to the Pasha of Baghdad.
1870: May – Left Karachi for the Euphrates with two barges. Had to put into a Guader, now
    Gwadar in Pakistan, for repairs after being disabled in a storm.
No record of her ultimate fate is available.

241: *Ruby* (1854)

Number in Williamson's list: 192
Built: 1854
174 tons. Length 172.9 feet, later 177.4 feet
Builders: J. Henderson & Son, Renfrew
Engine builders: McNab & Clark, Greenock. Engine type: oscillating; 90 hp
Hull material: Iron
Owners: J. Henderson

There may be confusion with another *Ruby*, which went blockade running.

1854: Entered service from Glasgow to Rothesay.

1860: Sold to G. Reed, Bridgwater. Operated from Burnham-on-Sea to Cardiff.

1863: Sold to P. L. Henderson.

1863: Sold to George Wigg for Alexander Collie & Co. Used as a blockade runner.

1863: February–March – Made three successful return trips from Nassau to Charleston.

1863: 11 June – Chased ashore on Folly Island and destroyed while trying to reach Charleston off Lighthouse Inlet, South Carolina.

242: *Vulcan* (1854)

Number in Williamson's list: 193
Built: 1854
129 tons. Length 167.9 feet
Builders: Robert Napier & Sons, Govan
Engine builders: Robert Napier & Sons, Govan. Engine type: oscillating; 80 hp
Hull material: Flush-decked
Owner: J. W. Napier
1854: Entered service from Glasgow to Rothesay.
1859: Sold to J. McIntyre.
1864: Sold to A. and T. McLean.
1872: Sold to J. & G. Thomson, used as a workers ferry from Govan to their new shipyard at Clydebank.
1879: Broken up.

243: *Express* (1854)

Number in Williamson's list: 194
Built: 1854
113 tons. Length 179 feet
Builders: J. Barr, Kelvinhaugh
Engine builders: Robert Napier & Sons, Govan. Engine type: steeple; 70 hp
Hull material: Iron
Owner: Captain Bob Campbell (the father of Peter and Alex Campbell of Bristol Channel fame)
1854: Entered service from Glasgow to Kilcreggan and Kilmun.
1864: Broken up, engines fitted in *Vesper* (No. 304).

244: *Cygnus*

Built: 1854
250 tons. Length 182 feet
Builders: J. Henderson & Son, Renfrew
Engine builders: McNab & Clark, Greenock
Hutson and Corbett. Engine type: two-cylinder oscillating; 120 hp
Hull material: Iron, flush-decked

Owners: North of Europe Steam Navigation Co.

1854: Entered service from Harwich to Antwerp.

1857: Sold to the Weymouth & Channel Islands Steam Packet Co. Operated from Weymouth to the Channel Islands.

1889: Sold to the Southport, Preston & Blackpool Steam Packet Co. (T. Holden).

1870: Operated from Southport to Douglas and Llandudno, also on excursions from Southport.

1874: Re-boilered.

1890: December – Sold to David MacBrayne.

1891: Operated on the Glasgow–Inveraray cargo service, also later from Oban to Loch Sunart, and on various relief sailings including on the Clyde.

c. 1892: Re-boilered and rebuilt with a single funnel instead of two. Renamed *Brigadier*.

1896: 7 December – Wrecked on Duncan's Rock near Rodel, Harris, while on her the outer islands service to join the blockade..

245: *Iona* (1855)

Number in Williamson's list: 196
Built: 1855
368 tons. Length 225.2 feet
Builders: J. & G. Thomson, Govan
Engine builders: J. & G. Thomson, Govan. Engine type: oscillating; 220 hp
Hull material: Flush-decked
Owners: D. Hutcheson & Co.

1855: 22 March – Launched.

1855: Entered service from Glasgow to Ardrishaig.

1862: Sold to G. Wigg for the Navigation Company for blockade running.

1862: 2 October – Sank off Gourock after a collision with the steamer *Chanticleer*, which was on trials.

246: *Sir Colin Campbell*

Number in Williamson's list: 197
Built: 1855
119.8 tons. Length 166.7 feet
Builders: J. Barr, Kelvinhaugh
Engine builders: J. Barr, Kelvinhaugh. Engine type: steeple; 85 hp
Hull material: Flush-decked
Owner: J. Barr

1855: Entered service from Glasgow to Ardrishaig. Was a double-ended steamer.

1857: Sold to H. Curtiss and others. Operated from Hull to Grimsby.

1867: Last mention of this steamer in the public records.

247: *Alma*

Number in Williamson's list: 198
Built: 1855
146 tons. Length 157.3 feet
Builders: Barr & McNab, Renfrew
Engine builders: J. Barr, Kelvinhaugh. Engine type: steeple; 80 hp
Hull material: Flush-decked
Owner: D. Stewart
1855: Entered service from Glasgow to Rothesay.
1855: Sold to R. Salmond, Glasgow.
1865: Broken up. Engines fitted in *Argyle* (No. 302).

248: *Nelson*

Number in Williamson's list: 199
Built: 1855
113.72 tons. Length 150.1 feet
Builders: T. B. Seath & Co., Rutherglen
Engine builders: T. Wingate & Co., Whiteinch, from *Eclipse*. Engine type: steeple; 60 hp
Hull material: Iron
Owner: A. McKellar
1855 June: Entered service from Glasgow to Kilmun.
1862: Operated from Glasgow to Garelochhead .
1863: January – Sold to P. L. Henderson and E. Blackman.
1863: Operated from Glasgow to Arrochar in this and part of the following year.
1864: Returned to the Glasgow–Garelochhead service.
1868: April – Sold to T. B. Seath. Operated from Glasgow to Helensburgh.
1868: May: Sold to W. Baird, Glasgow.
1870: May: Sold to W. Buchanan, Rothesay.
1870: May: Sold to J. C. R. Grove, London. Service not known.
1871: 11 March – Lost on the River Niger.

249: *Clansman*

Built: 1855
414 tons. Length 191.3 feet
Builders: J. & G. Thomson, Govan
Engine builders: J. & G. Thomson, Govan. 180 hp
Hull material: Iron
Owners: D. Hutcheson & Co.
1855: Entered service from Glasgow to Oban, Portree and Stornoway.
1869: 21 July – Wrecked on Deep Island, near Sanda.

250: *Mail* (1856)

Built: 1856
138 tons. Length 183 feet
Builders: J. Barr, Kelvinhaugh
Engine builders: J. Barr, Kelvinhaugh. Engine type: steeple; 85 hp
Hull material: Iron
Owner: J. Barr
1856: Entered service from Glasgow to the Holy Loch and Greenock to Rothesay.
1857: Sold to Henderson and Handyside.
1857: Sold to unknown Russian owners.

251: *Jupiter* (1856)

Number in Williamson's list: 201
Built: 1856
171 tons. Length 184.9 feet
Builders: Tod & McGregor, Meadowside
Engine builders: Tod & McGregor, Meadowside. Engine type: steeple; 90 hp
Hull material: Iron
Owners: J. Reid, D. and A McKellar
1856: Entered service from Glasgow to Largs, Millport and Lamlash
1863: July – Sold for blockade running
1863: 13 September – Captured in Wassaw Sound, Georgia, by the gunboat USS *Cimmaron*
     en route to Savannah on her first trip.
1865: October – Sold at a prize court.
1877: Abandoned.

252: *Artizan*

Built: 1856
34 tons. Length 113.3 feet
Builders: T. B. Seath & Co., Rutherglen
Engine builders: T. B. Seath & Co., Rutherglen. Engine type: two-cylinder; 40 hp
Hull material: Iron, flush-decked
Owners: T. B. Seath, J. Reid and T. Steele
1856: Entered service from Rutherglen to Glasgow (Hutchesonstown Bridge).
1857: Sold to the Midland Great Western Railway Co., Dublin. Moved to the River Shannon.
     Sailed to Limerick, cut in half and transported to Athlone, where she was joined together
     again. Operated on the River Shannon from Athlone to Killaloe.
1860: Owners taken over by the Great Southern & Western Railway Co., Dublin.
1861: Laid up.
1863: Broken up.

253: *Caledonia* (1856)

Built: 1856
183 tons. Length 162.8 feet
Builders: Tod & McGregor, Meadowside
Engine builders: Tod & McGregor, Meadowside. Engine type: geared; 90 hp
Hull material: Iron
Owners: Glasgow & Stranraer Steam Packet Co., Stranraer
1856: Entered service from Glasgow to Stranraer, and occasionally Stranraer to Belfast.
Late 1863: Sold for blockade running.
1864: 10 February – Made a successful return trip from Bermuda to Wilmington, South Carolina.
1864: 30 May – Attempted to run the blockade from Bermuda to Wilmington. Captured by USS *Keystone State* and USS *Massachusetts* south of Cape Fear.
c. 1864: According to some sources, sold to Brazilian owners and renamed *Torre de Belem*. Other sources state renamed *Island City*.
No further information as available.

254: *Royal Burgh*

Number in Williamson's list: 202
Built: 1857
63 tons. Length 102.2 feet
Builders: T. B. Seath & Co., Rutherglen
Engine builders: ? Engine type: two-cylinder; 45 hp
Hull material: Iron
Owners: T. B. Seath & Co.
1857: Entered service from Rutherglen to Glasgow (Hutchesonstown Bridge).
1858: Sold for use on the Rhine.
No further information is available.

255: *Alliance*

Number in Williamson's list: 203
Built: 1857
113 tons, 407 tons (1863). Length 140 feet, 174 feet (1863)
Builders: Tod & McGregor, Meadowside
Engine builders: Seaward & Capel, Millwall, new engines (1863). Engine type: two trunk, one in each hull, with centre wheel, converted to conventional side wheel (1863); 170 hp, 180 hp (1863)
Hull material: twin hull; deck saloons
Owners: G. Mills, The Clyde Improved Steam Packet Co. Ltd
1857: 4 April – Maiden voyage from Glasgow to Garelochhead. Built as a double-ended twin-hull centre wheel steamer (with one large wheel for propulsion and two small wheels for steering).
1857: August – Moved to the Greenock–Lochgoilhead service.
Late 1858: Owners went into liquidation.
1859: Made occasional Sunday excursions.

1860: Laid up.

1861: July – Chartered to D. Hutcheson & Co. for two months. Operated from Banavie to Inverness.

1862: December – Sold to W. J. Glazebrook, Liverpool, for blockade running.

1863: Spring – Rebuilt at a Clyde yard with conventional side wheels and a new engine. Some sources say the engine was upgraded and not replaced. Now witted with three funnels athwartships.

1863: December – Sold to L. G. Watson, Nassau.

1864: April – Ran aground on her first blockade running trip from Nassau to Savannah. Towed off and taken to Boston.

1864: 11 June – Sold at auction at Boston to Isaac Taylor. Probably resold to a New Zealand owner.

1865: Renamed *New Zealand*. Moved to New Zealand and operated from Dunedin to Lyttleton.

1865: 7 August – Wrecked at Hokitia.

256: *Spunkie*

Number in Williamson's list: 204
Built: 1857
165.8 tons. Length 191.3 feet
Builders: Tod & McGregor, Meadowside
Engine builders: Tod & McGregor, Meadowside. Engine type: steeple; 100 hp
Hull material: Deck saloons
Owners: Tod & McGregor

1857: Entered service from Glasgow to Largs, Millport and Lamlash.

1859: Laid up.

1860: Sold to A. Denny, Dumbarton.

1861: Returned to her original route.

1863: Sold to E. Lomnitz, Manchester, for blockade running.

1863: September to January 1864 – Ran as a blockade runner, made four return trips between Nassau and Wilmington.

1864: 9 February – Sank while attempting to enter Old Inlet, off Fort Caswell, North Carolina.

257: *Kelpie*

Number in Williamson's list: 205
Built: 1857
165.8 tons. Length 192.5 feet
Builders: Tod & McGregor, Meadowside
Engine builders: Tod & McGregor, Meadowside. Engine type: steeple; 100 hp
Hull material: Deck saloons
Owners: Tod & McGregor

1857: Entered service from Glasgow to the Kyles of Bute.

1858: Sold to W. Dargan, Limerick. Operated across the Shannon Estuary from Foynes to Kilrush Kilkee in connection with the new railway from Limerick to Foynes.

1858: 15 August – Made her first trip from Foynes to Kilrush. Carried 14,000 passengers in her first four months of operation.

1862: Sent across the Atlantic for blockade running.

1862: December – Lost entering Nassau before she could attempt to run the blockade.

258: *Carradale*

Built: 1857

37 tons, 45 tons (1861), 51 tons (1865). Length 44 feet, 61.6 feet (1861), 80.3 feet (1865)

Builders: J. & R. Swan, Maryhill

Engine builders: Smith Brothers. Engine type: two-cylinder side-lever; 60 hp

Hull material: Iron

Owners: J. & R. Lyle, Glasgow

1860: Entered service as a cargo steamer from Glasgow to the West Highlands.

1861: Lengthened by 17.6 feet.

1862: Sold to A. Montague, Glasgow.

1865: Lengthened again by a further 18.7 feet.

1866: Sold to R. Tennant.

1866: Ran ashore at Luing, then converted to a screw steamer.

1868: Sold to R. Rintoul, Leith. Moved to operate on the Forth.

1869: September – Sold to P. Brash, Leith.

1873: July – Sold to unknown owners at St Paul de Loanda, Angola.

No information is available after this date.

259: *Druid*

Built: 1857

229 tons. Length 160.1 feet

Builders: R. Barclay & Curle, Stobcross

Engine builders: R. Barclay & Curle, Stobcross. Engine type: two-cylinder; 150 hp

Hull material: Iron, flush-decked

Owners: Campbeltown & Glasgow Steam Packet Joint Stock Co. Ltd

1857: Entered service from Glasgow to Campbeltown.

1863: Sold to H. C. Drinkwater, Manchester, for blockade running.

1863: Sold to the Steamship Druid Co., Charleston, South Carolina, USA.

1 July 1864–1865: Made four return trips as a blockade runner from Nassau to Charleston.

1868: Sold to J. Robertson, Greenock. Engines removed and converted to a schooner.

1871: Sold to T. Redhead, Birkenhead.

1871: Sold to W. S. Martin, Porthcawl.

1880: 5 April – Lost in Bay of Biscay en route from Irvine to Lisbon with coal.

260: *Dumbarton* (1858)

Number in Williamson's list: 206

Built: 1858

115 tons. Length 143.5 feet

Builders: Smith & Rodger, Govan

Engine builders: Smith & Rodger, Govan. Engine type: 65 hp

Hull material: Flush-decked
Owners: Dumbarton Steamboat Co. (G. Burns and others).
1858: Entered service from Glasgow to Dumbarton.
1862: Sold to J. Watson.
No further information is available and there are no records of this steamer after this date.

261: *Hero* (1858)

Number in Williamson's list: 207
Built: 1858
157.9 tons. Length 181 feet
Builders: T. Wingate & Co., Whiteinch
Engine builders: T. Wingate & Co., Whiteinch. Engine type: steeple; 80 hp
Hull material: Iron
Owners: T. Wingate, J. McClymont
1858: Entered service from Glasgow to Rothesay.
1861: Sold to J. & R. Brown, Belfast. Operated from Belfast to Bangor.
1863: May – Returned to the Glasgow–Rothesay service.
1865: Sold to A. Watson, Glasgow.
1866: Sold to G. & J. Ferguson, Glasgow.
1871: Sold to M. McIntyre. Route extended to Kilchattan Bay and Arran for one year only.
1873: Sold to D. Chalmers. Operated from Glasgow to Rothesay.
1876: January – Sold to Keith and Campbell. Operated from Glasgow to Garelochhead.
1878: Operated from Glasgow to Arran for one year only.
1884: Sold to Capt. W. Buchanan. Re-boilered and a deck saloon added. Used as a spare
    steamer.
1886: May – Sold to the River Tay Steamboat Co. Operated from Broughty Ferry to Perth.
1887: Operated on excursions from Dundee.
1888: Laid up.
1889: February – Sold to J. Orr. Operated on excursions from Dumbarton and Paisley.
1890: June – Sold to David MacBrayne. Rebuilt with a deck saloon and clipper bow. Operated
    from Ardrishaig to Glasgow.
1891: Operated on sailings out of Oban from now onwards. Occasionally used on the early
    morning newspaper run from Greenock to Rothesay.
1892: Renamed *Mountaineer*.
1909: Scrapped.

262: *Pearl*

Number in Williamson's list: 209
Built: 1858
167.7 tons. Length 182.2 feet
Builders: J. Henderson & Son, Renfrew
Engine builders: J. Henderson & Son, Renfrew. Engine type: diagonal oscillating, four
    cylinders, one crank; 120 hp
Hull material: composite, flush-decked
Owner: J. Henderson
1858: Entered service from Glasgow to Rothesay.

1862: Sold to G. Wigg for the Navigations Company for blockade running.

1863: January – Captured off the Bahamas while sailing on her first run from Nassau to Charleston.

No further information is available.

263: *Prince of Wales* (1858)

Built: 1858
142 tons. Length 153.8 feet
Builders: Laurence Hill & Co., Port Glasgow
Engine builders: Scott Sinclair & Co., Greenock. Engine type: two-cylinder diagonal; 75 rhp
Hull material: Iron; fore saloon
Owners: Loch Lomond Steamboat Co.
1858: Entered service on Loch Lomond, operating from Balloch to Ardlui.
1860: 11 September – Struck a submerged rock off the north-east shore of Inchmurrin, now known as the Prince of Wales rock. A 10-foot gash was sustained in her hull. Taken to Cameron Bay, near Balloch, where the damage was examined, and then down the River Leven to Scott, MacGill & Duncan's yard at Bowling, where the hull was repaired.
1888: Taken over by the North British Steam Packet Co.
1895: Owners now the Dumbarton & Balloch Joint Line Committee (North British and Caledonian railways).
1899: Sold for Jebb Bros., Glasgow for use as a coal hulk at Newry.

264: *Loch Long* (1859)

Number in Williamson's list: 208
Built: 1859
116 tons. Length 150.4 feet
Builders: Alex Denny, Dumbarton
Engine builders: Alex Denny, Dumbarton. Engine type: oscillating; 60 hp
Hull material: Iron
Owners: Loch Goil & Loch Long Steamboat Co.
1859: Entered service from Glasgow to Lochgoilhead.
1864: Sold to unknown owners in Copenhagen.
No further information is available.

265: *Windsor Castle* (1859)

Number in Williamson's list: 210
Built: 1859
191 tons. Length 191 feet
Builders: Caird & Co., Greenock
Engine builders: John Penn, Blackheath. Engine type: double diagonal; 115 hp
Hull material: Steel hull, flush-decked, deck saloons
Owners: Caird & Co.
1859: Entered service from Glasgow to Rothesay. Was the first Clyde steamer built with a steel hull.

1860: Sold to unknown owners in India, intended for service on the River Hooghly.

1860: 27 September – Ran aground on Sanda on delivery voyage to India under sail. Her engines were salvaged and later fitted in a new hull, named *Indus*.

266: *Royal Reefer*

Built: 1859
tons. Length 133 feet
Builders: T. B. Seath & Co., Rutherglen
Engine builders: T. B. Seath & Co., Rutherglen. Engine type: two-cylinder; 60 hp
Hull material: Iron
Owners: T. B. Seath & Co.
1859: Entered service from Rutherglen to Glasgow (Hutchesonstown Bridge).
1859: July – Sold to unknown owners in St Petersburg, Russia. Renamed *Royal Rodger*.

CHAPTER 6
Steamers Built 1860–69

267: *Earl of Arran*

Number in Williamson's list: 211
Built: 1860
144 tons. Length 140 feet
Builders: Blackwood & Gordon, Paisley
Engine builders: Blackwood & Gordon, Paisley. Engine type: double steeple; 80 hp
Hull material: Flush-decked
Owners: Ardrossan Steamboat Co.
1860: Entered service from Ardrossan to Arran.
1869: Laid up.
1871: Sold to West Cornwall S. S. Co. Operated from Penzance to St Mary's, Isles of Scilly.
1872: 16 July – Ran aground off St Martins en route from Penzance to St Mary's. Beached at Normour, broke in two and was abandoned.

268: *Ruby* (1860)

Number in Williamson's list: 212
Built: 1860
175.6 tons. Length 188.4 feet
Builders: J. Henderson & Son, Renfrew
Engine builders: J. Henderson & Son, Renfrew. Engine type: diagonal oscillating; 100 hp
Hull material: Flush-decked
Owner: P. L. Henderson
1860: 8 May – Launched.
1860: Operated from Glasgow to Rothesay.
1860: November – Sold to Indian owners for a proposed service on the River Hooghly at Calcutta. Left the Clyde under sail but was lost off the Copeland Islands. Her engine was salvaged and fitted in a new hull by her builders, named *Soane*.

269: *Juno* (1860)

Number in Williamson's list: 213
Built: 1860
341 gross tons. Length 188.9 feet
Builders: Tod & McGregor, Meadowside
Engine builders: Tod & McGregor, Meadowside. Engine type: steeple; 110 hp

Hull material: Flush-decked
Owners: D. McKellar
1860: Entered service from Glasgow to Largs, Millport and Arran.
1863: May – Sold to H. Wigg, Nassau, for blockade running.
1863: 8 July – Arrived at Charleston from Nassau on her one and only trip through the blockade. Taken over by the Confederacy. Remained at Charleston and was used as a dispatch, picket and flag-of-truce boat. Fitted with a howitzer and outfitted with a spar torpedo.
1863: August – Rammed a launch from USS *Wabash*.
1863: December – Renamed *Helen*. Became a Confederate Gunboat in Charleston Harbour.
1864: 9 March – Made another trip running the blockade out of Charleston with a cargo of cotton.
1864: 10 March – Lost in a gale en route from Charleston for Nassau. Only two survivors: the engineer and the pilot.

270: *Mail* (1860)

Number in Williamson's list: 214
Built: 1860
291 tons. Length 179.5 feet
Builders: Tod & McGregor, Meadowside
Engine builders: Tod & McGregor, Meadowside. Engine type: steeple; 85 hp
Hull material: Raised quarter deck
Owners: J., A. and R. Campbell
1860: Entered service from Glasgow to Kilmun.
1863: 29 April – Sold to S. H. Bigland for use as a blockade runner.
1863: September – Made one run from Havana to St Marks, Florida.
1863: 15 October – Captured near Bayport, Florida, on her return journey from St Marks, by USS *Honduras*.
1864: Sold to unknown owners. Returned to operation as a blockade runner. Renamed *Susanna*, also known as *Susanna Mail*. Made five successful return runs from Havana to Galveston between June and November.
1864: 27 November – Captured at Campeche Banks by USS *Metacomet*, on her return trip from Galveston to Havana. Half of her cargo of cotton was thrown overboard. She was regarded by Rear Admiral Farragut as 'their fastest steamer'.
No further information is available.

271: *Albion* (1860)

Built: 1860
307 tons. Length 165 feet
Builders: Tod & McGregor, Meadowside
Engine builders: Tod & McGregor, Meadowside. Engine type: two-cylinder; 150 hp
Hull material: Iron
Owners: Glasgow & Stranraer Steam Packet Co.
1860: Entered service from Ayr, Girvan and Ballantrae to Stranraer and from Ayr to Campbeltown.
1861: Used on the Stranraer–Belfast service.
1865: May – Chartered to the Somerset & Dorset Railway. Operated from Poole to Cherbourg.

1867: February – Charter ended, sold to J. Pool, Hayle. Operated from Hayle to Swansea, Ilfracombe and Bristol.
1868: August – Made one excursion trip from Hayle, Penzance and Plymouth to Jersey and Guernsey.
1869: Sold to M. Langlands & Sons. Operated from Belfast to Stranraer.
1877: Laid up.
1880: Sold to Readhead, Liverpool.
1882: Converted to a sailing vessel.
No further information is available.

272: *St Clair of the Isles*

Number in Williamson's list: 214
Built: 1860
358 tons. Length 185.5 feet
Builders: J. Reid & Co., Port Glasgow
Engine builders: McNab & Co., Greenock. Engine type: two-cylinder oscillating; 120 hp
Hull material: Iron
Owners: Companhia Lusitania, Lisbon
1860: 25 March – Launched.
1860: Entered service from Lisbon to Oporto as *Lisboa*.
1873: Following completion of the railway from Lisbon to Oporto, service withdrawn and sold to the Western Isles Steam Packet Co. Ltd (J. McCallum). Renamed *St Clair of the Isles*. Entered service from Glasgow to Dunvegan or Uig, Lochmaddy and Lochboisdale.
1874: Autumn – Operated from Glasgow to Loch Swilly.
1875: Sold at auction to Harris & Goodwin, Birmingham.
1879: Sold to unknown owners in the Dutch East Indies. Renamed *Mangkor Almansoer*.
There is no further information available about her career after that date and her eventual fate.

273: *Sultan* (1861)

Number in Williamson's list: 215
Built: 1861
124 tons. Length 166 feet, 176 feet (1865), 148.3 feet (1895)
Builders: R. Barclay & Curle, Stobcross
Engine builders: Barclay Curle & Co., Whiteinch. Engine type: steeple; 60 hp
Hull material: Flush-decked, saloon added 1895
Owner: A. McKellar
1861: 9 May – Launched.
1861: Entered service from Glasgow to Dunoon and Kilmun. Fitted with the engine from *Wellington* (No. 231).
1862: 28 February – Sold to Alexander Williamson. Operated from Glasgow to Rothesay and the Kyles of Bute.
1865: Lengthened by 10 feet.
1877: Re-boilered.
1891: September – Sold to the Glasgow & South Western Railway. Operated on rail-connected services from Greenock (Princes Pier).

1893: March – Sold to John Williamson. Renamed *Ardmore*. Used on sailings out of Glasgow.

Late 1894: Sold to David MacBrayne. Renamed *Gairlochy*.

1895: Shortened by 28.7 feet, deck saloon added. Operated from Banavie to Inverness.

1919: 24 December – Destroyed by fire when lying at Fort Augustus. Her remains were visible at low water for many years.

274: *Ruby* (1861)

Number in Williamson's list: 216
Built: 1861
200.51 tons. Length 209.3 feet
Builders: Henderson, Coulborn & Co., Renfrew
Engine builders: Henderson, Coulborn & Co., Renfrew. Engine type: diagonal oscillating; 120 hp
Hull material: Flush-decked
Owner: P. L. Henderson
1861: Entered service from Glasgow to Rothesay.
1862: Sold to R. C. Heddell (or Keddell) for blockade running.
1862: 15 November – Left the Clyde for Havana.
1864: 27 February – Captured on first run from Havana to St Marks, Florida, by USS *Proteus*.
1874: Abandoned.

275: *Neptune* (1861)

Number in Williamson's list: 217
Built: 1861
260 tons. Length 201.7 feet
Builders: Robert Napier & Sons, Govan
Engine builders: Robert Napier & Sons, Govan. Engine type: double diagonal; 100 hp
Hull material: Flush-decked
Owners: J. & W. Napier
1861: Entered service from Glasgow to Rothesay.
1863: Sold to J. H. Wilson for Fraser, Trenholm & Co. for blockade running.
1863: April–June – made two return trips from Havana to Mobile, Alabama.
1863: 14 June – Captured entering Mobile, Alabama, by USS *Lackawanna*. Taken to Key West, then to New York and taken over by the US Navy.
1863: Renamed USS *Clyde*. Patrolled the western Florida coast.
1865: 25 October – Sold to unknown private owners. Renamed *Indian River*.
1865: Early December – Wrecked at Indian River, Florida.

276: *Rothesay Castle* (1861)

Number in Williamson's list: 218
Built: 1861
177.62 tons. Length 191.5 feet
Builders: W. Simons & Co., Renfrew

Engine builders: W. Simons & Co., Renfrew. Engine type: oscillating; 110 hp
Hull material: Flush-decked
Owners: A. Watson
1861: Entered service from Glasgow to Rothesay.
1863: June – Sold to D. McNutt, for blockade running.
1864: January – Made one return trip from Nassau to Wilmington.
1864: April – Made one return trip from Nassau to Charleston.
1866: Sold to C. Heron and T. Leach, Halifax. Operated from Toronto to Queenston (Niagara River).
1867: Operated from Gulf of St Lawrence ports to Northumberland Strait ports.
1872: Sold to Mrs S. Boomer, Yorkville (Toronto).
1874: Operated from Toronto to Hamilton.
1875: 10 February – Damaged by fire at Shediac, New Brunswick. Later rebuilt.
1875: 16 August – Grounded in Toronto Harbour. Later rebuilt with deck saloons.
1876: Purchased by T. Leach, Toronto. Renamed *Southern Belle*. Operated from Toronto to Hamilton and Oakville.
1876: Chartered by the Canada Southern Railway.
1879: Purchased by D. S. Keith, Toronto.
1885: Laid up.
1887: Taken to Napanee and slipped. It was the intention to place her on the route from Belleville to Charlotte.
1892: Scrapped.

277: *Fairy* (1861)

Built: 1861
151 tons. Length 149.4 feet
Builders: J. & G. Thomson, Govan
Engine builders: J. & G. Thomson, Govan. Engine type: two-cylinder oscillating; 75 hp
Hull material: Iron, deck saloon
Owners: D. Hutcheson & Co.
1861: Entered service on the Caledonian Canal.
1862: Operated from Oban to Staffa and Iona.
1863: Sold to J. Proudfoot and M. Gray, Glasgow for blockade running.
1863–64: Ran the blockade from Havana to Matamoras, Mexico.
1866: Sold to unknown owners at Montevideo, Uruguay. Operated from Montevideo to the River Uruguay and on the River Parana to Santa Fe.
No record of her fate has survived.

278: *Kingstown*

Number in Williamson's list: 219
Built: 1862
153 tons. Length 151 feet
Builders: T. Wingate & Co., Whiteinch
Engine builders: T. Wingate & Co., Whiteinch. Engine type: diagonal; 86 hp
Hull material: Deck saloons
Owners: Dublin and Kingstown S. P. Co.

1862: Entered service from Dublin to Kingstown (Dun Laoghaire). Was built as a double-ended steamer.

1876: Sold to Willoughby, Liverpool. Operated across the Mersey from Liverpool to Tranmere.

1885: Sold to A. McFarlane. Operated a Sunday service from Glasgow to Greenock in this and the following year.

1888: Scrapped.

279: *Briton* (1862)

Built: 1862
184 tons, 486 tons (1876). Length 175.7 feet, 207.1 feet (1876)
Builders: Tod & McGregor, Meadowside
Engine builders: Tod & McGregor, Meadowside. Engine type: two-cylinder steeple; 150 hp
Hull material: Iron, raised quarterdeck
Owners: Glasgow & Stranraer Steam Packet Co., Stranraer
1862: Entered service from Glasgow to Stranraer.
1862: August – Moved to the Stranraer–Belfast service.
1862: October – Moved to the Stranraer–Larne route.
1864: January – Sold to the Bristol General Steam Navigation Co. Operated from Bristol to Waterford with calls at Tenby and Carmarthen.
1866: Used on the Bristol–Ilfracombe route.
1867: Ran from Bristol to Cork in this year only. Moved to the Bristol–Wexford service with calls at Tenby and Pembroke.
1876: Lengthened by 31.4 feet.
1890: Sold to the Waterford Steamship Co.
1892: 8 March – Stranded on North Bar, Wexford. Got off on the nest tide and was sold for breaking up.

280: *Prince Consort*

Built: 1862
169 tons. Length 151.3 feet
Builders: Caird & Co., Greenock.
Engine builders: Caird & Co., Greenock. Engine type: two-cylinder diagonal; o hp
Hull material: Iron; deck saloons
Owners: Loch Lomond Steamboat Co.
1862: 19 April – Launched.
1862: Entered service on Loch Lomond from Balloch to Ardlui. The sponsons ran the full length of the steamer, a feature that was repeated on subsequent Loch Lomond steamers until *Prince Edward* in 1911.
1864: 11 August – Conveyed the Prince and Princess of Wales from Balloch to Inversnaid.
1869: 4 September – Carried Queen Victoria and Princesses Louise and Beatrice on a 4½-hour cruise on the loch from Inversnaid.
1888: Taken over by the North British Steam Packet Co. Ltd.
1896: Owners now the Dumbarton & Balloch Joint Line Committee (NBR and CR).
1899: Broken up.

281: *Iona* (1863)

Number in Williamson's list: 220
Built: 1863
367.7 tons. Length 249.2 feet
Builders: J. & G. Thomson, Govan
Engine builders: J. & G. Thomson, Govan. Engine type: oscillating; 180 hp
Hull material: Deck saloons
Owners: D. Hutcheson & Co.
1863: 19 May – Launched.
1863: Operated from Glasgow to Ardrishaig.
1864: Sold to D. McNutt for use as a blockade runner. Deck saloons removed. Later sold to
    C. H. Boster, Richmond, Virginia.
1864: 2 February – Sank off Lundy on her delivery voyage.

282: *Eagle* (1863)

Built: 1863
235 tons. Length 201.3 feet
Builders: Charles Connell & Co., Scotstoun
Engine builders: Charles Connell & Co., Overnewton shipyard, Kelvinhaugh. Engine type: 110 hp
Hull material: Flush-decked
Owners: Eagle Steamer Co.
1863: Intended route Glasgow–Rothesay. Sold while on the stocks to G. Wigg for blockade
    running and renamed *Mary Ann*.
1863: 19 May – Launched.
1864: February – Made two round trips from Nassau to Wilmington, and a single trip to
    Wilmington.
1864: 6 March – Captured by USS *Grand Gulf* after leaving Wilmington and sent to Boston,
    Massachusetts.
1864: 25 July – Sold at Prize Court and renamed *Russia*.
1865: Abandoned.

283: *Victory*

Number in Williamson's list: 221
Built: 1864
126 tons. Length 176.7 feet
Builders: Barclay Curle, Whiteinch
Engine builders: J. Barr, Kelvinhaugh. Engine type: steeple; 75 hp
Hull material: Flush-decked
Owners: D. Stewart
1863: Entered service from Glasgow to Rothesay.
1865: Sold to the Wemyss Bay Steamboat Co. Used on rail-connected sailings from Wemyss
    Bay.
1869: January – Sold to Gillies & Campbell.
1869: February – Sold to A. Chalmers, Clynder.
1871: Sold to Duncan Dewar, Dumbarton. Renamed *Marquis of Lorne*.

1872: Used as a Sunday breaker.

1882: Sold to Hill & Co., Largs. Renamed *Cumbrae*. Operated from Fairlie to Millport and Kilchattan Bay.

1892: Spring – Sold to W. R. Fairlie, Glasgow. Used for excursions from Paisley.

1897: Sold to J. Carvill, Newry. Used as a coal hulk at Newry.

284: *Iona* (1864)

Number in Williamson's list: 222
Built: 1864
393 tons. Length 255.5 feet
Builders: J. & G. Thomson, Govan
Engine builders: J. & G. Thomson, Govan. Engine type: two-cylinder oscillating; 180 hp
Hull material: Deck saloons
Owners: D. Hutcheson & Co.

1864: 10 May – Launched.

1864: 21 June – Entered service from Glasgow to Ardrishaig. Fitted with deck saloons from *Iona* (1863) (No. 281). Was the first Clyde steamer to be fitted with a with steam whistle.

Winter 1870/1: Navigating bridge, the first on a Clyde steamer, erected between the paddle boxes.

1873: Claimed to be the first steamer in the world to have steam steering gear fitted. Became the first Clyde steamer to be fitted with engine-room telegraphs.

1875: Spring – Re-boilered and rebuilt with new accommodation similar to that fitted previously.

1879: Owners now David MacBrayne.

1880: June – Moved to the Oban–Corpach service. Continued to operate the Glasgow–Ardrishaig service for short spells in spring and autumn each year until the end of her career.

1886: Moved to the Ardrishaig–Glasgow service, departing Ardrishaig in the mornings.

1891: Accommodation again rebuilt. Re-boilered. Surface condenser replaced the original jet type.

1903: Now making a double run from Ardrishaig to Wemyss Bay and Greenock (Princes Pier) and, on some days, making a short afternoon cruise from Ardrishaig to Loch Fyne.

1905: Owners became David MacBrayne Ltd.

1914: July – Collided with Rothesay Pier, cutting 3 feet into the timbers and damaging her hull plating.

1914: August – Extra services withdrawn on the outbreak of war.

1915: Operated from Wemyss Bay to Ardrishaig due to the boom between the Cloch and Dunoon.

1916: August – Chartered to the Caledonian Steam Packet Co. Operated from Wemyss Bay to Rothesay.

Winter 1918/19: New deck saloons added, the forward one extending 10 feet further forward than previously.

1919: 1 July – 1 September – Again chartered to the Caledonian Steam Packet Co., operating from Wemyss Bay to Rothesay.

1922: Operated from Glasgow to Lochgoilhead and Arrochar.

1928: Owners became David MacBrayne (1928) Ltd. Moved to the Oban–Fort William service.

1934: Owners became David MacBrayne Ltd again.

1935: Withdrawn from service at the end of the summer season after a record-breaking career of seventy-two years.

1936: Scrapped at Dalmuir alongside *Columba*.

285: *Vivid*

Number in Williamson's list: 223
Built: 1864
156.7 tons. Length 188.3 feet
Builders: Barclay Curle, Whiteinch
Engine builders: Barclay, Curle & Co.. Engine type: steeple; 80 hp
Hull material: Flush-decked
Owners: J. & R. Campbell
1864: 8 April – Launched.
1864: Entered service from Glasgow to Kilmun.
1871: Owners became Keith and Campbell.
1872: Route extended to Lochgoilhead on certain days.
1876: July–September – Operated from Glasgow to Millport.
1878: Returned to the Glasgow–Kilmun service.
1881: Operated from Glasgow to Garelochhead on summer Saturday afternoons.
1884: Moved to the Glasgow–Rothesay service.
1885: Sold to Capt. W. Buchanan.
1891–92: Made some excursion sailings from Paisley.
1902: Broken up, by which time she was the last surviving steeple-engined steamer on the Clyde.

286: *Eagle* (1864)

Number in Williamson's list: 224
Built: 1864
208 tons. Length 189 feet
Builders: Charles Connell & Co., Scotstoun
Engine builders: (1) Anchor Line (D. & W. Henderson); (2) W. King and Co. (1876). Engine type: (1) double diagonal, 103 hp; (2) single diagonal (1877); 85 hp
Hull material: Raised quarter deck
Owner: Captain William Buchanan
1864: 25 April – Launched.
1864: Entered service from Glasgow to Rothesay.
1866: Lengthened by 15 feet.
1877: Lengthened by 14.5 feet and re-engined. Original engine placed in *Brodick Castle* (No. 347). Reduced from two funnels to one funnel.

1887: Saloon added above raised quarter deck, the only Clyde steamer to have this feature. Service extended to Arran.
1889: Re-boilered.
1892: Route now just from Glasgow to Rothesay.
1894: Sold to the Ship Canal Passenger Steamer Co. (1893) Ltd, Liverpool. Operated trips on the Manchester Ship Canal.
1898: Sold to Eastham Ferry Pleasure Gardens and Hotel Ltd.
1899: Sold for scrapping.

287: *Largs* (1864)

Number in Williamson's list: 225
Built: 1864
153 tons. Length 161.4 feet
Builders: T. Wingate & Co., Whiteinch
Engine builders: T. Wingate & Co., Whiteinch. Engine type: double oscillating; 80 hp
Hull material: Flush-decked
Owners: Wemyss Bay Steamboat Co.
1864: 17 September – Launched.
1865: April – Entered service from Glasgow to Largs, Millport and Lamlash.
1865: 15 May – On the opening of Wemyss Bay Pier, operated from Wemyss Bay to Largs, Millport and Lamlash.
1865: October – Now operated from Wemyss Bay to Millport and from Wemyss Bay to Rothesay.
1869: Sold to Gillies & Campbell.
1875: Sold to the Waterford Steam Ship Co. Renamed *Mermaid*. Operated by the Lower Shannon Steamship Company on the Shannon Estuary from Limerick, Tarbert and Foynes to Cappa Pier, Kilrush.
1892: Following the opening of the South Clare Railway (narrow gauge) to Cappa Pier, a connecting train was run to Kilkee.
1898: 2 December – In collision with the cargo steamer *Premier*, which sank fifteen minutes later.
1903: Scrapped.

288: *Leven* (1864)

Number in Williamson's list: 226
Built: 1864
65.4 tons. Length 139.4 feet
Builders: Clyde Shipbuilding Co., Greenock
Engine builders: Rankin & Blackmore, Greenock. Engine type: oscillating; 40 hp
Hull material: Raised quarter deck
Owners: Dumbarton Steamboat Co. (Denny)
1864: Entered service from Glasgow to Dumbarton.
1866: December – Sold to the Bahia Steam Navigation Co., Bahia, Brazil. Renamed *Sevaros*.
1867: 20 March – Sank on delivery voyage to Brazil under sail off Irish Coast.

289: *Chancellor* (1864)

Number in Williamson's list: 227
Built: 1864
171 tons. Length 163.2 feet
Builders: Blackwood & Gordon, Port Glasgow
Engine builders: Blackwood & Gordon, Port Glasgow. Engine type: double diagonal; 80 hp
Hull material: Deck saloons
Owners: Loch Long Steamboat Co.
1864: 7 May – Launched.
1864: Entered service from Helensburgh to Arrochar. Built with full-length sponsons like the Loch Lomond steamers.
1867: Owners became the Loch Long & Loch Lomond Steamboat Co.
1880: Sold to Keith and Campbell. Operated from Glasgow to Garelochhead.
1881: Also operated from Glasgow to Kilmun.
1882: Renamed *Shandon*.
1884: Purchased by Capt. W. Buchanan.
1885: Re-boilered.
Late 1886: Moved to the Glasgow–Rothesay service.
1890: Moved to the Greenock–Helensburgh service.
1891: Started making occasional excursions from Paisley.
1893: Sold to Ship Canal Passenger Steamer Co. (1893) Ltd, Liverpool. Renamed *Daniel Adamson*.
1894: Started operating excursions on the Manchester Ship Canal.
1895: Sold to J. Orr, Glasgow. Operated from Glasgow to the Clyde Coast for a few weeks.
1896: Scrapped.

290: *Lennox*

Number in Williamson's list: 228
Built: 1864
87 tons. Length 139.4 feet
Builders: Clyde Shipbuilding Co., Greenock
Engine builders: Rankin & Blackmore, Greenock. Engine type: oscillating; 40 hp
Hull material: Raised quarter deck
Owners: Dumbarton Steamboat Co. (Denny)
1864: Entered service from Glasgow to Dumbarton.
1866: December – Sold to the Bahia Steam Navigation Co., Bahia, Brazil. Renamed *Taviros Bastor*.
1867: 17 March – Ran aground near Kingstown on her delivery voyage to Brazil under sail.

291: *Arran Castle* (1864)

Number in Williamson's list: 229
Built: 1864
224 tons. Length 220.5 feet
Builders: Kirkpatrick, McIntyre & Co., Greenock
Engine builders: Rankin & Blackmore, Greenock. Engine type: oscillating; 130 hp

Hull material: Deck saloons aft
Owners: A. Watson and W. Brown
1864: 20 July – Launched.
1864: Entered service from Glasgow to Rothesay. She had been built on spec as a blockade runner.
1866: 21 March – Sailed to the Thames for a proposed service from London to Gravesend.
1866: 22 March – Sank off Portpatrick with all hands after a boiler explosion en route to Thames.

292: *Carham*

Built: 1864
159 tons. Length 141.8 feet
Builders: A. & J. Inglis, Pointhouse
Engine builders: A. & J. Inglis, Pointhouse. Engine type: twin steeple oscillating; 40 hp
Hull material: Iron, flush-decked
Owners: North British Steam Packet Co.
1864: 7 September – Launched.
1864: Entered service from Silloth to Dumfries and Annan.
1867: Transferred to the Clyde. Operated from Helensburgh to Garelochhead.
1871: Sold to the Dingwall & Skye Railway. Operated from Strome Ferry to Portree.
1872: Owners taken over by the Highland Railway.
1880: Sold to the Bournemouth & South Coast Steam Packet Co. Operated on excursions from Bournemouth.
1883: Sold to the Ramsgate Steamboat Co. Renamed *Queen of Thanet*. Operated sailings from Ramsgate.
1884: 2–21 September – Chartered to Paine & Collard, Hastings. Operated excursions from Hastings, including to Boulogne.
1889: Scrapped.

293: *Hattie*

Built: 1864
284 tons. Length 219.4 feet
Builders: Caird & Co., Greenock
Engine builders: Caird & Co., Greenock. Engine type: twin oscillating; 260 hp
Hull material: Iron
Owners: Wemyss Bay Steamboat Co.
1864: Launched.
1864: Intended for rail-connected services from Wemyss Bay, but sold on stocks to J. L. Martin for blockade running.
1865: 8 May – Lost en route from Cork to Nassau.

294: *Kyles*

Number in Williamson's list: 230
Built: 1865
171.25 tons. Length 219.4 feet
Builders: Caird & Co., Greenock
Engine builders: Caird & Co., Greenock. Engine type: oscillating; 120 hp
Hull material: Iron; deck saloons
Owners: Wemyss Bay Steamboat Co.
1864: 15 October – Launched.
1865: May – Entered service from Wemyss Bay to Rothesay and Tighnabruaich.
1865: June–August – Operated from Glasgow and Wemyss Bay to Ardrishaig.
1867: Sold to The Waterman's Steam Packet Co., London. Renamed *Albert Edward*. Operated on the Thames from London to Gravesend, Southend and Sheerness. Fore and aft deck saloons added.
1871: Sold to the Woolwich Steam Packet Co., London.
1871: 27 July – Made a special trip to Clacton with dignitaries on board for the official opening of Clacton Pier.
1876: Sold to the London Steamboat Co.
1885: Sold to the River Thames Steamboat Co.
1889: Scrapped.

295: *Undine*

Number in Williamson's list: 231
Built: 1865
172 tons. Length 200 feet
Builders: Henderson, Coulborn & Co., Renfrew
Engine builders: Henderson, Coulborn & Co., Renfrew. Engine type: single diagonal; 90 hp
Hull material: Flush-decked
Owners: Henderson, Coulborn & Co.
1865: Entered service from Glasgow to Rothesay.
1879: Sold to unknown owners in Italy or Russia.
No further information is available.

296: *Bute*

Number in Williamson's list: 232
Built: 1865
171.03 tons. Length 219.4 feet
Builders: Caird & Co., Greenock
Engine builders: Caird & Co., Greenock. Engine type: oscillating; 120 hp
Hull material: Flush-decked
Owners: Wemyss Bay Steamboat Co.
1865: 29 March – Launched.
1865: June–August – Entered service from Lamlash to Wemyss Bay and Glasgow.
1867: Sold to The Waterman's Steam Packet Co., London. Renamed *Princess Alice*. Operated on the Thames from London to Gravesend, Southend and Sheerness.

1870: Sold to the Woolwich Steam Packet Co., London.

1875: Sold to the London Steamboat Co.

1878: Sank after a collision with the collier *Bywell Castle* in the Thames near Woolwich on her return sailing from Sheerness. Over 650 lives lost, the worst peacetime disaster in British pleasure steamer history.

297: *Rothesay Castle* (1865)

Number in Williamson's list: 233
Built: 1865
203 tons. Length 203 feet
Builders: Henderson, Coulborn & Co., Renfrew
Engine builders: J. Barr, Kelvinhaugh. Engine type: steeple; 80 hp
Hull material: Deck saloons
Owner: A. Watson
1865: Entered service from Glasgow to Rothesay.
1866: Owners now Barr, Watson and Campbell.
1867: Sold to Capt. W. Buchanan.
1879: Sold to the Compagnie Maritime Gironde et Garonne, Bordeaux. Renamed *Gironde-et-Garonne No. 1ére*. Operated from Bordeaux to Royan.
c. 1900: Owners renamed Compagnie Bordeaux-Océan, Bordeaux.
Early 1900s: Reduced to a mooring hulk at Lormont, Gironde.

298: *Vale of Clwyd*

Number in Williamson's list: 234
Built: 1865
155 tons. Length 186.5 feet
Builders: T. B. Seath & Co., Rutherglen
Engine builders: A. Campbell & Son, Anderston. Engine type: two-cylinder ; one cylinder steeple, one cylinder diagonal; 90 hp
Hull material: Flush-decked
Owner: R. W. Preston, Liverpool
1865: Entered service from Liverpool to Rhyl.
1866: Sold to Seath and Steele. Operated from Glasgow to Ayr.
1870: Operated from Ayr to Glasgow for this year only.
1877: Chartered to Gillies & Campbell. Operated services out of Wemyss Bay.
1878: Moved to the Glasgow–Largs and Millport service.
1881: Sold to the Thames & Channel Steam Ship Co. Operated from London to Clacton, Walton, Harwich, and Ipswich.
1882: Sold to the London Steamboat Co.
1888: Scrapped after her owners were taken over by the Victoria Steamboat Association.

299: *Fairy* (1865)

Built: 1865
25 tons. Length 59.9 feet
Builders: J. Patterson, Port Glasgow
Engine builders: W. Smith & Co., Greenock. Engine type: two-cylinder; 15 hp
Hull material: Iron
Owners: Inveraray Ferry & Coach Co.
1865: Entered service from Inveraray to St Catherines.
1870: Sold to Inveraray & St Catherines Ferry Co.
1881: Sold to the Inveraray Steam Ferry Co.
1893: Sold to D. McGregor, Leith. There is no record of her service from this date onwards.
1894: Sold to J. Lindsay, Edinburgh.
1894: Sold to J. Cromarty, Berwick-on-Tweed.
1896: Sold to A. Lindsay, Lochgilphead.
1899: Sold to J. Giffen, Campbeltown.
1900: Scrapped.

300: *Flying Foam*

Built: 1865
88 tons. Length 96.5 feet
Builders: Blackwood & Gordon, Port Glasgow
Engine builders: (1) Scott, Sinclair & Co., Greenock (1848); (2) Carr Fowler & Co.,
    Sunderland. Engine type: (1) side-lever, 50 hp; (2) side-lever; 25 hp
Hull material: Iron tug/tender
Owners: Clyde Shipping Co.
1865: January – Launched.
1865: May – Entered service as a tug and tender at the Tail of the Bank.
1874: April – Sold to J. P. Rennoldson, North Shields. Converted to a screw tug, re-engined.
1874: December – Sold to J. Brodie, N. Shields.
1875: Sold to unknown Russian owners.
No further information is available.

301: *Chevalier* (1866)

Built: 1866
292 tons. Length 211 feet
Builders: J. & G. Thomson, Govan
Engine builders: J. & G. Thomson, Govan. Engine type: two-cylinder oscillating; 150 hp
Hull material: Deck saloons
Owners: D. Hutcheson & Co.
1866: 12 April – Launched.
1866: Entered service from Crinan to Oban and Corpach in the summer months, and Glasgow
    to Ardrishaig in the winter months.
1879: Owner became David MacBrayne.
1886: Re-boilered.
1901: Re-boilered.

1905: Owners became David MacBrayne Ltd.

1912: Operated on the Glasgow–Lochgoilhead route.

1915: Chartered to the Caledonian Steam Packet Co. Ltd. Operated from Wemyss Bay to Rothesay and Millport until 1918.

1919: Laid up in the summer months.

1927: 25 February – Wrecked on Barmore Island, Loch Fyne. Later salvaged and taken to Troon for breaking up.

302: *Argyle* (1866)

Number in Williamson's list: 236
Built: 1866
141 tons. Length 177.3 feet
Builders: Barclay Curle & Co., Whiteinch
Engine builders: J. Barr, Kelvinhaugh. Engine type: (1) steeple; 75 hp; (2) steeple
Hull material: Flush-decked
Owner: D. Stewart

1866: Entered service from Glasgow to Rothesay, for two weeks only. Fitted with the engine from *Alma* (No. 247).

1866: April – Purchased by the Wemyss Bay Steamboat Co. Operated from Wemyss Bay to Rothesay and Millport.

1869: Sold to Gillies & Campbell.

1880: Re-boilered.

1890: Sold to D. Edwards, Dundee. Operated from Dundee to Perth.

1899: Sold to the Dundee & Perth Passenger Steamboat Ltd.

1902: Sold to the Tay Passenger Steamship Co.

1904: Sold to Spanish owners. Renamed *Ares*. Service not known.

1908: Broken up.

303: *Athole*

Number in Williamson's list: 237
Built: 1866
165.1 tons. Length 192.2 feet
Engine builders: Barclay Curle & Co., Whiteinch
Engine type: steeple; 80 hp
Hull material: Poop deck aft
Owner: D. Stewart

1866: 8 March – Launched.

1866: Entered service from Glasgow to Rothesay.

1870: Sold to the Greenock & Ayrshire Railway. Operated on rail-connected services from Greenock (Princes Pier) to Rothesay and Kilmun. Was the first steamer to sail from Princes Pier.

1871: Retuned to the Glasgow–Rothesay service.

1872: Sold to A. and T. McLean.

1889: Sold to the Bute Steam Packet Ltd.

1898: Sold to Capt. James Williamson.

1898: Scrapped.

304: *Vesper* (1866)

Number in Williamson's list: 238
Built: 1866
135 tons. Length 173.8 feet
Builders: Barclay Curle & Co., Whiteinch
Engine builders: Barr's 'Express Engine'. Engine type: steeple; 75 hp
Hull material: Poop deck aft
Owners: J. & R. Campbell
1866: Entered service from Glasgow to Kilmun.
1866: December – Sold to the Bahia Steam Navigation Co., Bahia, Brazil. Renamed *Leitao Cunha*.
1867: 19 January – Sank off St Ives on her delivery voyage to Brazil under sail.

305: *Dandie Dinmont* (1866)

Number in Williamson's list: 239
Built: 1866
215 tons. Length 197.2 feet
Builders: A. & J. Inglis, Pointhouse
Engine builders: A. & J. Inglis, Pointhouse. Engine type: double diagonal oscillating; 110 hp
Hull material: Deck saloons
Owners: North British Steam Packet Co.
1866: 11 April – Launched.
1866: 1 May – Entered service from Helensburgh to Ardrishaig. This lasted only until the end of the end of the summer season, when she was laid up.
1868: Operated from Granton to Burntisland.
1869: Operated from Broughty Ferry to Tayport.
1869: May – Operated from Craigendoran to Dunoon and the Holy Loch.
1887: Sold to the Southsea, Ventnor, Sandown & Shanklin Steamboat Co. Operated excursions from Portsmouth, Southsea and Ryde round the Isle of Wight and to Bournemouth.
1901: Sank in Portsmouth Harbour. Raised and towed to Bembridge, where she was broken up.

306: *Meg Merrilies* (1866)

Number in Williamson's list: 240
Built: 1866
213.4 tons. Length 192.1 feet
Builders: A. & J. Inglis, Pointhouse
Engine builders: A. & J. Inglis, Pointhouse. Engine type: double diagonal oscillating; 110 hp
Hull material: Deck saloons
Owners: North British Steam Packet Co.
1866: 27 March – Launched.
1866: Entered service from Helensburgh to Ardrishaig. This lasted only until the end of the summer season, when she was laid up.
1869: Sold to Fevaid-i Osmaniye, Constantinople. Renamed *Nuzhutiye*. Operated from Constantinople to the Princes' Islands.

1910: Transferred to the Constantinople–Bandirma route.
1913: Broken up.

307: *Ardencaple*

Number in Williamson's list: 241
Built: 1866
89 tons; 127 gross tons (1875). Length 150 feet, 159.1 feet (1875)
Builders: R. Duncan, Port Glasgow
Engine builders: Rankin & Blackmore, Greenock. Engine type: oscillating; 50 hp
Hull material: Raised quarter deck
Owners: Greenock & Helensburgh Steamboat Co. Ltd.
1866: Entered service from Greenock to Helensburgh and Garelochhead.
1868: Operated from Greenock to Lochgoilhead.
1869: Sold to Keith and Campbell. Operated from Glasgow to Dumbarton briefly and then from Glasgow to Garelochhead.
1875: Re-boilered and lengthened by 9.1 feet.
Late 1875: Sold to the London Steamboat Co. Ltd. Renamed *Duke of Connaught*. Operated from London to Ipswich.
1885: Sold to the River Thames Steamboat Company.
1888: Scrapped when taken over by the Victoria Steamboat Association.

308: *Vale of Doon*

Number in Williamson's list: 242
Built: 1866
179 tons. Length 197 feet
Builders: T. B. Seath & Co., Rutherglen
Engine builders: A. Campbell & Son, Anderston. Engine type: steeple; 110 hp
Hull material: Iron; flush-decked
Owners: Seath and Steele, Ayr
1866: Entered service from Glasgow to Ayr.
1868: Sold to Mensajeries Fluviales a Vapor (Saturnino Ribes), Buenos Aires. Renamed *Meteoro*. Operated on the River Plate.
1877: Sold to the La Platense Flotilla Co. (William Denny & Paddy Henderson).
1890: December – Owners went into liquidation. Laid up.
1895: Scrapped.

309: *Rosneath*

Number in Williamson's list: 243
Built: 1866
88.7 tons. Length 150 feet
Builders: R. Duncan, Port Glasgow
Engine builders: Rankin & Blackmore, Greenock. Engine type: oscillating; 50 hp
Hull material: Raised quarter deck
Owners: Greenock & Helensburgh Steamboat Co. Ltd.

1866: Entered service from Greenock to Helensburgh and Garelochhead.

1869: Operating from Glasgow to Dumbarton and from Glasgow to the Gareloch.

1870: Sold to unknown foreign owners and renamed *Rosolio*.

1872: Sold to the Citizens' River Steamer Co., Cork. Renamed *Erin*. Operated from Cork to Queenstown (Cobh).

1890: April – Sold to the Cork, Blackrock & Passage Railway.

1890: July – Scrapped.

310: *Levan*

Number in Williamson's list: 244
Built: 1866
93.2 tons. Length 150.2 feet
Builders: Kirkpatrick, McIntyre & Co., Greenock
Engine builders: Rankin & Blackmore, Greenock. Engine type: oscillating; 50 hp
Hull material: Raised quarter deck
Owners: Greenock & Helensburgh Steamboat Co. Ltd.

1866: Operated excursions and special sailings including some to Ardrishaig and Inveraray.

1869: Sold to G. Brymner.

1870: Operated from Greenock to Helensburgh and Garelochhead.

1871: October – Sold to Keith and Campbell. Operated from Glasgow to Kilmun.

1874: Operated from Glasgow to Millport.

1875: Sold to the London Steamboat Co., London. Renamed *Duke of Teck*. Operated from London to Ipswich.

C. 1889: Broken up.

311: *Ardgowan*

Number in Williamson's list: 245
Built: 1866
92.4 tons. Length 150.9 feet
Builders: Laurence Hill & Co., Port Glasgow
Engine builders: Rankin & Blackmore, Greenock. Engine type: oscillating; 50 hp
Hull material: Raised quarter deck
Owners: Greenock & Helensburgh Steamboat Co. Ltd.

1866: Entered service between Greenock, Helensburgh and Garelochhead, also operated from Glasgow to Rothesay.

1868: Now operated from Helensburgh to Dunoon and Rothesay.

1869: Sold to G. Brymner. Operated from Glasgow to Largs and Millport.

1870: Back on the route from Greenock to Helensburgh and Garelochhead.

1871: October – Sold to Keith and Campbell.

1875: Sold to the London Steamboat Co., London. Renamed *Duke of Cambridge*. Operated from London to Ipswich.

1885: Sold to the River Thames Steamboat Company.

1890: Sold to the Victoria Steamboat Association.

1897: Owners became Victoria Steamboats Ltd.

1898: Broken up.

312: *Flying Scud*

Built: 1866
100 tons. Length 98.5 feet
Builders: J. P. Rennoldson, North Shields
Engine builders: J. P. Rennoldson, North Shields. Engine type: side-lever; 80 hp
Hull material: Wood tug/tender
Owners: Clyde Shipping Co.
1866: Entered service as a tug and tender at the Tail of the Bank.
1873: May – Sold to J. M. Hewitt, Liverpool.
1878: September – Sold to T. Gray, Hull.
1895: 7 October – Collided with trawler *Sledmore* and sank in the River Humber.

313: *Gondolier*

Built: 1866
173 tons. Length 148.2 feet
Builders: J. & G. Thomson, Clydebank
Engine builders: J. & G. Thomson, Clydebank. Engine type: two-cylinder oscillating; 80 hp
Hull material: Deck saloons
Owners: D. Hutcheson & Co.
1866: 3 May – Launched.
1866: Entered service on the Caledonian Canal from Banavie to Inverness.
1878: May – Chartered for the funeral of the Duchess of Argyll, sailing from Wemyss Bay to Rosneath.
1879: Owners became David MacBrayne.
1905: Owners now David MacBrayne Ltd.
1928: Owners became David MacBrayne (1928) Ltd.
1930: Boiler replaced with one from *Grenadier*.
1935: Owners now David MacBrayne Ltd. Deck saloons rebuilt with large windows.
1936: Deckhouse added over the aft companionway.
1939: Ceased operation on the outbreak of war, after seventy-three years' service on the same route.
1940: Purchased by the Admiralty. Her machinery, deck saloons and paddle boxes were removed and she was sunk as a blockship in Scapa Flow.

314: *Herald*

Built: 1866
329 tons. Length 221.69 feet
Builders: Caird & Co., Greenock.
Engine builders: Caird & Co., Greenock. Engine type: oscillating; 150 hp
Hull material: Iron
Owners: J. Little & Co.
1866: May–September – Operated from Glasgow to Campbeltown.
1867: Sold to the Barrow Steam Navigation Co. Operated from Barrow-in-Furness to the Isle of Man.
1891: Registered by Lord Cavendish, Sir J. Ramsden, J. Allport, J. & H. Little. Operated for

J. & H. Little from Fairlie to Carradale and Campbeltown.

1892: Sold to the Workington and Isle of Man Steamship Co., Workington. Operated from Workington to Ramsey, Isle of Man.

1893: Laid up.

1894: Broken up.

315: *Princess of Wales*

Built: 1866

256 tons. Length 142.6 feet

Builders: Aitken & Mansel, Glasgow

Engine builders: J. Aitken & Co., Glasgow. Engine type: two-cylinder oscillating; 0 hp

Hull material: Iron; flush-decked

Owners: Loch Lomond Steamboat Co.

1866: Entered service on Loch Lomond from Balloch to Ardlui.

1881: October – Sold to Matthew Brydie, Alloa. Moved to the River Forth and operated from Leith to Stirling.

1883: May – Sold to J. Cran, Alloa.

1884: April – Sold to W. Beveridge, Alloa.

1885: Sold to W. B. Ritchie, Dundee. Operated from Broughty Ferry to Perth.

1886: Sold to the Dundee, Perth & Newburgh Steam Boat Co., Dundee.

1886: Sold to J. C. Forbes, Dundee.

1887: Sold to T. S. Blakeney, Dundee.

1887: Sold to J. K. Henderson, Dundee.

1888: Laid up.

1891: Sold to D. Nicoll, Dundee. Resumed operation from Broughty Ferry to Perth.

1894: Sold to Dundee Pleasure Boat Co., Dundee.

1896: Sold to W. T. Rogers, Dundee. Renamed *Albion*.

1899: Sold to Dundee & Perth Passenger Steam Boat Co., Dundee.

1901: Sold to North Eastern Passenger Steamers Ltd, Newcastle. May have operated on the Tyne.

1902: Chartered to W. Horton, operated from Rhyl and Rhos-on-Sea to Llandudno.

1903: Sold to G. Martin, Dundee. Renamed *Shamrock*. Resumed operation again from Broughty Ferry to Perth.

1909: Sold to E. W. C. Abbott, London.

1910: Sold to Foreland Steam Boat Co., London 1910.

1912: August – Sold to unknown owners in France. There is no record of this steamer after this date.

316: *Dunoon Castle* (1867)

Number in Williamson's list: 246
Built: 1867
172 tons. Length 191.7 feet
Builders: T. Wingate & Co., Whiteinch
Engine builders: T. Wingate & Co., Whiteinch. Engine type: steeple; 90 hp
Hull material: Flush-decked
Owners: Dunoon & Rothesay Carriers (D. Lennox)
1867: Entered service from Glasgow to Rothesay, mainly carrying cargo. Had the last single steeple engine to be built for a Clyde steamer. Was the last Clyde paddle steamer to be built with the funnel aft of the paddles.
1871: Sold to R. Morrison and others.
1874: Sold to Henry Sharp.
1875: Commenced offering Sunday excursions.
1883: Sold to Hill & Co. Renamed *Arran*. Operated from Fairlie to Millport.
1884: Operated from Glasgow to Rothesay.
1885: Sold to A. Campbell
1885: July–September – Chartered to person or persons unknown and operated from Liverpool to Llandudno.
1886: Resumed the Glasgow–Rothesay service.
1891: Sold to the Thames & Medway Saloon Steamship Co. Operated from London to Southend.
1892: Sold to unknown owners in Ireland and used as a tug on the River Shannon.
1896: Scrapped.

317: *Lochlomond* (1867)

Number in Williamson's list: 247
Built: 1867
91 tons. Length 129 feet
Builders: Archibald Denny, Dumbarton
Engine builders: M. Paul & Co. 56 hp
Hull material: Iron
Owner: Peter Denny
1867: Entered service from Glasgow to Dumbarton.
1869: Laid up.
1870: Sold to unknown owners, Trieste. Renamed *Telegrafo*.
No further information is available.

318: *Elaine*

Number in Williamson's list: 248
Built: 1867
128 tons. Length 175 feet
Builders: R. Duncan, Port Glasgow
Engine builders: Rankin & Blackmore, Greenock. Engine type: oscillating; 70 hp
Hull material: Raised quarter deck

Owners: Graham Brymner & Co.
1867: 6 April – Launched.
1867: Entered service from Glasgow to Millport.
1872: Sold to Capt. D. Stewart. Operated from Glasgow to Rothesay and the Kyles of Bute.
1878: August – Ran aground in the Kyles of Bute, later salvaged.
1879: Sold to Capt. William Buchanan.
1880: Re-boilered.
1890: Operated from Greenock to Helensburgh.
1891: Also made some excursions from Paisley.
1894: Moved to the Greenock–Garelochhead route.
1899: Broken up.

319: *Great Western*

Built: 1867
466 tons. Length 220.4 feet
Builders: W. Simons & Co., Renfrew
Engine builders: W. Simons & Co., Renfrew. Engine type: compound oscillating; 190 hp
Hull material: Iron
Owners: Ford & Jackson, Milford
1867: 3 March – Launched.
1867: Entered service from Milford to Cork.
1872: Purchased by the Great Western Railway.
1878: Moved to the Weymouth–Cherbourg service.
1885: 30 June – Now operated from Milford to Waterford and Cork.
1887: Chartered to the Weymouth & Channel Islands Steam Packet Co. Operated from Weymouth to the Channel Islands.
1890: 30 May – Sold to N. Miller, Preston. Operated from Preston to Douglas and Glasgow.
1891: Sold to David MacBrayne. Operated from Strome Ferry to Stornoway.
1893: Renamed *Lovedale*. Re-boilered and rebuilt with one funnel rather than two.
1897: With the opening of the railway to Kyle of Lochalsh, operated from there to Stornoway.
1900: Moved to the service from Kyle of Lochalsh to Portree, extended to Lochinver on Saturdays.
1903: Operated from Glasgow to Islay.
1904: Scrapped.

320: *Islay* (1867)

Built: 1867
362 tons, 201 tons (1882). Length 192.8 feet, 206.6 feet (1882)
Builders: Barclay Curle, Whiteinch
Engine builders: Barclay Curle, Whiteinch. Engine type: two-cylinder steeple; 145 hp
Hull material: Iron
Owners: J. Ramsay and others, Islay
1867: Entered service from Glasgow to Islay.
1875: Sold to D. Hutcheson & Co.
1879: Owner now David MacBrayne.

c. 1880: Route extended to Portrush.
1882: Now operating from Oban to Gairloch.
1890: December – Wrecked at Red Bay, Cushendall, Co. Antrim.

321: *Gael*

Built: 1869
497 tons. Length 211 feet
Builders: Robertson & Co., Greenock
Engine builders: Rankin & Blackmore, Greenock. Engine type: two-cylinder oscillating; 150 hp
Hull material: Flush-decked
Owners: Campbeltown & Glasgow Steam Packet Joint Stock Co. Ltd
1867: Entered service from Glasgow to Campbeltown.
1879: Re-boilered. Surface condenser replaced jet condenser. Aft deck saloon added.
1884: Sold to the Great Western Railway. Operated from Weymouth to Cherbourg.
1885: Operated from Portishead to Ilfracombe in the summer months only in this and the following year.
1887: Chartered to the West Cornwall Steamship Co. Operated from Penzance to the Isles of Scilly.
1889: Served as a relief steamer at Milford and Weymouth until 1891.
1891: Sold to David MacBrayne. Operated from Oban to Gairloch.
1892: Re-boilered, aft cargo hold removed and new full-width aft deck saloon added.
Early 1900s: Raised foc'sle added.
1903: Operated from Oban to Staffa and Iona for this summer only, then returned to the Gairloch service.
1914: Laid up.
1916–19: March – Chartered to the Glasgow & South Western Railway. Operated the winter service from Ardrossan to Arran.
1920: April – From now on operated the Ardrishaig Mail service in the winter months, from Mallaig to Stornoway and as the director's yacht.
1924: May – Broken up.

322: *Lancelot*

Number in Williamson's list: 249
Built: 1868
141.78 tons. Length 191.2 feet
Builders: R. Duncan, Port Glasgow
Engine builders: Rankin & Blackmore, Greenock. Engine type: oscillating; 90 hp
Hull material: Raised quarter deck
Owners: Graham Brymner & Co.
1868: Entered service from Glasgow to Millport and Arran.
1871: Now sailed via Kilchattan Bay instead of Millport.
1874: Operated from Wemyss Bay to Millport and Arran.
1875: Taken over by Gillies & Campbell. Operated from Wemyss Bay to Rothesay and Millport.
1877: Re-boilered.
1890: Also operated some excursions from Paisley.

1892: Sold to Idare-e Mahsusa, Constantinople. Renamed *Erenköy*. Sailed to Turkey and operated from Constantinople to the Bosporus.

1906: Withdrawn from service.

1909: Broken up.

323: *Sultana*

Number in Williamson's list: 250
Built: 1868
177 tons. Length 188.1 feet
Builders: Robertson & Co., Greenock
Engine builders: W. King & Co., Glasgow. Engine type: single diagonal; 80 hp
Hull material: Flush-decked
Owner: Captain Alexander Williamson

1868: 13 February – Launched.

1868: Entered service from Glasgow to Rothesay and the Kyles of Bute.

1869: Call introduced at Greenock (Princes Pier).

1886: Re-boilered.

1891: Purchased by the Glasgow & South Western Railway. Operated from Greenock (Princes Pier) to Kilmun.

1892: Moved to the service from Fairlie to Millport.

1897: Sold to Captain John Williamson. Operated from Glasgow to Rothesay.

1899: July – Sold to the Lochfyne & Glasgow Steam Packet Ltd. Operated from Glasgow to Ardrishaig via Skipness.

1900: March – Sold to M. Clavel, Cherbourg. Probably operated out of Cherbourg.

1907: Broken up.

324: *Marquis of Bute* (1868)

Number in Williamson's list: 251
Built: 1868
173 tons. Length 196.6 feet
Builders: Barclay Curle & Co., Whiteinch
Engine builders: Barclay Curle & Co., Whiteinch. Engine type: single diagonal; 85 hp
Hull material: Flush-decked
Owners: A. & T. McLean

1868: 3 March – Launched.

1868: Entered service from Glasgow to Rothesay.

1889: Sold to Capt. Alexander Williamson, Sr. Route extended to the Kyles of Bute.

1891: Sold to the Glasgow & South Western Railway. Aft deck saloon added. Operated rail-connected services from Princes Pier and Fairlie.

1892: Re-boilered.

1893: Now operated from Fairlie to Millport.

1904: Sold to Capt. John Williamson. Chartered to an unknown company and operated from Belfast to Bangor.

1906: Sold to J. Gordon, Newry. Operated on Carlingford Lough.

1907: Sold to D. Monk, Preston. Operated excursions from Preston.

1908: Broken up.

325: *The Lady Mary*

Number in Williamson's list: 252
Built: 1868
179 tons. Length 173.4 feet
Builders: Blackwood & Gordon, Port Glasgow
Engine builders: Blackwood & Gordon, Port Glasgow. Engine type: oscillating; 110 hp
Hull material: Flush-decked
Owner: The Duke of Hamilton
1868: 5 June – Launched.
1868: Entered service from Ardrossan to Arran.
1871: Sold to A. Watson, but chartered back to previous owner.
1873: Laid up.
1875: Sold to Boyle's Cardiff & Bristol Channel Steamships Ltd., Bristol. Operated from
    Cardiff to Bristol.
1876: 16 August – Operated an excursion from Neath to Weston.
1882: Operated from Cardiff to Burnham on Sea.
1883: April – Returned to the Bristol–Cardiff route.
1887: Sold to William Lewis, Cardiff. Continued on the same service.
1890: Scrapped.

326: *Guinevere*

Number in Williamson's list: 253
Built: 1869
169 tons. Length 200.3 feet
Builders: R. Duncan, Port Glasgow
Engine builders: Rankin & Blackmore, Greenock. Engine type: oscillating; 85 hp
Hull material: Raised quarter deck
Owners: Graham Brymner & Co.
1869: Entered service from Glasgow to Largs, Millport, Brodick and Lamlash.
1872: Now operated to Arran via Rothesay and Kilchattan Bay.
1876: Sold to Keith and Campbell.
1885: Sold to Captain William Buchanan. Operated from Glasgow to Rothesay.
1891: Made some excursions from Paisley.
1891: Sold to J. Garvie, London.
1892: Sold to the Ottoman Government, Turkey.
1892: Lost with all hands in Bay of Biscay while on delivery voyage to Constantinople.

CHAPTER 7
Steamers Built 1870–79

327: *Bonnie Doon* (1870)

Number in Williamson's list: 254
Built: 1870
217 tons. Length 209 feet 5 inches
Builders: T. B. Seath & Co., Rutherglen
Engine builders: A. Campbell & Son, Anderston. Engine type: single diagonal; 96 hp
Hull material: Deck saloon aft
Owners: T. Seath and Steele
1870: April – Entered service from Glasgow to Millport and Ayr.
1873: Laid up.
1874: Sold to J. F. Braeunlich, Stettin. Renamed *Kronprinz Friedrich Wilhelm*.
1876: Operated from Stettin, now Szczecin, to Swinemünde, now Swinoujscie, Lauterbach and Bornholm. Also operated Swinemünde to Sassnitz, and on excursions from Stettin to Swinemünde and various bathing resorts.
1901: Sold to C. Feuerloh, Stettin.
1902: Broken up. Hull used as a lighter.

328: *Craigrownie*

Number in Williamson's list: 255
Built: 1870
122.3 tons. Length 175 feet
Builders: R. Duncan, Port Glasgow
Engine builders: Rankin & Blackmore, Greenock. Engine type: oscillating; 70 hp
Hull material: Raised quarter deck
Owners: Greenock & Helensburgh Steamboat Co.
1870: Entered service from Glasgow to Largs and Millport.
1871: October – Sold to Keith and Campbell.
1872: Operated from Glasgow and Greenock to Helensburgh and Garelochhead.
1873: 7 December – Sank off Greenock after a collision. Raised and returned to service.
1875: Back on the Glasgow–Largs and Millport service.
1876: Sold to the London Steamboat Co. Renamed *Duke of Edinburgh*. Operated from London to Ipswich.
1885: Sold to the River Thames Steamboat Company.
1890: Owners merged into the Victoria Steamboat Association.
1897: Owners became Victoria Steamboat Ltd.
c. 1898: Scrapped.

329: *Carrick Castle*

Number in Williamson's list: 256
Built: 1870
175 tons. Length 192.1 feet
Builders: J. Fullerton & Co., Paisley
Engine builders: W. King & Co., Glasgow. Engine type: single diagonal; 85 hp
Hull material: Flush-decked
Owners: Loch Goil & Loch Long Steamboat Co.
1870: 30 April – Launched.
1870: Entered service from Glasgow to Lochgoilhead.
1881: May – Sold to Matthew & Matheson, Leith. Operated on excursions from Leith.
1884: September – Withdrawn from service.
1885: April – Sold to the Hastings & St Leonards Steamship Co. (A. Paine), Hastings.
1885: 18 May – Commenced operation on excursions from Hastings.
1888: May – Sold to Edwards & Robertson, Cardiff (Bristol Channel Passenger Services Ltd.).
    Renamed *Lady Margaret*. Operated from Cardiff to Weston-Super-Mare.
1895: October – Sold to J. Gunn, Cardiff. Renamed *Lord Tregedar*. Continued on the same
    service.
1898: Sold to P. Baker, Cardiff, and scrapped.

330: *Lorne*

Number in Williamson's list: 257
Built: 1871
255 tons. Length 212.5 feet
Builders: A. McMillan, Dumbarton
Engine builders: J. & J. Thomson, Glasgow. Engine type: two-cylinder diagonal oscillating;
    120 hp
Hull material: Flush-decked
Owner: Captain Duncan Stewart
1871: 18 April – Launched.
1871: Entered service from Glasgow to Rothesay.
1873: January – Sold to Ångfartyg AB Öresund, Malmö, Sweden. Renamed *Öresund*.
    Operated from Copenhagen to Malmö.
1873: June – Sold to Det Forenede Öresundska Ångfartygs A/B, Malmö. Continued on same
    route.
1874: May – Sold to A/S D/S Kjøbenhaven-Malmø, Copenhagen, Denmark. Renamed
    Øresund. Continued on same route.
1874: July – Sold to DFDS, Copenhagen. Continued on same route.
1875: Deck saloons added. Engine rebuilt and re-boilered by Burmeister & Wain,
    Copenhagen.
1900: 31 March – Sold to A/S D/S Øresund, Copenhagen. Continued on same route.
1900: 30 June – Sold to A/S D/S Kysten, Copenhagen. Continued on same route.
1901: December – Sold to W. & O. E. Potenberg, Swinemünde, Germany, for scrapping.
1902: Scrapped.

331: *Heather Bell*

Number in Williamson's list: 258
Built: 1871
268 tons. Length 207 feet 7 inches
Builders: Blackwood & Gordon, Port Glasgow
Engine builders: Blackwood & Gordon, Port Glasgow. Engine type: double diagonal; 100 hp
Hull material: Flush-decked
Owners: The Duke of Hamilton Trustees
1871: 1 May – Launched.
1871: Entered service from Ardrossan to Arran.
1876: Sold to the Port of Portsmouth and Ryde United Steam Packet Ltd. Operated on excursions from Portsmouth and Ryde round the Isle of Wight, and to Cherbourg, Bournemouth, Brighton, etc.
Winter 1878/9: Re-engined and re-boilered.
1880: May – Taken over by the South Western & Brighton Railway Companies Steam Packet Service.
1899: November – Sold to T. Ward shipbreakers.
1900: July – Sold to South Coast & Continental Services Ltd. (Sir C. E. Scott, London).
1900: 13–29 July – Chartered to person or persons unknown. Operated from Glasgow to Dunoon including Sunday sailings.
1900: 30 July – Chartered to her master, Captain Sims.
1900: 2 August – Commenced operating from Liverpool to North Wales.
1900: 24 August – Chartered to W. Horton, Colwyn Bay. Operated from Liverpool to Rhyl, Rhos-on-Sea and Llandudno.
1900: 8 September – Taken back by T. Ward because of non-payment of instalments of purchase price, charter fees, etc.
1901: April – Sold to E. Hunt, Towcester. Operated excursions on the Bristol Channel including trips to Chepstow and Newport.
1902: 26 August – Ran ashore at the entrance to Newport, Mon.
1903: May – Scrapped.

332: *Conqueror*

Built: 1871
233 tons. Length 136.5 feet
Builders: Henderson, Coulborn & Co., Renfrew
Engine builders: (1) Henderson, Coulborn & Co., Renfrew (2) J. & R. Weir, Montreal (1893). Engine type: (1) compound; 150 hp (2) compound (1893); 143 hp (1893)
Hull material: Iron tug/tender
Owners: Clyde Shipping Co.
1871: Built for service as a tug/tender at the Tail of the Bank.
1872: June – Sold to J. G. Ross and W. Ross, Quebec, and W. Ferrier-Kerr, Glasgow.
1873: March – Owners now J. G. Ross and W. Ross, Quebec.
1875: March – Owner now solely J. G. Ross, Quebec.
1876: Sold to M. McNamara, Quebec.
1881: Sold to H. Dinning, Quebec.
1885: Owner now Mrs E. C. Dinning, Quebec.

1887: Sold to J. Walsh, Quebec.
1891: October – Sold to A. K. Hanson, Montreal, then to F. Dupre, Montreal.
1891: December – Sold to the Sincennes McNaughton Line Ltd, Montreal.
1893: Re-engined.
1907: Scrapped.

333: *Gareloch* (1872)

Number in Williamson's list: 259
Built: 1872
172 tons. Length 180 feet
Builders: H. Murray & Co., Port Glasgow
Engine builders: D. Rowan & Son, Glasgow. Engine type: two-cylinder oscillating; 85 hp
Hull material: Raised quarter deck
Owners: North British Steam Packet Co.
1872: 28 March – Launched.
1872: Entered service from Helensburgh to Garelochhead.
1882: May – Started operating from Craigendoran on the opening of the pier there.
1888: Now used as a spare vessel for the NBSP Clyde services.
1891: Transferred to the Galloway Saloon Steam Packet Co., Leith, another subsidiary of the North British Railway. Renamed *Wemyss Castle*. Operated on Firth of Forth services, including excursions to the Isle of May.
1906: Scrapped.

334: *Lady Gertrude*

Number in Williamson's list: 260
Built: 1872
167.7 tons. Length 190 feet
Builders: Blackwood & Gordon, Port Glasgow
Engine builders: Blackwood & Gordon, Port Glasgow. Engine type: single diagonal; 82 hp
Hull material: Flush-decked
Owners: Gillies & Campbell
1872: 11 June – Launched.
1872: Entered service from Wemyss Bay to Rothesay.
1877: 13 January – Wrecked at Toward Pier, engine salved and fitted in *Adela* (No. 344).

335: *Islay* (1872)

Built: 1872 as *Princess Louise*.
497 tons. Length 211.4 feet
Builders: Tod & McGregor, Meadowside
Engine builders: Tod & McGregor, Meadowside. Engine type: two-cylinder steeple; 200 hp
Hull material: Iron; flush-decked
Owners: Larne & Stranraer Steamboat Co. Ltd
1872: 7 May – Launched.
1872: 1 July – Entered service from Stranraer to Larne.

1889: March – Owners became the Larne & Stranraer Steamship Joint Committee.

1890: February – Sold to David MacBrayne. Renamed *Islay*. Operated from Glasgow to Islay.

1902: 15 July – Wrecked on Sheep Island, Port Ellen, in fog.

336: *Windsor Castle* (1875)

Number in Williamson's list: 261
Built: 1875
195.1 tons. Length 195.8 feet
Builders: T. B. Seath & Co., Rutherglen
Engine builders: W. King & Co., Glasgow. Engine type: single diagonal jet condenser; 85 hp
Hull material: Flush-decked
Owners: Loch Goil & Loch Long Steamboat Co.

1875: Entered service from Glasgow to Lochgoilhead.

1900: Sold to Idar-e-Mahsusa, Constantinople. Renamed *Eser I Sevket*. Operated from Constantinople to the Bosphorus.

1918: Scrapped.

337: *Viceroy*

Number in Williamson's list: 262
Built: 1875
218 tons, 236 tons (1892). Length 194.7 feet, 208.9 feet (1891)
Builders: D. & W. Henderson, Meadowside
Engine builders: (1) D. & W. Henderson, Meadowside (2) Hutson and Corbett. Engine type: (1) single Diagonal jet condenser; 194 hp (2) two cylinders; 320 hp
Hull material: Raised quarter deck
Owner: Captain Alex Williamson Sr.

1875: Entered service from Glasgow to the Kyles of Bute. Also ran from Greenock (Princes Pier) in connection with trains.

1883: Operated from Glasgow to Tarbert and Ardrishaig until 1886.

1886: Re-boiled, surface condenser added.

1888: Re-engined.

1891: March – Lengthened by 14.2 feet. Normal aft deck saloon replaced raised quarter deck and small forward deck saloon added.

1891: September – Sold to the Glasgow & South Western Railway. Operated rail connected sailings from Greenock (Princes Pier).

1895: Now operated from Fairlie to Millport.

1897: Re-boiled.

1907: Sold to Mersey Trading Co. Ltd. Renamed *Rhos Colwyn*. Operated from Liverpool to Colwyn Bay, Llandudno and Beaumaris or Caernarvon.

1908: Sold to W. Hawthorn, Rhyl.

1911: Scrapped.

338: *Glendale*

Built: 1875
483 tons. Length 220 feet
Builders: John Elder & Co., Govan
Engine builders: John Elder & Co., Govan. Engine type: compound oscillating; 775 hp
Hull material: Iron
Owners: London, Brighton & South Coast Railway Co.
1875: 15 June – Launched as *Paris*.
1875: Entered service from Newhaven to Dieppe.
1888: Sold back to Fairfield Ship Building Co. (successors to J. Elder), Govan. Re-boilered.
1890: Sold to R. Barnwell (a director of Fairfield's), chartered to New North Wales Steamship Co. Operated from Liverpool to Llandudno, Beaumaris and Menai Bridge.
1892: April – Chartered to A. Ballinn/Hamburg Amerika Line. Operated from Hamburg to Helgoland. Renamed *Flamingo*.
1895: Charter ended.
1897: Sold to W. M. Rhodes, London. Renamed *La Belgique*. Chartered to New Palace Steamers, London. Operated from Tilbury to Ostend for one season only.
1898: Laid up.
1902: Sold to David MacBrayne. Renamed *Glendale*.
1903: Operated from Oban to Gairloch and Ullapool or Lochinver.
1904: Operated from Oban to Stornoway.
1905: Operated from Glasgow to Islay.
1905: 20 July – Wrecked on Cove Point, Kintyre, en route from Glasgow to Islay.

339: *Benmore*

Number in Williamson's list: 263
Built: 1876
235.1 tons. Length 201.2 feet
Builders: T. B. Seath & Co., Rutherglen
Engine builders: W. King & Co., Glasgow. Engine type: single diagonal jet condenser; 85 hp
Hull material: Raised quarter deck
Owner: Captain Bob Campbell, Kilmun
1875: 5 May – Launched.
1876: Entered service from Glasgow to Kilmun.
1885: Sold to Captain William Buchanan.
1886: Operated from Glasgow to Rothesay.
1887: Re-boilered and a second funnel added, also a fore saloon.
1888: Returned to a single-funnelled condition.
1891: October – Sold to Captain John Williamson. Continued on the Glasgow–Rothesay service, only now based at Rothesay, with occasional excursions to Ayr.
1903: Now on a service from Helensburgh to Kilcreggan, Strone, Kirn and Dunoon, starting on certain days at Garelochhead and connecting at Dunoon with the turbine steamers.
1915: Operated from Dunoon and Kirn to Glasgow.
1915: Chartered to the Caledonian Steam Packet Co. Ltd. Operated from Gourock to Kilmun and Wemyss Bay to Millport.
1919: Owners became Williamson-Buchanan Steamers Ltd.
1919: 27 September – Final day on charter to the Caledonian Steam Packet Co.

1920: 30 September – Returned to service for Williamson-Buchanan on the Glasgow–Rothesay service.

1920: 19 October – Laid up at Greenock because of the threat of a miners' strike.

1920: 11 November – Damaged by fire while laid up and never returned to service.

1923: Scrapped.

340: *Bonnie Doon* (1876)

Number in Williamson's list: 264

Built: 1876

272 tons. Length 218 feet

Builders: T. B. Seath & Co., Rutherglen

Engine builders: A. Campbell & Son, Anderston. Engine type: single diagonal surface condenser; 96 hp

Hull material: Deck saloon aft

Owners: Seath, Robertson and Steel

1876: 17 April – Launched.

1876: June – Entered service from Glasgow to Ayr. Also offered afternoon and evening excursions from Ayr, Irvine and Ardrossan to Ailsa Craig, Turnberry, round the Cumbraes and to Arrochar.

1877: 1 June – Made a trip from Ayr to Campbeltown.

1881: April – Sold to the Liverpool, Llandudno & Welsh Coast Steamboat Co. Operated from Liverpool to Llandudno, Beaumaris and Bangor.

1881: 25 July – Route extended to Menai Straits.

1882: July – Sold to Gilles and Campbell. Operated from Wemyss Bay to Rothesay and on other rail-connected services and excursions from Wemyss Bay.

1886: Chartered to Bristol Steam Yachting & Excursion Company, Bristol. Operated on excursions from Bristol to Bristol Channel piers including some to Ilfracombe.

1887: Purchased by G. Nurse and others, Bristol. Re-boilered. Continued to operate on the Bristol Channel. Chartered by the British Cruising Association for a trip to Spithead for the Jubilee Naval Review.

1889: Chartered to the Belfast, Bangor & Larne Steamboat Co. Operated from Belfast to Bangor.

1890: May – Sold to Edwards and Robertson, Cardiff. Returned to Bristol Channel sailings including trips to Ilfracombe.

1892: Operated out of Cardiff.

1895: Sold to J. Gunn, Cardiff.

1899: March – Sold to P. & A. Campbell, Bristol.

1906: Operated from the South Coast out of Brighton until 1910.

1911: Operated Bristol Channel sailings from Newport, Mon, in this and the following season.

1913: September – Sold to W. Pugsley, Bristol, and scrapped at Rotterdam.

This steamer was notoriously unreliable and supposedly earned herself the sobriquet '*Bonnie Breakdoon*'.

341: *Lord of the Isles* (1877)

Number in Williamson's list: 265
Built: 1877
427.4 tons. Length 246 feet
Builders: D. & W. Henderson, Meadowside
Engine builders: D. & W. Henderson, Meadowside. Engine type: two-cylinder diagonal oscillating, surface condenser; 326 hp
Hull material: Deck saloons
Owners: Glasgow & Inveraray Steamboat Co.
1877: 30 May – Launched.
1877: 2 July – Entered service on a day-return sailing from Greenock to Inveraray.
1881: Commenced operating from Glasgow to Inveraray in July and August.
1886: Re-boilered.
1890: September – Sold to the Victoria Steamboat Association, London. Fitted with telescopic funnels to enable her to sail above London Bridge.
1891: Operated on the Thames from London (Old Swan Pier) to Harwich.
1896: Sold to Mrs C. Black. Renamed *Jupiter*. Operated from London (Old Swan Pier) to Southend and Margate.
1898: Owner now P. B. Black. Owner soon bankrupt and steamer laid up.
1903: April – Sold to unknown owners in Rotterdam.
1903: May – Sold to A. Dawson Reid.
1903: May – Owned by the Isles Steamship Co. Renamed *Lady of the Isles*. Operated from Glasgow to the Kyles of Bute, including Sunday sailings.
1903: 29 August – Broke down off Greenock with boiler failure. Never sailed again.
1905: Scrapped at Dumbarton.

342: *Sheila*

Number in Williamson's list: 266
Built: 1877
255.9 tons. Length 205.5 feet
Builders: Caird & Co., Greenock
Engine builders: Caird & Co., Greenock. Engine type: single diagonal surface condenser; 120 hp
Hull material: Raised quarter deck
Owners: Gillies & Campbell
1877: 19 April – Launched.
1877: Entered service from Wemyss Bay to Rothesay with a sailing to Lamlash on Wednesdays.
1878: Lamlash sailing operated daily from this year.
1882: Sold to the North British Steam Packet Co., Craigendoran. Operated from Craigendoran to Rothesay.
1883: Renamed *Guy Mannering*.
1891: Re-boilered.
1893: Deck saloon fitted aft.
1894: Sold to Captain William Buchanan. Renamed *Isle of Bute*. Operated from Glasgow to Rothesay. Forward deck saloon added about this date.
1912: July – Sold to W. Cordingley, Morecambe. Operated excursions from Morecambe.
1913: October – Scrapped after she was damaged by hitting the pier at Morecambe.

343: *Glen Rosa* (1877)

Number in Williamson's list: 267
Built: 1877
254 tons. Length 206 feet
Builders: Caird & Co., Greenock
Engine builders: Caird & Co., Greenock. Engine type: single diagonal surface condenser;
    120 hp
Hull material: Raised quarter deck
Owners: Shearer and Ritchie
1877: May – Launched.
1877: Entered service from Glasgow to Lamlash via Rothesay and Kilchattan Bay.
1880: Sailed on alternate days to Skipness instead of Lamlash.
1881: Sold to the Thames & Channel Steam Ship Company, London. Operated on the
    Thames Estuary and was used for charters.
1881: July – Chartered to carry dignitaries, including the President of the Board of Trade and
    the Mayor of Ipswich, to the opening of a new lock at Ipswich.
1883: Sold to the London Steam Boat Co.
1885: Sold to the River Thames Steamboat Company.
1890: Sold to the Victoria Steamboat Association. Telescopic funnel fitted. Operated from
    London (Old Swan Pier) to Harwich, Walton-on-the-Naze, Clacton and Ipswich.
1891: Re-boilered.
1892: 14 July – Chartered to the Hastings, St Leonards & Eastbourne Steamboat Co. Ltd.
    Operated on excursions from Hastings until the end of the season.
1893: 2 July – Commenced operating from Harwich to Great Yarmouth with a ferry call at
    Lowestoft, connecting with the London steamer *Koh-I-Noor* at Harwich.
1897: Sold to P. & A. Campbell, Bristol.
1898: Operated excursions from Southampton, and on some dates from Bournemouth.
1899: Commenced operating in the Bristol Channel.
1903: Moved to operate excursions from Brighton.
1913: Back on the Bristol Channel.
1914: 26 August – 28 September – Final spell operating on the South Coast.
1915: Operated from Cardiff to Weston-super-Mare in this and the following summer.
1917: 26 May – Requisitioned by the Admiralty. Converted to a minesweeper. Operated out
    of Swansea, in the Bristol Channel and off the south-east coast of Ireland.
1919: 23 March – Completed Admiralty service.
1919: Scrapped by Pugsley & Co. at Bristol.

344: *Adela*

Number in Williamson's list: 268
Built: 1877
206 tons. Length 197 feet
Builders: Caird & Co., Greenock
Engine builders: Blackwood & Gordon, Port Glasgow (1872). Engine type: single diagonal;
    90 hp
Hull material: Flush-decked
Owners: Gillies & Campbell
1877: Entered service from Wemyss Bay to Rothesay. Fitted with the engines from *Lady*

Gertrude (No. 334). Was the final flush-decked steamer to be built for service on the Clyde.

1890: Chartered to the Birkdale, Southport & Preston Steamship Co. Ltd. Operated excursions from Southport to Llandudno, Beaumaris and the Menai Straits, New Brighton and Liverpool, Blackpool, etc. Also sailed on Sundays from Liverpool to Llandudno.

1891: Sold to the Brighton, Worthing & South Coast Steam Boat Co. Renamed *Sea Breeze*. Operated excursions from Brighton.

1893: Chartered to P. & A. Campbell. Operated from Cardiff to Weston-Super-Mare.

1897: Sold to La Banque Transatlantique, Marseilles. Renamed *La Corse*. Operated out of Marseilles.

c. 1898: Scrapped.

345: *Seagull*

Built: 1877
107 tons. Length 121 feet
Builders: John Softley & Sons, North Shields
Engine builders: Hepple & Co., South Shields. Engine type: side lever; 50 hp
Hull material: Flush-decked
Owners: J. Steel and K. McCaskill, Glasgow
1877: Built as a tug.
1877: Owners became Steele and Bennie.
1886: July – Chartered to the Wemyss Bay Steamboat Co. Used for one week only as a passenger steamer from Wemyss Bay to Toward and Innellan during Glasgow Fair.
1889: Laid up.
1890: Sold to unknown owners at South Shields.
1891: Sold to the Hastings, St Leonards & Eastbourne Steamboat Co. Converted from a tug to a passenger steamer. Operated excursions from Hastings, Eastbourne, etc.
1896: Scrapped.

346: *Columba*

Number in Williamson's list: 269
Built: 1878
543.3 tons. Length 301.4 feet
Builders: J. & G. Thomson, Clydebank
Engine builders: J. & G. Thomson, Clydebank. Engine type: Oscillating, surface condenser; 220 hp
Hull material: Steel, deck saloons
Owners: David Hutcheson & Co.
1877: Entered service from Glasgow to Ardrishaig. Was the longest and finest of the Clyde and West Highland paddle steamers. Normally only operated in the peak summer months. She had a hairdressing saloon and post office on board.
1879: Owner became David MacBrayne.
1884: Original, stumpy, funnels lengthened.
1900: Re-boilered. New funnels fitted.
1901: Companionway cover added. Later a smoking room was erected aft of this.

1905: Owners became David MacBrayne Ltd.

1915: Laid up for one summer due to the war.

1916: July – Commenced operating from Wemyss Bay to Ardrishaig due to the boom between the Cloch and Dunoon.

1919: 16 May–5 September – Back on the Glasgow–Ardrishaig service. The post office was removed at this time.

1928: Owners became D. MacBrayne (1928) Ltd.

1934: Owners name reverted to David MacBrayne Ltd.

1935: Withdrawn from service at the end of the season.

1936: April – Broken up at Dalmuir alongside *Iona* (1864) (No. 284).

347: *Brodick Castle*

Number in Williamson's list: 270

Built: 1878

283 tons. Length 207.6 feet

Builders: H. McIntyre & Co., Paisley

Engine builders: W. King & Co., Glasgow (1864). Engine type: double diagonal jet condenser; 90 hp

Hull material: Raised quarter deck; raised fo'csle and shelter deck forward

Owner: Captain William Buchanan

1878: 18 April – Launched.

1878: Entered service from Ardrossan to Arran. Fitted with the original engine from *Eagle* (1864) (No. 286).

1887: Sold to the Bournemouth, Swanage & Poole Steam Packet Co. Operated from Bournemouth to Swanage and on excursions from Bournemouth.

1887: 23 July – Was present at the Jubilee Naval Review at Spithead.

1894: May – Chartered to Bristol & Ilfracombe Pleasure Steamers Ltd. Operated from Bristol to Ilfracombe.

1894: July – Operated in conjunction with the Edwards & Robertson steamers from Cardiff to Weston-Super-Mare and on excursions to Newport, Chepstow and Clevedon.

1895: Returned to Bournemouth.

1897: 26 June – Operated an excursion from Swanage and Bournemouth to the Diamond Jubilee Naval Review at Spithead.

1897: 2 September – Was hit while lying at Weymouth by the Great Western Railway's Channel Island steamer *Reindeer*. The port lifeboat was wrecked and the sponson house containing the gentleman's toilet was destroyed. One passenger who was using these facilities was extricated from the damaged area unhurt apart from some bruising. Returned to Poole without passengers after emergency repairs were made by Cosens' shore staff.

1898: Owners renamed Bournemouth & South Coast Steam Packets Ltd.

1901: March – Sold to Cosens & Co., Weymouth. Continued on the same service.

1910: Used on fleet tendering at Weymouth and Portland.

1910: 9 July – Withdrawn from service due to the need for a new boiler.

1910: Sold to unknown owners in Argentina. Towed to the Netherlands and converted to a cattle-carrying barge. Renamed *Paca Nova*.

1910: 31 October – Sank off Portland under tow while on her delivery voyage to Argentina.

348: *Carabinier*

Built: 1878
269 tons. Length 169.4 feet
Builders: Oswald, Mordaunt & Co., Southampton
Engine builders: Oswald, Mordaunt & Co., Southampton. Engine type: compound oscillating;
    120 hp
Hull material: Iron, aft saloon
Owners: Port of Portsmouth & Ryde United Steam Packet Company Ltd.
1878: Entered service from Portsmouth to Ryde as *Albert Edward*.
1880: Sold to the London & South Western and London, Brighton & South Coast Railways
    Joint Committee. Continued on same service.
1893: Sold to David MacBrayne. Renamed *Carabinier*. Operated from Oban to the Sound of
    Mull, Tobermory and Loch Sunart.
1905: Owners became David MacBrayne Ltd.
1909: Scrapped.

349: *Edinburgh Castle* (1879)

Number in Williamson's list: 271
Built: 1879
234 tons, later 261 tons. Length 205.3 feet
Builders: R. Duncan, Port Glasgow
Engine builders: Rankin & Blackmore, Greenock. Engine type: single diagonal jet condenser;
    83 hp
Hull material: Deck saloon aft
Owners: Loch Goil & Loch Long Steamboat Co.
1879: 27 April – Launched.
1879: Entered service from Glasgow to Lochgoilhead. Was fitted with extremely large paddle
    wheels and boxes.
1879: Owners became the Loch Goil & Inveraray Steamboat Co.
1893: Re-boilered.
1912: Taken over by Turbine Steamers Ltd.
1913: Scrapped.

Jupiter leaves an unknown Clyde pier, while some of her crew attend to the ropes..

Juno in CSP livery with a full complement of passengers, *c.* 1930.

Caledonia off Rothesay in her inaugural season, 1934.

Jeanie Deans in dazzle camouflage in Govan dry dock preparing for war service in late 1939, showing how her stern had been built up to promenade deck level for this, a feature she retained after the war.

Talisman in dazzle camouflage. She was used as an anti-aircraft vessel and escort vessel and her engines performed far better than they had in peacetime.

Eagle III on the beach at Dunkirk at low tide. She made five trips there and rescued about 5,000 men.

Eagle III, worn out after war service, being broken up with the Isle of Man Steam Packet's *Snaefell* aft of her.

Lucy Ashton in 1945 in yellow ochre war paint.

Marchioness of Lorne in a lighter overall paint condition leaving Hunter's Quay.

The paddle box of *Duchess of Fife*, seen in her penultimate season in 1952.

Jupiter off Gourock in the 1950s.

Caledonia off Bridge Wharf in summer 1964.

Waverley off Dunoon in 1948 with brown deck saloons.

Waverley off Gourock in the mid-1950s, now with white deck saloons.

Waverley in the mid-1950s off Brodick.

Waverley departing Gourock in 1959, now with white paddle boxes.

Bowling was for many years the favoured winter lay-up berth for many Clyde steamers, as seen here in this image from the 1920s with *Iona* and *Columba* sandwiching the 1899 *Waverley*.

Waverley sporting buff funnels in 1972.

Glen Sannox in GSWR colours on the slipway at Blackwood & Gordon's yard at Port Glasgow.

Columba in dry dock at Govan prior to her final season in 1935.

Lord of the Isles being scrapped at Smith & Co., later Smith & Houston, at Port Glasgow in 1928.

The end of the greatest; demolishing the paddle box of *Columba* in 1936 at Arnott Young's at Dalmuir.

Grenadier cut down to deck level at Ardrossan on 2 June 1928.

Columba, passing Greenock, *c.* 1895.

Ivanhoe (1880) between 1912 and 1914, with thin black tops on her funnels.

Grenadier (1886) going astern out of Oban in her later years with large funnels, post-1913 with more lifeboats.

Victoria (1886) departing Craigmore.

Lucy Ashton (1888).

A stern view of *Lord of the Isles* (1891) in mid-Firth.

Lord of the Isles (1891).

Glen Sannox (1892) at speed off Mount Stuart on a VIP cruise in her initial season.

Duchess of Rothesay (1895) in 1925 or later off Dunoon.

Glen Rose with her tartan lum.

Waverley (1899) between 1920, when her promenade deck was extended to the bow, and 1932, after which she received an observation saloon forwards, in Loch Goil.

Duchess of Fife (1903) arriving at Dunoon in 1923 with the 'tartan lum'.

Queen Empress (1912) between 1920 and 1924 leaving Dunoon.

Jeanie Deans (1931) off Rothesay in 1948 with the dark saloon window frames.

Caledonia (1934) at Gourock in May 1968, dressed overall for a CRSC charter.

Above: Jupiter (1937) in her inaugural season of 1937.

Left: Waverley (1947) at Craigendoran in the mid-1960s.

Maid of the Loch (1953) arriving at Ardlui in the 1960s.

The 1962 *Comet* replica on her plinth at Port Glasgow, complete with Christmas decorations, in the late 1970s.

CHAPTER 8
Steamers Built 1880–89

350: *Chancellor* (1880)

Number in Williamson's list: 272
Built: 1880
272 tons. Length 199.7 ft
Builders: R. Chambers Jr, Dumbarton
Engine builders: M. Paul & Co., Dumbarton. Engine type: Double Diagonal, surface condenser
    140 hp. (2) 1892, Compound Diagonal, 199 hp
Hull Material: Steel, Deck saloon
Owners: Loch Lomond & Loch Long Steamboat Co.
1880: 21 April – Launched
1880: 1 June – Entered service from Helensburgh to Lochgoilhead and Arrochar. Was the third
    Clyde steamer to be built of steel and the last to be built with alleyways round the saloons.
    Had full length sponsons, like the Loch Lomond steamers.
1882: Sailed from Craigendoran from this year, after the pier was opened there.
1884: 17 May: Made an excursion from Dumbarton (Old Quay) to Arrochar.
1885: March – Sold to the Loch Goil & Loch Long Steamboat Co.
1887: Now operated from Glasgow to Lochgoilhead & Arrochar.
1891: July – Sold to the Glasgow & South Western Railway. Operated from Greenock
    (Princes Pier) to Lochgoilhead.
1892: Compounded and reboiled.
1892: Also made some sailings from Greenock (Princes Pier) to Kilmun.
1901: early – Sold to La Herculana Ferolana, El Ferrol, Spain. Operated out of Corunna.
    Renamed *Comercio*.
1910: Converted to a coaling barge at El Ferrol.
No details are available as to when she was broken up.

351: *Scotia* (1880)

Number in Williamson's list: 273
Built: 1880
260 tons. Length 211.2 ft
Builders: H. McIntyre & Co., Paisley
Engine builders: W. King & Co., Glasgow. Engine type: Double Steeple, Surface condenser;
    135 hp
Hull Material: Poop and saloon aft, shelter deck forward
Owner: Captain William Buchanan
1880: 14 January – Launched.

1880: Entered service from Glasgow to Rothesay.

1885: Moved to the Glasgow to Arran service.

1886: A raised foc'sle was added.

1887: Operated from Ardrossan to Arran.

1891: July – Sold to the Glasgow & South Western Railway.

1892: Reboilered.

1892: Operated excursions from Ayr.

1893: Sold to Edwards & Robertson, Cardiff. Operated from Cardiff to Bristol.

1895: Sold to John Gunn, Cardiff. Continued on the same service.

1899: March: Sold to P. & A. Campbell Ltd, Bristol. Continued on the same service.

1903: Sold to Societa Industriale e Commerciale Italiana, Castellamare. Operated from Naples to Sorrento and Capri. Renamed *Principessa Mafalda*.

1907: Sold to Societa Napoletana di Navigazione a Vapore, Naples. Renamed *Epomeo*. Continued on the same service.

1911: Sold to T. Astarita, Napoli. Now operated on cargo services in the Bay of Naples.

1913: Scrapped.

352: *Ivanhoe*

Number in Williamson's list: 274

Built: 1880

281.9 tons. Length 225.3ft

Builders: D. & W. Henderson, Meadowside

Engine builders: D. & W. Henderson, Meadowside. Engine type: Diagonal Oscillating, Surface condenser; 123 hp

Hull Material: Deck saloons

Owners: The Frith of Clyde Steam Packet Ltd (sic)

1880: 25 February – Launched

1880: Entered service from Helensburgh and Greenock to Arran via the Kyles of Bute. Operated as a teetotal steamer with no alcoholic drink being sold on board.

1882: Sailed from Craigendoran from this year, after the pier was opened there.

1888: Call at Gourock added, in the year before the railway was opened to there.

1894: 23 March – 22 May – Chartered to the Ship Canal Passenger Steamer Co. (1893) Ltd. Operated on the Manchester Ship Canal.

1897: Sold to the Caledonian Steam Packet Co. Ltd. Bar installed and alcoholic drinks served. Operated on rail connected services from Gourock.

1898: Now operated excursion sailings from Gourock, Mondays to Arrochar, Tuesdays and Thursdays to Millport, continuing on Tuesdays round Arran and on Thursdays round Ailsa Craig, on Wednesdays and Fridays round the lochs, and sailing as a general relief steamer on Saturdays.

1906: Operated from Gourock to the Kyles of Bute with an afternoon cruise from the Kyles piers.

1911: Sold to the Firth of Clyde Steam Packet Ltd. Operated from Glasgow to Rothesay.

1914: June: Sold to Turbine Steamers Ltd. Operated from Glasgow to Lochgoilhead.

1914: September: Laid up.

1916: June: Chartered to the Caledonian Steam Packet Co. Ltd. Operated from Wemyss Bay to Rothesay until September.

1917: February: Again chartered to the Caledonian Steam Packet Co. Ltd. Operated from Gourock and Dunoon to Kilmun.

1918: February – Laid up.
1918: April to September – Operated from Gourock to Dunoon, Wemyss Bay and Rothesay.
1918: September – Laid up.
1919: September – Scrapped.

353: *Flying Javelin*

Built: 1882
132 tons. Length 108.4 ft
Builders: J. T. Eltringham, South Shields
Engine builders: J. P. Rennoldson & Sons, South Shields. Engine type: side lever; 80 hp
Hull Material: Iron tug/tender
Owners: Clyde Shipping Co.
1882: Entered service as a tug.
1887: May – Sold to A. & W. McKinnon, Greenock. Renamed *Champion*. Also operated a
   service with mail and newspapers from Greenock to the Firth of Clyde ports.
1896: 12 December – Sank after a collision with the Caledonian Steam Packet's *Caledonia* in
   fog south of Dunoon.

354: *Meg Merrilies* (1883)

Number in Williamson's list: 275
Built: 1883
244 tons. Length 210.3 ft
Builders: Barclay Curle Ltd, Whiteinch
Engine builders: Barclay Curle Ltd, Whiteinch. Engine type: Double Diagonal, Jet condenser,
   surface condenser from 1888, compounded 1898; 205 hp
Hull Material: Iron hull; Deck saloon aft
Owners: North British Steam Packet Ltd
1883: 21 April – Launched
1883: Entered service from Craigendoran to Rothesay. Rejected by her owners after the
   season as being too slow. Was the final iron-built steamer built for Clyde service.
1884: Chartered to the Belfast, Bangor & Larne Steamboat Co., Belfast, after her hull was
   remodelled to increase speed.
1885: Sold to Captain Bob Campbell, Kilmun. Operated from Glasgow to Kilmun. Plans to
   renamed her *Blairmore* were not followed up.
1887 to 1888: winter – Reboilered and reduced from two funnels to one funnel.
1888: April – Owner became P. & A. Campbell, Kilmun after Captain Bob died. Continued
   on the Kilmun service.
1889: 1 January – Sold to the Caledonian Railway Company. Continued on the Kilmun
   service.
1889: 5 May – Now owned by the newly formed Caledonian Steam Packet Co. Ltd. Operated
   on rail connected services from Gourock to Dunoon and Rothesay and in winter from
   Gourock to Kilmun.
1893: Reboilered.
1897: 29 January – While en route from Wemyss Bay to Largs was hit from behind by the
   Royal Navy torpedo-boat destroyer HMS *Electra*, which was on trials on the Skelmorlie
   measured mile. Her stern bulwarks and the after end of the saloon was damaged, but she

was able to continue her trip to Millport and back to Wemyss Bay before going for repairs. Some sources erroneously state that she was fitted at this time with two second-hand boilers at this time from *Marchioness of Lorne* (No. 370).

1898: April – Haythorn experimental high-pressure water-tube boilers fitted. Engine compounded. Fore saloon added.

1900: 29 January – Explosion in the boiler-room caused by a bursting tube. New conventional boiler fitted.

1902: Late July – Used on extra sailings from Largs to Rothesay.

1902: Early summer – Sold to the Leopoldina Railway Co., Brazil. Renamed *Maua*. Turtle deck built over the open bow for the transatlantic crossing. Operated in Rio de Janiero harbour.

1921: Scrapped.

355: *The Queen*

Built: 1883
237 tons. Length 165.1 ft
Builders: Caird & Co., Greenock
Engine builders: Caird & Co., Greenock. Engine type: 2-cylinder diagonal; 86Rhp hp
Hull Material: Steel; deck saloons
Owners: Loch Lomond Steamboat Co.
1883: 17 November – Launched.
1883: 31 December – Ran trials.
1883: Spring – Entered service on Loch Lomond from Balloch to Ardlui.
1888: Sold to the North British Steam Packet Co.
1896: Owners now the Dumbarton & Balloch Joint Line Committee (NBR/CR)
1896: 15 June – Ran aground on a sandbank off Rossdhu Point. Was towed off by *Empress* and *Prince of Wales* on 10 July after water levels had risen in the loch.
1911: Scrapped.

356: *Jeanie Deans* (1884)

Number in Williamson's list: 276
Built: 1884
234 tons. Length 210 ft
Builders: Barclay Curle Ltd, Whiteinch
Engine builders: Barclay Curle Ltd., Whiteinch. Engine type: Single Diagonal, Jet Condenser, surface condenser 1889; 106 hp
Hull Material: Steel; raised poop deck
Owners: North British Steam Packet Ltd
1884: Entered service from Craigendoran to Rothesay.
1894: Fore and aft deck saloons added.
1896: Sold to the Derry & Moville Steam Packet Co. Operated from Londonderry to Moville.
1897: Sold to The Clyde Steamers Ltd. Operated on excursions from Glasgow.
1898: Sold to The Glasgow Steamers Ltd (A. Dawson Reid). Renamed *Duchess of York*.
1900: Laid up.
1900: December – Sold to Reid Ltd.

1901: Operated on excursions from Glasgow, mainly to Tighnabruaich and the Gareloch (including Sunday trips).

1903: Laid up.

1904: Sold to Buchanan Steamers Ltd. Renamed *Isle of Cumbrae*. Operated from Glasgow to Garelochhead.

1904: Operated from Glasgow to Rothesay.

1905: Returned to the Glasgow to Garelochhead service.

1916: Chartered to the Glasgow and South Western Railway. Operated on sailings from Princes Pier.

1919: Owner became Williamson-Buchanan Steamers Ltd.

1920: Scrapped.

357: *Waverley* (1885)

Number in Williamson's list: 277

Built: 1885

258 tons. Length 205 ft

Builders: H. McIntyre & Co., Paisley

Engine builders: Hutson & Corbett, Kelvinhaugh. Engine type: Single Diagonal, Surface condenser; 99 hp

Hull Material: Steel hull; Deck saloon aft

Owner: Captain Bob Campbell

1885: Entered service from Glasgow to Kilmun.

1886: Operated from Glasgow to Millport and Ayr after she was found too large for the Holy Loch service.

1887: Chartered to Bristol Channel Marine Excursion Co., Bristol. Operated excursions from Bristol.

1888: Owners now P. & A. Campbell, following the death of Captain Bob Campbell. Operated by Captain Alec Campbell from Bristol to Ilfracombe, Weston-super-Mare, etc.

1889: Owners moved to the Bristol Channel. Continued to operate excursions from Bristol.

1896: Operated from Weston-super-Mare to Cardiff.

1911: Operated from Hastings for this year only.

1915 & 1916: Operated from Weston-super-Mare to Cardiff.

1917: 26 May – Requisitioned by the Admiralty. Renamed HMS *Way*. Used as a minesweeper, initially at Swansea and later on the Thames

1919: 17 March – Returned to her owners.

1920: 1 October – Scrapped at Bristol.

358: *Diana Vernon*

Number in Williamson's list: 278

Built: 1885

192.78 tons. Length 180.5 ft

Builders: Barclay Curle Ltd, Whiteinch

Engine builders: Barclay Curle Ltd, Whiteinch. Engine type: Single Diagonal, Surface condenser; 103 hp

Hull Material: Iron and steel hull; Deck saloon aft

Owners: North British Steam Packet Ltd

1885: 2 June – Launched.

1885: Entered service on rail connected services from Craigendoran.

1888: Moved to the Craigendoran to Garelochhead service.

1890: Reboilered.

1901: Sold to Lee Ltd, Brighton. Operated excursions from Brighton. Renamed *Worthing Belle*. Operated short trips to sea and sailings to Eastbourne and Worthing.

1914: March – Sold to Administration de Navires â Vapeur, Constantinople, renamed *Tuzla*. Operated from Constantinople to the Bosphorus.

1915: 30 August – Was a war loss at Canakkale. Some sources state she was raised and returned to service until scrapped in 1926.

359: *Grenadier*

Number in Williamson's list: 279

Built: 1885

371.9tons. Length 222.9 ft

Builders: J. & G. Thomson, Clydebank

Engine builders: J. & G. Thomson, Clydebank. Engine type: Compound Diagonal Oscillating; 150 hp

Hull Material: Steel hull; Deck saloons fore and aft

Owner: David MacBrayne

1885: 19 March – launched.

1885: May – Entered service from Glasgow to Ardrishaig.

1885: June – Operated from Oban to Loch Scavaig, Portree and Gairloch. Was fitted with the first compound engine on a Clyde or West Highland steamer.

1886: Moved to the Oban to Staffa and Iona service in the summer months and Glasgow or Greenock to Ardrishaig in winter.

1889: Early – Collided with the schooner *Lady Margaret* while berthing at Colintraive. The schooner's mast fell across the deck of the *Grenadier*, killing one passenger and severely injuring another.

1901 – 1902: Winter – Reboilered. Fitted with wider diameter funnels.

1902: Summer – Operated from Rothesay to Glasgow and from Glasgow to Rothesay and the Kyles of Bute with an afternoon cruise round Bute on Saturdays.

1903: Summer – Returned to the Oban to Staffa and Iona service.

1906: Owners became David MacBrayne Ltd.

1915: Operated from Wemyss Bay to Ardrishaig in this and the following year year-round.

1916: September – Requisitioned by the Admiralty as HMS *Grenade*. Used as a minesweeper in the North Sea.

1919: 17 October – Released from Admiralty control, returned to her pre-war service to Ardrishaig.

1927: 5-6 September – Seriously damaged by fire while lying overnight at Oban. 3 crew members, including her former master, Captain McArthur, died.

1928: May – Refloated and towed to Ardrossan for scrapping.

360: *Victoria* (1886)

Number in Williamson's list: 280
Built: 1886
341 tons. Length 222.4 ft
Builders: Blackwood & Gordon, Port Glasgow
Engine builders: Blackwood & Gordon, Port Glasgow. Engine type: Double Diagonal, Surface
    condenser; 160 hp
Hull Material: Steel hull; Deck saloon aft
Owners: Gillies & Campbell
1886: 20 May – Launched.
1886: Entered service on excursions from Wemyss Bay.
1890: May – Made one sailing from Liverpool to Llandudno.
1890: Chartered to the Belfast, Bangor & Larne Steamboat Co. Operated from Belfast to
    Bangor.
1891: 29 July – Chartered to Gunning, Naerup & le Boulanger, Swansea. Operated from
    Swansea to Ilfracombe until 27 August.
1892: Reboilered.
1892: Purchased by the Scottish Excursion Steamer Co. Operated from Fairlie to
    Campbeltown.
1893: Moved to a thrice weekly service from Greenock (Princes Pier) to Millport and
    Campbeltown.
1894: Sold to the London & East Coast Express Steamship Service Co. Operated from
    London to East Anglian Resorts.
1897: Sold to The Clyde Steamers Ltd (A. Dawson Reid). Operated from Glasgow to Skipness
    and on Sunday Excursions from Glasgow round Bute.
1900: September – Scrapped. Claims in certain sources that she was sold to Bermuda are
    erroneous.

361: *Madge Wildfire*

Number in Williamson's list: 281
Built: 1886
220 tons. Length 190 ft
Builders: S. McKnight & Co. Ltd., Ayr
Engine builders: Hutson & Corbett, Kelvinhaugh. Engine type: Single Diagonal Tandem
    Compound 1891; 95 hp
Hull Material: Steel hull; Deck saloon aft
Owner: Captain Bob Campbell
1886: 25 May – Launched.
1886: Entered service from Glasgow to Kilmun with occasional sailings to Lochgoilhead.
1888: June – Now owned by P. & A. Campbell following the death of Captain Bob Campbell.
1888: December – Sold to the Caledonian Steam Packet Co. Ltd. Continued to operate from
    Glasgow to Kilmun.
1889: January – Calls at Gourock added after the opening of the pier. Also relieved on other
    sailings from Gourock and Wemyss Bay.
1889: 28 September – Collided with the small steam yacht *Osprey*, which was carrying no
    lights, off Gourock, cutting her in two with three fatalities on the yacht.
1890: A fore saloon was added.

1901 to 1902: Winter – The Kilmun service was cut back to start from Gourock.

1903: Reboilered.

1910: Laid up.

1911: April – Sold to the Vale of Clyde Steam Packet Co. (A. W. Cameron), Dumbarton. Operated on excursions from Glasgow.

1911: June – Now operated from Glasgow to Rothesay, Largs and Millport with a cruise round Cumbrae.

1913: January – Sold to Buchanan Steamers Ltd. Renamed *Isle of Skye*. Operated from Glasgow to Rothesay.

1915: Operated from Glasgow to Garelochhead.

1916: May – Requisitioned by the Admiralty. Used as a Naval tender and as a minesweeper at Invergordon until April 1919.

1919: 10 May – Resumed sailings from Glasgow to Dunoon, Rothesay and Port Bannatyne with a Loch Striven Cruise added from July until early September. Was the first steamer to operate from Glasgow after the end of the First World War.

1920: March – Owners now Williamson-Buchanan Steamers Ltd. Operated from Glasgow to Lochgoilhead.

1922: Back on the Glasgow to Rothesay service.

1927: March – Sold to the Grangemouth & Forth Towing Co. Renamed *Fair Maid*. Operated from Leith to Aberdour and Kirkcaldy.

1939: Service ceased on the outbreak of war.

1940: November – Requisitioned by the Admiralty. Used as a Naval tender and a decontamination vessel at Greenock.

1944: 21-30 March – Operated from Craigendoran to Dunoon as a relief to *Lucy Ashton*, which was undergoing repairs. Also operated from Gourock to Kilmun for one day around this period.

1946: December – Scrapped at Troon.

362: *Fusilier*

Number in Williamson's list: 282

Built: 1888

251.5 tons. Length 202 ft

Builders: J. McArthur & Co., Paisley

Engine builders: Hutson & Corbett, Kelvinhaugh. Engine type: Single Diagonal surface condenser; 133 hp

Hull Material: Iron and Steel hull; deck saloon aft

Owner: David MacBrayne.

1888: 14 April – Launched.

1888: Entered service from Oban to Gairloch.

1889: Moved to the route from Oban to Fort William.

1901: Reboilered.

1906: Owners became David MacBrayne Ltd.

1916: July to August – Operated from Glasgow to Dunoon.

1917: Chartered to the Caledonian Steam Packet Co. Ltd. Operated from Wemyss Bay to Rothesay. Funnel painted in CSP yellow for a while.

1919: Charter ceased. Returned to her pre-war duties.

1928: Owners now David MacBrayne (1928) Ltd. Operated from Oban to Staffa and Iona in summer and from Greenock to Ardrishaig in winter.

1931: Operated from Mallaig to Portree.

1934: July – Sold to Redcliffe Shipping Ltd, Hull. Operated on excursions from Granton to Kirkcaldy and on non-landing cruises to the Forth Bridge, the Bass Rock, etc.

1934: December – Sold to Cambrian Shipping Co. Ltd, Blackpool. Renamed *Lady Orme*.

1935: June – Operated from Llandudno to Menai Straits.

1936: Sold to F Perry. Operated on excursions from Ramsgate.

1937: Sold to the Ormes Cruising Co. Ltd. Operated on non-landing cruises from Llandudno thrice daily

1938: July – Sold to J. H. Oliver – Renamed *Crestawave*. Continued to operate from Llandudno.

1938: August – Withdrawn from service and laid up.

1939: October – Scrapped.

363: *Lucy Ashton*

Number in Williamson's list: 283

Built: 1888

271.3 tons. Length 190 ft

Builders: T. B. Seath & Co., Rutherglen

Engine builders: (1) Hutson & Corbett, Kelvinhaugh; (2) A. & J. Inglis Ltd. Engine type: (1) Single Diagonal 150 hp; (2) Compound Diagonal; 174 hp

Hull Material: Steel hull, deck saloon aft, narrow fore saloon

Owners: North British Steam Packet Ltd

1888: 24 May – Launched.

1888: Entered service from Craigendoran to Kilmun.

1894: Pursers office and new bridge above it, replacing the bridge across the paddle boxes, added. The steering wheel was moved from a small raised platform on the promenade deck to this new bridge.

1895: Now used as a spare steamer and for excursions.

1901: Reboilered. Now operating to Greenock and Garelochhead rather than Kilmun.

1902: Owners now the North British Railway.

1902: Re-engined and again reboilered. The year-old boilers were transferred to another steamer.

1903: Deck saloons enlarged. Stairways in sponsons replaced by conventional stairs from the promenade deck and new lavatories installed in the sponsons.

1908: Forward companionway shelter added. Combined Captain's Cabin, Pursers Office and deck shelter replaced the old Pursers Office below the bridge.

1918: Back on the Craigendoran to Kilmun route for this year only.

1923: Reboilered.

1923: Owners now the London & North Eastern Railway.

1939: September – Now operated from Craigendoran to Clynder and to Greenock.

1940: April – Now sailed to Gourock instead of Greenock.

1942: September – Now operated from Craigendoran to Gourock and Dunoon.

1945: July – Operated from Craigendoran to Rothesay until the return of *Jeanie Deans* from war service in June 1946.

1948: 1 January – Owners became the British Transport Commission on nationalisation of the railways.

1949: February – Final sailing from Dunoon to Craigendoran.

1949: After a career of sixty-one years on the Firth of Clyde, sold for scrapping. Engines, paddles and paddle boxes removed.

1949–1950: Hull used of experiments with jet propulsion by British Ship-Building Research
  Association and later scrapped.
The paddle box carving from *Lucy Ashton* has survived and is on display at the National
  Railway Museum at York.

364: *Empress*

Built: 1888
229 tons. Length 165 ft
Builders: Napier, Shanks & Bell, Yoker
Engine builders: D. Rowan & Son, Glasgow. Engine type: 2-cylinder diagonal; 138 hp
Hull Material: Steel hull, deck saloons
Owners: Loch Lomond Steamboat Co.
1888: Taken over whilst on the stocks by the North British Steam Packet Co.
1888: 6 November – Launched.
1888: 28 December – Ran trials on the Gareloch.
1890: 11-14 January – Moved up the River Leven to Balloch after low water had made this
  impossible for the previous 12 months.
1890: Entered service on Loch Lomond from Balloch to Ardlui.
1895: Owners now the Dumbarton & Balloch Joint Line Committee (North British Railway
  and Caledonian railways).
1900: Now worked both winter and summer services on the loch.
1919: 3-10 February – Commandeered by the Admiralty for an unknown reason.
1923: Owners now the Dumbarton & Balloch Joint Line Committee (London & North
  Eastern and London, Midland & Scottish Railways). By now used as a reserve steamer.
1925: December – Final sailing from Balloch to Ardlui and back.
1925: Laid up.
1933: Scrapped at Balloch.

365: *Caledonia* (1889)

Number in Williamson's list: 284
Built: 1889
244.44 tons. Length 200.4 ft
Builders: J. Reid & Co., Port Glasgow
Engine builders: Rankin & Blackmore, Greenock. Engine type: Single crank tandem
  Compound; 140 hp
Hull Material: Steel hull, deck saloon aft
Owners: Caledonian Steam Packet Co. Ltd.
1889: 6 May – Launched.
1889: Entered service from Gourock to Rothesay. Was the first Clyde steamer to be fitted with
  docking telegraphs.
1890: 1 May – Moved to the route from Wemyss Bay to Millport.
1893: Converted experimentally to oil firing.
1894: Spring – Returned to coal firing after the price of oil increased.
1896: 17 December – Collided with and sank the tug *Champion* (No. 353), which was
  carrying mail and newspapers, south of Dunoon.
1897: Again experimentally converted to oil firing for a short period.

1902: Moved to Gourock to Kilmun service.

1903: Reboilered.

1910: Used as a spare steamer.

1911: Late in the year – Bridge moved forward of the funnel.

1916: Operated from Gourock to Dunoon as well as to Kilmun.

1917: April – Requisitioned by the Admiralty – Converted for use as a minesweeper in the English Channel.

1919: Early – Involved in a collision in the River Seine. Little damage.

1919: April – Released by the Admiralty.

1919: November – Returned to service in the Clyde.

1933: November – Withdrawn form service and sold for scrapping.

The paddle box crest from *Caledonia* was on display at Wemyss Bay station until the late 1970s, but its present location is unknown.

366: *Galatea*

Number in Williamson's list: 285

Built: 1889

331 tons. Length 230.2 ft

Builders: Caird & Co., Greenock

Engine builders: Caird & Co., Greenock. Engine type: Double Diagonal Compound; 250 hp

Hull Material: Steel hull, deck saloon aft

Owners: Caledonian Steam Packet Co. Ltd.

1889: 31 May – Launched.

1889: 9 July – Entered service from Gourock to Rothesay with an afternoon cruise round Bute.

1890: Operated from Wemyss Bay to Rothesay with a variety of longer excursions to Lochranza, Lochgoilhead, Arrochar, round Arran, Skipness, Ayr and Campbeltown.

1891: Moved to a service from Rothesay to Dunoon and Arrochar.

1893: Operated from Gourock to Rothesay and a round Bute cruise for this summer onwards.

1898: From this season operated form Gourock to Rothesay and the Kyles of Bute rather than round Bute.

1903: Now used as a relief steamer.

1906: July – Sold to Soc. Anon di Navigazione 'Tirrenia', Genoa, Italy. Operated from Genoa to San Remo, Monte Carlo and Nice.

1914: Broken up at Palermo.

CHAPTER 9
Steamers Built 1890–99

367: *Marchioness of Breadalbane* (1890)

Number in Williamson's list: 286
Built: 1890
246.22 tons. Length 200.4 ft
Builders: J. Reid & Co., Port Glasgow
Engine builders: Rankin & Blackmore, Greenock. Engine type: Tandem Compound Diagonal; 140 hp
Hull Material: Steel hull, deck saloon aft
Owners: Caledonian Steam Packet Co. Ltd
1890: 15 April – Launched.
1890: Entered service from Wemyss Bay to Rothesay & Millport.
1901–1902: Winter – Reboilered.
1909: Continued on same service, but mainly carrying cargo.
1915: Operated from Gourock to Rothesay and on other sailings inside the boom.
1916: Operated on sailings out of Wemyss Bay, to Millport and to Rothesay.
1917: April – Requisitioned by the Admiralty. Renamed HMS *Marquis of Breadalbane*. Used as a minesweeper based at Troon and later in the English Channel.
1919: 1 May – Returned to her owners.
1921: Returned to service after an overly long refit, including a complete renewal of her electrical installation. Continued on the same service as previously.
1933: Moved to the Gourock to Kilmun service.
1935: February – Sold to Smith & Houston Ltd. for scrapping.
1935: 23 May – Resold to Redcliffe Shipping, Hull. Used on excursions from Great Yarmouth and Lowestoft.
1936: May–July – Used on excursions from Newcastle, then returned to operations from Great Yarmouth.
1937: Scrapped.

368: *Marchioness of Bute*

Number in Williamson's list: 287
Built: 1890
246.22 tons. Length 200.4 ft
Builders: J. Reid & Co., Port Glasgow
Engine builders: Rankin & Blackmore, Greenock. Engine type: Tandem Compound Diagonal; 140 hp
Hull Material: Steel hull, deck saloon aft

Owners: Caledonian Steam Packet Co. Ltd

1890: 6 May – Launched.

1890: Entered service from Gourock to Rothesay.

1895: Afternoon trip to the Kyles of Bute added to her schedule until 1897.

1900–1901: Winter – Reboilered.

1903: By now on the Wemyss Bay to Millport and Rothesay services.

1908: July – Sold to D. & J. Nicol, Dundee. Operated from Dundee to Newburgh and Perth, and to Arbroath and cruises to the Bell Rock.

1914: August – Laid up on the outbreak of war.

1917: Requisitioned by the Admiralty and converted to a minesweeper.

1919: Sold to the Admiralty. Used as a transport ship and hospital ship at Archangel in the White Sea, in support of White Russian forces fighting the Bolsheviks.

1920: Laid up at Inverkeithing.

1923: Scrapped at Inverkeithing.

369: *Duchess of Hamilton*

Number in Williamson's list: 288

Built: 1890

552.7 tons. Length 250 ft

Builders: W. Denny & Bros, Dumbarton

Engine builders: W. Denny & Bros Ltd, Dumbarton. Engine type: Double Diagonal Compound; 268 hp

Hull Material: Steel hull, deck saloon aft, promenade deck extended to bow

Owners: Caledonian Steam Packet Co. Ltd

1890: April – Launched

1890: 30 May – Entered service from Ardrossan to Arran

1898: Made excursions from Ayr for this season only

1899: Returned to the Ardrossan to Arran service.

1906: Now operated excursions from Gourock.

1907: Reboilered

1909: Moved to the service from Gourock to Arran via the Kyles.

1910: Commenced operating on excursions from Gourock including a weekly trip to Ayr.

1911: Operated from Gourock to Arrochar.

1912: Returned to operating excursions from Gourock

1915: February – Requisitioned by the Admiralty. Converted to a minesweeper, operating out of Harwich.

1915: 29 November – Sunk by a mine off Harwich.

The paddle box crest from *Duchess of Hamilton* was on display at Gourock station until the late 1970s, but its present location is unknown.

370: *Marchioness of Lorne* (1891)

Number in Williamson's list: 289

Built: 1891

294.8 tons. Length 200 ft

Builders: Russell & Co., Port Glasgow

Engine builders: Rankin & Blackmore, Greenock. Engine type: Twin crank Tandem Triple

Expansion; 140 hp

Hull Material: Steel hull, deck saloon aft, promenade deck extended to bow

Owners: Caledonian Steam Packet Co. Ltd

1891: 25 April – Launched.

1891: Entered service on rail connected services from Wemyss Bay in the summer months and from Ardrossan to Arran in the winter months. Also operated excursions from Gourock.

1897: Reboilered.

1898: Relieved *Duchess of Hamilton* on the Ardrossan to Arran service on the days that she operated excursions from Ayr.

1900: Moved to the winter Rothesay service.

1902: Returned to the winter Arran run.

1904: Operated from Gourock to Rothesay and the Kyles of Bute.

1909: Fore saloon extended forwards to give extra accommodation to steerage passengers. Moved to the Wemyss Bay and Fairlie to Millport route.

1916: Requisitioned by the Admiralty. Converted to a minesweeper.

1917: Used at Malta and in the Suez Canal.

1921: 18 March – Laid up on her return from war service.

1923: December – Scrapped.

The paddle box crest from *Marchioness of Lorne* was on display at Gourock station until the late 1970s, but its present location is unknown. The mast was used as a flagpole at Glasgow High School's playing fields at Anniesland until destroyed in the early 1980s.

371: *Lady Rowena*

Number in Williamson's list: 290

Built: 1891

314 tons. Length 200.6 ft

Builders: S. McKnight & Co. Ltd, Ayr

Engine builders: Hutson & Corbett, Kelvinhaugh. Engine type: Single Diagonal; 166 hp

Hull Material: Iron hull, deck saloons

Owners: North British Steam Packet Co.

1891: 31 May – Launched.

1891: July – Entered service from Craigendoran to Arrochar.

1901: Reboilered.

1902: Owners now the North British Railway.

1903: Chartered to the Loch Goil & Loch Long Steamboat Co. Operated from Greenock to Lochgoilhead.

1903: Late June – Sold to Societa di Navigazione a Vapore della Peninsula Sorrentine, Castellamare. Operated from Naples to Sorrento & Capri.

1908: Sold to R. R. Collard, Newhaven. Operated from Newhaven to Eastbourne and Hastings. At some time also operated out of Ostend.

1909: Operated excursions in the Solent.

1912: April to July – Chartered to Wilson & Reid, Belfast. Operated from Belfast to Bangor.

1912: August – Sold to Capt. A. W. Cameron, Dumbarton. Operated excursions from Glasgow.

1916: 12 April – Requisitioned by the Admiralty. Used on the Firth of Forth as a tender, to carry horse-fodder and as a hospital ship.

1917: 12 August – Converted to a minesweeper. Used in the English Channel and then in the Mediterranean, based at Malta and later at Alexandria.

1919: 6 February – Returned to her owners.

1919: April – Sold to the Goole & Hull Steam Packet Co. Ltd. Laid up at Goole, never operated for them.

1920: Sold to W. K. David, Swansea. Operated from Swansea to Ilfracombe, also on trips from Mumbles and Llanelly.

1920: July – Hit quay and collided with a couple of mud barges while berthing at Swansea. Towed to Bristol for repairs which bankrupted her owner.

1920: 15 August – Returned to Swansea, and completed the season under the management of a consortium of local businessmen.

1921: July – Sold to F. C. Deering, Brighton (The South Coast Shipping Company). Operated excursions from Brighton.

1922: November – Scrapped.

372: *Lord of the Isles* (1891)

Number in Williamson's list: 291
Built: 1891
465.9 tons. Length 255.3 ft
Builders: D. & W. Henderson, Meadowside
Engine builders: D. & W. Henderson, Meadowside. Engine type: 2-cylinder Diagonal Oscillating; 280 hp
Hull Material: Steel hull, deck saloons
Owners: Glasgow & Inveraray Steamboat Co.

1891: 25 April – Launched.

1891: 20 May – Entered service from Glasgow to Inveraray. Was the final Clyde steamer to be built with oscillating engines.

1899 (or earlier): Promenade deck extended to the bow.

1908: Reboilered.

1909: Owners became the Loch Goil & Inveraray Steamboat Co.

1912: Purchased by Turbine Steamers Ltd. Placed on a service from Glasgow to Rothesay and a cruise round Bute.

1914: Moved to the Glasgow to Lochgoilhead service.

1919: Returned to the cruise round Bute from Glasgow.

1928: Service extended to Arrochar.

1928 – late: Scrapped.

373: *Lady Clare*

Number in Williamson's list: 292
Built: 1891
257 tons. Length 180.5 ft
Builders: J. McArthur & Co., Paisley
Engine builders: Hutson & Corbett, Kelvinhaugh. Engine type: Single Diagonal; 108 hp
Hull Material: Steel hull, deck saloons
Owners: North British Steam Packet Co.

1891: 24 June – Launched.

1891: Entered service from. Craigendoran to Garelochhead.

1895: Moved to the service from Craigendoran to Greenock (Prince Pier) in connection with the new West Highland Railway.

1897: Back on the Garelochhead service.
1902: Owners now the North British Railway.
1904: Laid up.
1906: Sold to the Moville Steamship Co. Ltd., Londonderry. Operated from Londonderry to Moville, and was also used as a tender to liners calling at Moville.
1915: Laid up.
1914: May – Requisitioned by the Admiralty. Converted to a minesweeper and operated out of Belfast.
1918: December – Returned to her owners.
1919: Resumed Lough Foyle service.
1921: Laid up at Londonderry.
1922: Resumed operation.
1925: Laid up.
1928: March – Scrapped at Dumbarton.

374: *Seamore*

Built: 1891
262 tons. Length 132 ft
Builders: J. P. Rennoldson & Son, South Shields
Engine builders: J. P. Rennoldson & Son, South Shields. Engine type: single cylinder side lever; 98 hp
Hull Material: Iron
Owners: Clyde Shipping Co.
1891: January – Entered service as the tug/tender *America* at Queenstown/Cobh.
1912: Tendered to the White Star liner *Titanic* on her only call at Queenstown, taking 123 passengers on board.
1915: September – Chartered to the Admiralty, Continued to be used as a tender.
1920: May – Returned to her owners.
1928: April – Sold to J. & L. Vercammen, Burght, Belgium for demolition.
1928: May – Sold to Anchor Line (Henderson Bros.), Glasgow. Renamed *Seamore*. Operated as a tender on Lough Foyle, also offered excursions.
1935: May – Owners now Anchor Line (1935) Ltd.
1936: September – Owners became Anchor Line Ltd.
1939: Now used as a tender on the Clyde.
1945 – early: Operated for one day for the Caledonian Steam Packet Co. Ltd from Gourock to the Holy Loch in lieu of *Marchioness of Lorne* (1935) (No: 413).
1945: November: Broken up at Port Glasgow.

375: *Glen Sannox*

Number in Williamson's list: 293
Built: 1892
609.6 tons. Length 260.5 ft
Builders: J. & G. Thomson Ltd, Clydebank
Engine builders: J. & G. Thomson Ltd, Clydebank. Engine type: Double Diagonal Compound; 326 hp
Hull Material: Steel hull, deck saloons fore and aft, promenade deck extended to bow
Owners: Glasgow & South Western Railway
1892: 26 March – Launched.

1892: 6 June – Entered service from Ardrossan to Arran with excursions round Arran, round Ailsa Craig and to Campbeltown Loch during her mid-day layover. These excursions lasted ten years or so.

1910: Laid up.

1911: Returned to the Ardrossan to Arran service.

1912: Operated from Greenock (Princes Pier) to Arran via the Kyles.

1913: Returned to the Ardrossan to Arran service and continued there until 1915.

1915 – early: Requisitioned by the Admiralty – Used as a troopship from Southampton to France, but only made one trip and was returned to owners because of her inability to cope with heavy weather. Returned to the Ardrossan to Arran service.

1923: Owners absorbed into the London, Midland & Scottish Railway.

1924: September – Laid up.

1925: May – Broken up by Smith & Co., Port Glasgow.

376: *Isle of Arran* (1892)

Number in Williamson's list: 294

Built: 1892

313 tons. Length 210 ft

Builders: T. B. Seath & Co., Rutherglen

Engine builders: W. King & Co., Glasgow. Engine type: Single Diagonal, Surface condenser; 250 hp

Hull Material: Steel hull; deck saloons fore and aft. Had an fixed awning-cum-liferaft over the aft deck saloon

Owners: Buchanan Steamers Ltd

1892: 14 May – Launched.

1892: Entered service from Glasgow to Arran via Rothesay and Kilchattan Bay.

1894: Now operated from Glasgow to Rothesay with an afternoon cruise from there.

1902: Now operated from Glasgow to Rothesay and the Kyles of Bute.

1911: Reboilered.

1916: Operated on a service from Glasgow to the Gareloch, the only trip operating from Glasgow in that year.

1917: Spring – Requisitioned by the Admiralty – Used as a minesweeper and as a troop transport based at Portsmouth.

1918: November – Used to carry troops from Rouen and Le Havre to Portsmouth.

1919: Owners became Williamson-Buchanan Steamers Ltd.

1920: Released from Admiralty service. Bridge moved forward of the funnel and the forward part of the landing platform plated in. Awning replaced by a small upper deck. Operated from Glasgow to Rothesay, Largs, Millport and an Arran Coast Cruise.

1933: May – Sold to the General Steam Navigation Co. Ltd. Used on London River and Docks cruises and from London to Herne Bay and Margate and a cruise to the Nore Lightship.

1936: October – Scrapped.

377: *Mercury* (1892)

Number in Williamson's list: 295
Built: 1892
378 tons. Length 220.5 ft
Builders: Napier, Shanks & Bell, Yoker
Engine builders: D. Rowan & Son, Glasgow. Engine type: Double Diagonal Compound; 240 hp
Hull Material: Steel hull; deck saloons fore and aft
Owners: Glasgow & South Western Railway
1892: 18 April – Launched.
1892: Entered service from Greenock (Princes Pier) to Arran via the Kyles of Bute.
c. 1900: Service now Greenock (Princes Pier) to Rothesay and the Kyles of Bute.
1914: Reboilered.
1915: Operated from Fairlie to the Kyles of Bute, following the erection of the boom from the Cloch to Dunoon.
1915 – late: Requisitioned by the Admiralty and used as a minesweeper based at Harwich. Her bow was blown off by a mine, and only a day after she returned from repairs, her stern was blown off by a mine.
1920: January – Returned to commercial service after a refit. Operated from Greenock (Princes Pier) to Rothesay and the Kyles of Bute.
1923: Owners absorbed by the London, Midland & Scottish Railway. Started to be used on rail connected services from Princes Pier, Gourock and Wemyss Bay.
1933: December – Scrapped at Barrow-in-Furness.

378: *Neptune* (1892)

Number in Williamson's list: 296
Built: 1892
378 tons. Length 220.5 ft
Builders: Napier, Shanks & Bell, Yoker
Engine builders: D. Rowan & Son, Glasgow. Engine type: Double Diagonal Compound; 240 hp
Hull Material: Steel hull; deck saloons fore and aft
Owner: Glasgow & South Western Railway
1892: 10 March – Launched.
1892: 13 April – Entered service from Ardrossan to Arran.
1892: June – Moved to the Greenock (Princes Pier) to the Kyles of Bute service.
1896: Used on excursions from Ayr including some to Stranraer.
1898: Now used on excursions from Princes Pier, including weekly to Stranraer.
1902: Moved to the Princes Pier to Ayr service.
c. 1908: Forward observation windows of the fore deck saloon replaced by steel plating.
1909: Now operated from Princes Pier to Arrochar or the Kyles of Bute.
1912 – late: Reboilered. New charthouse and shelter over the aft stairway added, as was a small deck shelter over the forward companionway.
1915: September – Operated from Ardrossan to Arran, replacing *Glen Sannox*.
1915 – late: Requisitioned by the Admiralty. Renamed HMS *Nepaulin*. Converted to a minesweeper, stationed at Dover.
1917: 20 May – Sunk by a mine near the Dyck light vessel off Dunkirk with the loss of eighteen of her crew.

379: *Comet* (1892)

Built: 1892
37 tons. Length 87 ft
Builders: R. Rodger, Port Glasgow
Engine builders: Hanna, Donald & Wilson. Engine type: triple expansion
Hull Material: wood, flush-decked
Owner: H. McIntyre
1892: Built as a private yacht fort her owner, a shipbuilder.
1893: Summer – Used for short trips from Rothesay to Loch Striven landing, and to the Kyles of Bute and Loch Riddon.
1894: 7 March – Destroyed by fire at her owner's shipyard in Alloa.

380: *Culzean Castle*

Built: 1892
599 tons. Length 244.61895: ft
Builders: Southampton Naval Works, Southampton
Engine builders: Southampton Naval Works, Southampton. Engine type: Triple expansion diagonal, geared; 384 hp
Hull Material: Promenade deck to foremast, well deck, focsle
Owners: Bournemouth, Swanage & Poole Steam Packet Co.
1891: 13 June – Launched as *Windsor Castle*. Builders soon after went into liquidation and the steamer was completed by Day, Summers & Co. at Southampton.
1892: 30 July – Entered service on excursions from Bournemouth.
1895: Sold to the Glasgow, Ayrshire & Campbeltown Steamboat Co. Ltd. Renamed *Culzean Castle*. Well deck plated in. Operated from Princes Pier and Fairlie to Campbeltown. Was the first three-crank triple expansion-engined steamer to be utilised in Clyde services.
1898: Sold to Clyde Excursion Steamers Ltd. Renamed *Carrick Castle*. Operated on excursions from Glasgow.
1900: Sold to the Russian-owned Chinese Eastern Railway, Port Arthur. Renamed *Nagadon*. Operated on services from Port Arthur/Dalian, possibly to Shanghai and Japan.
1904: Captured by Japanese at Port Arthur in the Russo-Japanese war. Sold to Naksomura Goshi Kaisha, Kishwadahama, Japan. Renamed *Nagara Maru*. Operated on the Inland Sea in Japan.
1913: Sold to Sanyo Kisen Kabushiki Kaisha, Nishinomiya, Japan. Renamed *Tenri Maru*. Used on the same or a similar service.
1931: November – Ran aground near Matsu Shima, Japan.

381: *Minerva*

Number in Williamson's list: 297
Built: 1893
306.4 tons. Length 200 ft
Builders: J. & G. Thomson Ltd., Clydebank
Engine builders: J. & G. Thomson Ltd., Clydebank. Engine type: Double Diagonal Compound; 240 hp
Hull Material: Deck saloons fore and aft
Owners: Glasgow & South Western Railway

1893: 6 May – Launched.
1893: Entered service from Greenock (Princes Pier) to Arrochar and to the Kyles of Bute.
1902: Reboilered.
1908: Moved to the Fairlie to Millport service.
1914: Autumn – Operated from Greenock (Princes Pier) and Gourock to Kilmun until late 1915.
1916: 19 June – Purchased by the Admiralty. Renamed HMS *Minerva II*. Used as an Admiralty Patrol Paddler based at Malta and at Alexandria, also in the Suez Canal.
1917: Captured by the Turks.
1919: 20 April – Used as a minesweeper from now onwards.
1920: 7 April – Sold at Constantinople to unknown purchasers. Claims in certain sources and in Lloyds Register that she was sold to Turkish owners for use on the Bosphorus are not backed up by Turkish records.
1928: Deleted from Lloyds Register.

382: *Glen Rosa* (1893)

Number in Williamson's list: 298
Built: 1893
306.4 tons. Length 200 ft
Builders: J. & G. Thomson Ltd, Clydebank
Engine builders: J. & G. Thomson Ltd, Clydebank. Engine type: Double Diagonal Compound; 240 hp
Hull Material: Deck saloons fore and aft
Owners: Glasgow & South Western Railway
1893: 31 May – Launched.
1893: Entered service. Operated from Greenock (Princes Pier) to Ayr in the summer months and from Ardrossan to Arran in the winter months. Also offered excursions from Ayr until 1895.
1898: Moved to the services from Greenock (Princes Pier) to Arrochar and to the Kyles of Bute.
1908 – Late: Now operated from Fairlie to Millport. Kilchattan Bay and Rothesay.
1917: 12 June – Requisitioned by the Admiralty. Renamed HMS *Glen Cross*. Converted to a minesweeper. Used mainly in Belfast Lough.
1919: 12 September – Released from Admiralty service.
1920: Returned to the Fairlie to Millport. Kilchattan Bay and Rothesay service.
1923: Owners absorbed into the London, Midland & Scottish Railway.
1926: Reboilered and bridge placed forward of the funnel.
1937: Now used for special Excursions and as a spare steamer.
1938: Ownership transferred to the Caledonian Steam Packet Co. Ltd.
1939: Laid up.
1939: August – Scrapped at Dalmuir.

383: *Fairy* (1893)

Built: 1893
38 tons. Length 61.5 ft
Builders: D. M. Cumming, Blackhill, Glasgow
Engine builders: Lees Anderson & Co., Glasgow. Engine type: compound diagonal; 20 hp
Hull Material: flush-decked
Owners: Inveraray Burgh Council
1893: Entered service from Inveraray to St Catherines.
1908: Sold to G. Brown Greenock.
1909: Chartered to J. Dewar, Inveraray.
1912: By November – Blown from her moorings in a gale and blown ashore further up Loch Fyne, where she was wrecked.

384: *Duchess of Rothesay*

Number in Williamson's list: 299
Built: 1895
338 tons. Length 225.6 ft
Builders: J. & G. Thomson Ltd, Clydebank
Engine builders: J. & G. Thomson Ltd, Clydebank. Engine type: Double Diagonal Compound; 137 hp
Hull Material: Deck saloons fore and aft
Owners: Caledonian Steam Packet Co. Ltd
1895: 20 April – Launched.
1895: Entered service from Gourock and Wemyss Bay to Rothesay. Had a small weathercock at the top of her mast and was known as 'the Cock of the Walk'.
1897: Moved to the route from Gourock to Arran via the Kyles of Bute.
1897: 10 September – Carried the Duke and Duchess of York to the opening of the Cessnock Dock at Govan.
1907: April – Carried the Prince and Princess of Wales, also known as the Duke and Duchess of Rothesay, to the opening of Rothesay Dock in Clydebank.
1909: Back on the Gourock to Rothesay service.
1911: Peak summer season – Operated from Ardrossan to Arran.
1914: Reboilered.
1914: Peak summer season – Operated from Ardrossan to Arran.
1914: July – Carried King George V and Queen Mary from Fairfield's yard, Govan, to Beardmore's yard at Dalmuir to see the battleship HMS *Ramillies* under construction.
1915: 14 October – Requisitioned by the Admiralty. Converted for use as a minesweeper. Used in the Thames Estuary, based at Sheerness. During her time as a minesweeper towed the disabled Zeppelin airship *L15* into Margate and assisted in the salving of fourteen ships.
1917: Renamed HMS *Duke of Rothesay*. Now based at Portland.
1919: 1 June – Sank at her moorings as Merklands Wharf when mooring ropes were not slackened to take account of the falling tide and she canted over and filled with water, following which the mooring ropes broken and she settled on the river bed.
1919: 27 July – Raised and refloated.
1920: 29 March – Returned to service after reconditioning and repair.
1920: Summer – Commenced operating from Greenock (Princes Pier) and Gourock to Rothesay and the Kyles of Bute.
1939: Summer – Operated on certain dates from Gourock to Arran via the Kyles of Bute.

1939: October – Requisitioned by the Admiralty – Converted to a minesweeper; utilised initially on the Clyde and later at Dover.

1942: April – Used as an accommodation Ship at Brightlingsea.

1945: October – Returned to her owners and laid up.

1946: August – Scrapped in the Netherlands.

385: *Redgauntlet*

Number in Williamson's list: 300
Built: 1895
276.56 tons. Length 215 ft
Builders: Barclay Curle Ltd, Whiteinch
Engine builders: Barclay Curle Ltd, Whiteinch. Engine type: Single Diagonal, Surface condenser; 187 hp
Hull Material: Deck saloons fore and aft
Owners: North British Steam Packet Co. Ltd

1895: 4 April – Launched.

1895: Entered service operating from Craigendoran to Rothesay.

1898: Now operated excursions from Craigendoran.

1899: Now on longer distance excursions from Craigendoran including to Brodick, Lamlash, Ayr and round Arran.

1899: 14 August – Ran aground on the Iron Rocks at the south of Arran. Refloated on 24 August and repaired.

1902: Owners became the North British Railway.

1909: March – Transferred to subsidiary company the Galloway Saloon Steam Packet Co. Operated on excursions on the Firth of Forth, including to the Isle of May to land.

1916: 4 June – Requisitioned by the Admiralty. Converted to a minesweeper, based at Grimsby.

1917: 30 July – Purchased by the Admiralty.

1919: 16 April; Sold to Cie de Navires Olivier, Paris, France. Operated on services from Oran, Algeria.

1934: Deleted from Lloyds Register. Broken up then or before.

386: *Dandie Dinmont* (1895)

Number in Williamson's list: 301
Built: 1895
218.6 tons, 1912 343 tons. Length 197 ft,1912 209.6 f
Builders: A. & J. Inglis, Pointhouse
Engine builders: A. & J. Inglis, Pointhouse. Engine type: Single Diagonal, Surface condenser; 150 hp
Hull Material: Deck saloons fore and aft
Owners: North British Steam Packet Co. Ltd

1895: 10 May – Launched.

1895: Entered service from Craigendoran to Dunoon and the Holy Loch.

1902: Owners now the North British Railway. Used as a spare boat in this year.

1904: Operated from Craigendoran to Garelochhead and to Greenock.

1909: Used as a spare boat again until 1914.

1912: Lengthened by 12.6 feet and reboiled.
1917: Used on all services from Craigendoran, but only as far south as the boom at Dunoon, as the vast majority of her fleetmates had been called up for war service.
1918: Reboiled.
1919: Moved to the Craigendoran to Dunoon and Rothesay service.
1923: Owners absorbed into the London & North Eastern Railway.
1926: Laid up.
1928: Renamed *Frodingham*. Transferred to the service on the Humber from Hull to New Holland. Fore-saloon removed to carry cars and bridge placed forward of the funnel.
1936: January – Broken up at Ghent.

387: *Glenmore*

Number in Williamson's list: 302
Built: 1895
210.5 tons. Length 190.3 ft
Builders: Russell & Co., Greenock
Engine builders: Rankin & Blackmore, Greenock. Engine type: Double Diagonal Compound; 81 hp
Hull Material: Deck saloons fore and aft
Owners: J Williamson & Co.
1895: 9 April – Launched.
1895: Operated from Glasgow to the Kyles of Bute.
1896: Sold to Captain Joseph Wiggins. Renamed *Oryol* or *Orel*. Sailed for Siberia.
1896: 25 August – Arrived at Vardø, Norway, where the icebreaking steamer that was to escort her to the mouth of the Yenesei had already left. Laid up at Vardø for the winter.
1896: Sold to Balandin, Kitmanoff, Vestrotine & Co., Yenesei, Siberia. Operated on the Yenesei River.
No further information is available, although she is believed still to have been in existence in 1943.

388: *Jupiter* (1896)

Number in Williamson's list: 303
Built: 1896
394.3 tons. Length 230 ft
Builders: J. & G. Thomson Ltd, Clydebank
Engine builders: J. & G. Thomson Ltd, Clydebank. Engine type: Double Diagonal Compound; 172 hp
Hull Material: Deck saloons fore and aft
Owners: Glasgow & South Western Railway
1896: 21 March – Launched.
1896: Entered service from Greenock (Princes Pier) to Arran via the Kyles of Bute.
1902: For this season only, ran to Arran via Garroch Head, and made one trip on Saturdays from Whiting Bay to Ardrossan.
1909: Operated on longer excursions from Greenock (Princes Pier).
1910: Returned to sailing from Greenock (Princes Pier) to Arran via the Kyles of Bute.
1911: Operated on Excursions from Princes Pier, Gourock and Fairlie.

1912: Operated from Greenock (Princes Pier) to Ayr.

1914: Returned to the service from Greenock (Princes Pier) to Arran via the Kyles of Bute.

1915: 15 May – Requisitioned by the Admiralty and converted for use as the minesweeper *Jupiter II*, based at Dover.

1920: 29 May – Returned to service. Operated from Princes Pier to Ayr.

1923: Owners absorbed into the London Midland & Scottish Railway. Calls added at Gourock. Added a cruise Round the Lochs, also Saturday sailings from Greenock (Princes Pier) and Gourock to Rothesay and the Kyles of Bute, terminating at Ormidale.

1931: Moved to operate from Rothesay to Millport and to Loch Long.

1934: Now operated from Fairlie to Millport and Rothesay.

1935: December – Sold for scrapping at Barrow-in-Furness.

389: *Talisman* (1896)

Number in Williamson's list: 304
Built: 1896
278.8 tons. Length 215 ft
Builders: A. & J. Inglis, Pointhouse
Engine builders: A. & J. Inglis, Pointhouse. Engine type: Single Diagonal, Surface condenser; 183 hp
Hull Material: Deck saloons fore and aft
Owners: North British Steam Packet Co. Ltd

1896: 30 May – Launched.

1896: Entered service from Craigendoran to Rothesay and the Kyles of Bute.

1902: Owners became the North British Railway Co.

1906: Moved to the Craigendoran to Garelochhead service.

1908: Returned to the Craigendoran to Rothesay route.

1910: Reboilered. Fitted with a much taller funnel than previously.

1915: 6 May – Following the erection of the boom from the Cloch to Dunoon, now operated only as far as Dunoon, also serving the Holy Loch.

1916: Operated from Craigendoran to Lochgoilhead.

1917: 22 September – Requisitioned by the Admiralty. Renamed HMS *Talla*. Converted to a minesweeper, based at Troon. Later based at Portsmouth until the end of the war. Used for experimental work at Bournemouth in connection with mine-laying.

1919: 8 March – Returned to the Clyde and released from Admiralty control.

1919: 10 October – Returned to service after refurbishment. Bridge moved forward of her funnel and fore-saloon widened to the full width of the hull. Returned to the route from Craigendoran to Rothesay and the Kyles of Bute.

1923: Owners absorbed into the London & North Eastern Railway.

1934: September – Sold for scrapping at Barrow-in-Furness.

390: *Britannia* (1896)

Number in Williamson's list:
Built: 1896
459 tons. Length 230 ft
Builders: S. McKnight & Co. Ltd, Ayr
Engine builders: Hutson & Son. Engine type: compound diagonal; 304 hp
Hull Material: steel

Owners: P. & A. Campbell Ltd, Bristol

1896: 14 May – Launched.

1896: Entered service on the Bristol Channel. Was the flagship of the fleet until 1939.

1896: 17-20 July – Made a long distance trip from Bristol, Cardiff and Ilfracombe to Penzance, continuing on the second day to Falmouth, Penzance and the Isles of Scilly.

1896: 18-21 August – Made a long distance trip to Plymouth and the Channel Islands.

1897: 28 June – Visited the Diamond Jubilee fleet review at Spithead from Bournemouth and Southampton.

1901: 6 June: – Made single trip from Bristol, Cardiff, Penarth, and Mumbles to Greenock

1901: 7-8 June – Made an excursion from Gourock to follow a yacht race.

1901: 11 June – Made a single trip with passengers from Gourock on a cruise round the Lochs and Firth of Clyde, continuing to arrive at Mumbles, Cardiff and Bristol on the following morning.

1902: 28 June Visited the cancelled Coronation fleet review at Spithead from Bournemouth.

1902: 30 June – Carried passengers on her positioning run back from Bournemouth to Cardiff and Bristol.

1902: 16 August – Made a trip from Bournemouth to the rescheduled Coronation fleet review at Spithead. Left at 6 p.m. for Ilfracombe, Cardiff and Bristol carrying passengers.

1915: 27 January – Requisitioned by the Admiralty. Converted to the minesweeper HMS *Britain*.

1915: 5 February – Left Bristol for war service. Based in the Clyde area, serving off the north-west coast of Ireland, and later on the Moray Firth and then based at Granton.

1919: 8 April – Released from Admiralty service.

1921: Reboilered

1935: Reboilered – Fitted with a large oval funnel. Bridge deck added above the aft companionway.

1937: 11 May – Made a trip from Bournemouth to the Coronation fleet review at Spithead.

1939: September – Requisitioned by the Admiralty. Converted to the minesweeper HMS *Skiddaw*. Based at North Shields and at Granton.

1940: May – Held in reserve at Harwich for the Dunkirk evacuation, then returned to North Shields.

1942: Converted at North Shields to an Auxiliary Anti-aircraft Ship. Based at Sheerness. Used on the Thames.

1944: June – Moved to the South Coast to guard some of the components of the Mulberry Harbours used in the D-day invasion. Used during the invasion to provide hot meals for troops, of which some 14,500 were served.

1944: 27 November – Escorted the first military convoy up the River Schelde into Antwerp, where she was struck by a shell which damaged the wireless cabin, wounding the radio operator and damaging the equipment.

1945: 21 May – Returned to her owners.

1946: 1 June – Re-entered service on the Bristol Channel.

1948: Reboilered – Converted to oil fuel. Now had two funnels. Bridge deck removed.

1948: Operated excursions out of Brighton.

1951: Returned to Bristol Channel services.

1956: 7 December – Towed to Newport for scrapping.

391: *Strathmore*

Number in Williamson's list: 305
Built: 1897
315.6 tons. Length 200.5 ft
Builders: Russell & Co., Greenock
Engine builders: Rankin & Blackmore, Greenock. Engine type: Double Diagonal Compound; 93 hp
Hull Material: Deck saloons fore and aft; full length promenade deck, plated in underneath
Owners: J. Williamson & Co.
1897: 11 March – Launched.
1897: Entered service from Glasgow to the Kyles of Bute.
1898: May to September – Operated from Greenock (Princes Pier) and Fairlie to Campbeltown.
1899: Operated from Rothesay and Fairlie to Campbeltown.
1901: Returned to the route from Glasgow to the Kyles of Bute.
1908: Sold to the Admiralty. Renamed HMS *Harlequin*. Used as a naval tender and Ferry at Chatham and Sheerness.
1917: Converted for use as a minesweeper. Based at Swansea.
1918: Returned to her service in the Medway.
1942: June – Converted to an accommodation Ship at Chatham.
1943: March – Stranded in the Medway on passage to the Clyde.
1945: Broken up.

392: *Kylemore* (intended name)

Number in Williamson's list:
Built: 1897
319 tons. Length 200.5 ft
Builders: Russell & Co., Greenock
Engine builders: Rankin & Blackmore, Greenock. Engine type: compound diagonal; 0 hp
Hull Material: Full length promenade deck, plated in underneath
Owners: J Williamson & Co (sold on the stocks)
1897: Laid down for as *Kylemore*, a sister to *Strathmore*, but sold on the stocks to the Hastings, St Leonards-on-Sea & Eastbourne Steamboat Co. and named *Britannia*.
1897: 28 April – Launched.
1897: Entered service on excursions from Hastings.
1904: Sold to John Williamson & Co. Immediately resold to the Glasgow & South Western Railway. Renamed *Vulcan*. Operated from Fairlie to Millport.
1908: April – Sold to John Williamson & Co. Renamed *Kylemore*. Operated from Rothesay to Glasgow, berthing at Rothesay overnight.
1915: 1 July ot 4 September – Operated from Glasgow to Inveraray.
1915: 23 November – Requisitioned by the Admiralty. Converted to a minesweeper and was used in the English Channel based at Dunkirk and later at Harwich.
1919: Owners became Williamson-Buchanan Steamers.
1920: 20 February – Returned to her owners after reconditioning during which her bridge was moved forward of the funnel, returned to the Rothesay to Glasgow service and was also used on evening cruises from Rothesay and other Clyde piers. Also used as a tender to transatlantic liners anchored at the Tail of the Bank.

1936: Sold to Williamson-Buchanan Steamers (1936) Ltd.

1939: Late – Operated from Wemyss Bay to Millport and Rothesay.

1939: December – Requisitioned by the Admiralty. Converted to a minesweeper, later used as a net layer.

1940: 21 August – Sunk by bombing off Harwich.

393: *Juno* (1898)

Number in Williamson's list: 306

Built: 1898

592 tons. Length 245 ft

Builders: Clydebank Engineering & Shipbuilding Ltd., Clydebank (formerly J. & G. Thomson)

Engine builders: Clydebank Engineering & Shipbuilding Ltd.. Engine type: Double Diagonal Compound; 204 hp

Hull Material: Deck saloons fore and aft; full length promenade deck, plated in underneath

Owners: Ordered for Planet Steamers (Mrs C. Black), London

1898: Laid down as a consort for *Jupiter*, ex-*Lord of the Isles* (1877) (No. 341) but sold on the stocks after her owners became bankrupt. Purchased by the Glasgow & South Western Railway.

1898: 17 June; Launched

1898: Entered service on excursions from Ayr and Troon.

1915: 29 January – Requisitioned by the Admiralty. Renamed HMS *Junior*. Converted to a minesweeper. Operated in the Firth of Clyde from Troon and Ardrossan, and later in the Moray Firth and the Firth of Forth.

1919: 27 June – Released from Admiralty service.

1920: Resumed excursions from Ayr and Troon.

1923: Owners absorbed into the London, Midland & Scottish Railway.

1932: Spring: Scrapped at Alloa.

394: *Kenilworth*

Number in Williamson's list: 307

Built: 1898

333 tons. Length 215 ft

Builders: A. & J. Inglis, Pointhouse

Engine builders: A. & J. Inglis, Pointhouse. Engine type: Single Diagonal, Surface condenser; 190 hp

Hull Material: Deck saloons fore and aft

Owners: North British Steam Packet Co. Ltd

1898: 22 February – Launched.

1898: 31 May – Entered service from Craigendoran to Rothesay.

1902: Owners became the North British Railway Co.

1915: Reboilered; bridge moved forward of the funnel and fore-saloon enlarged.

1915: Services curtailed to Dunoon after the erection of the boom south of there.

1916: Operated from Craigendoran to Lochgoilhead.

1917: 18 June – Requisitioned by the Admiralty. Converted to a minesweeper. Initially based at Troon, then moved to Portsmouth. Used for experimental work at Bournemouth in connection with mine-laying

1919: 3 May – Returned to her owners. Resumed to the service from Craigendoran to Rothesay.

1919: 1 July until 13 September – Operated from Craigendoran to Lochgoilhead and Arrochar with morning and evening trips to the Holy Loch.

1920: Back on the Craigendoran to Rothesay and to the Holy Loch services, with an afternoon extension to the Kyles of Bute.

1923: Owners absorbed into the London & North Eastern Railway.

1936: Introduced a call at Largs into her sailings.

1938: January – Laid up and sold for scrapping by her builders, A. & J. Inglis at Pointhouse.

395: *Princess May*

Built: 1898
256 tons. Length 165.5 ft
Builders: A. & J. Inglis, Pointhouse
Engine builders: A. & J. Inglis, Pointhouse. Engine type: 2-cylinder diagonal; 130 hp
Hull Material: steel; deck saloons
Owners: Dumbarton & Balloch Joint Line Committee (NBR and CR)
1898: 11 October – Launched from her builder's yard.
1898: 8 November – Arrived at Balloch, having sailed up the River Leven.
1899: May – Entered service from Balloch to Ardlui.
1923: Owners came into LNER & LMSR joint ownership.
1933: Used as a spare vessel.
1936: Returned to regular service on the Loch.
1948: Owners nationalised, now British Railways.
1953: Scrapped at Balloch.

396: *Prince George*

Built: 1898
256 tons. Length 165.5 ft
Builders: A. & J. Inglis, Pointhouse
Engine builders: A. & J. Inglis, Pointhouse. Engine type: 2-cylinder diagonal; 130 hp
Hull Material: steel; deck saloons
Owners: Dumbarton & Balloch Joint Line Committee (NBR & CR)
1898: 17 October – Launched from her builder's yard.
1898: 7 December – Arrived at Balloch having sailed up the River Leven.
1899: May – Entered service on Loch Lomond from Balloch to Ardlui.
1923: Owners came under LMSR & LNER joint ownership.
1936: Became the spare steamer on the loch.
1941: Used as a static accommodation ship for Tank Pumping Station employees, evacuated from the Clydebank Blitz.
1942: Scrapped.

397: *Waverley* (1899)

Number in Williamson's list: 308
Built: 1899
448.5 tons. Length 235 ft
Builders: A. & J. Inglis, Pointhouse
Engine builders: A. & J. Inglis, Pointhouse. Engine type: Double Diagonal Compound; 350 hp
Hull Material: deck saloons fore and aft
Owners: North British Steam Packet Co. Ltd

1899: 29 May – Launched.

1899: July – Entered service from Craigendoran to Rothesay and a Round Bute cruise. Was described by G. M. Stromier in *The Craigendoran Story* (1979) as 'the apex of paddle steamer design'. Was the fastest steamer on the upper Firth with a speed of 20 knots.

1900: Now operated on long distance excursions including Campbeltown, Ayr and Inveraray.

1902 – autumn: Owners now the North British Railway Co.

1903: Back on the Round Bute sailings from Craigendoran.

1911: Operated excursions to Arran and round Ailsa Craig.

1912: Returned to the Round Bute cruises, with a Saturday afternoon cruise to Ayr, round Arran, or round Ailsa Craig.

1915: Operated from Craigendoran to Lochgoilhead and Arrochar.

1915: 21 September – Requisitioned by the Admiralty. Converted to a minesweeper, during which her promenade deck was extended to the bow.

1919: April – Returned to her owners. During her refit the extended promenade deck was retained.

1920: 12 July – Commenced operating from Craigendoran to Lochgoilhead and Arrochar, a route she served until 1937, also operating evening cruises.

1923: Owners absorbed into the London & North Eastern Railway.

1933: Promenade deck saloons added. Described by Stromier as 'disfigured with a hideous deck erection'.

1938: Operated from Craigendoran to Rothesay and the Kyles of Bute.

1939: Laid up.

1939: September – Evacuated schoolchildren to the Clyde Coast.

1939: October – Requisitioned by the Admiralty. Converted to a minesweeper, based at Harwich.

1940: 29 May – Bombed and sunk at Dunkirk on her first trip with around 600 men on board, 350 of whom lost their lives. She was lost on the forty-first anniversary of her launching.

CHAPTER 10
Steamers Built Since 1900

398: *Duchess of Montrose*

Built: 1902
321 tons. Length 210 ft
Builders: John Brown & Co. Ltd, Clydebank
Engine builders: John Brown & Co. Ltd, Clydebank. Engine type: 4-cylinder triple expansion tandem diagonal; 206 hp
Hull Material: deck saloons fore and aft, promenade deck extended to bow
Owners: Caledonian Steam Packet Co. Ltd
1902: 8 May – Launched.
1902: Summer – Entered service on excursions from Ayr. Also made relief sailings from Ardrossan to Arran on Saturdays.
1903: Operated from Gourock and Wemyss Bay to Rothesay.
1909: Moved to the Wemyss Bay to Millport route.
1915: February – Used as a transport from Southampton.
1915: 15 May – Requisitioned by the Admiralty. Converted to a minesweeper. Some sources state renamed HMS *Montrose*. Used from Dover to sweep off the Belgian Coast.
1917: 18 March – Sank after hitting a mine off Gravelines, France, near Dunkirk. twelve crewmen lost their lives.

399: *Mars* (1902)

Built: 1902
317 tons. Length 200.4 ft
Builders: John Brown & Co. Ltd., Clydebank
Engine builders: John Brown & Co. Ltd., Clydebank. Engine type: Compound 2-cylinder diagonal; 172 hp
Hull Material: Full length promenade deck, plated in underneath
Owners: Glasgow & South Western Railway
1902: 14 March – Launched.
1902: June – Entered service from Greenock (Princes Pier) to Rothesay, the Kyles of Bute and Ormidale.
1904: Moved to the Greenock (Princes Pier) to Arrochar service.
1916: 22 September – Requisitioned by Admiralty. Renamed HMS *Marsa*. Converter to a minesweeper.
1918: 18 November – Ran down by a British destroyer in darkness off Harwich. Settled on a sandbank but broke her back and was abandoned.

400: *Duchess of Fife*

Built: 1903
336 tons. Length 210.3 ft
Builders: Fairfield Shipbuilding & Engineering Ltd, Govan
Engine builders: Fairfield Shipbuilding & Engineering Ltd, Govan. Engine type: 4-cylinder
    tandem triple expansion diagonal; 199 hp
Hull Material: deck saloons fore and aft, promenade deck extended to bow
Owners: Caledonian Steam Packet Co. Ltd
1903: 9 May – Launched.
1903: Entered service from Gourock and Wemyss Bay to Rothesay and the Kyles of Bute.
1909: Now operating from Gourock and Wemyss Bay to Rothesay.
1915: Operated from Gourock to Dunoon, after the putting in place of the boom from the
    Cloch to Dunoon.
1916: 26 May – Requisitioned by the Admiralty. Renamed HMS *Duchess*. Converted to a
    minesweeper, based at Grimsby and Dover.
1919: April – Returned to her owners.
1919: September – Returned to service after reconditioning. Operated from Gourock and
    Wemyss Bay to Rothesay.
1923: Commence operating from Greenock (Princes Pier) and Gourock to Rothesay and the
    Kyles of Bute.
1928: Reboilered.
1936: Summer – Ran aground at Kirn at low water. Soon refloated and returned to service.
1937: Moved to the route from Wemyss Bay to Millport and Kilchattan Bay.
1939: 21 September – Requisitioned by the Admiralty. Converted to a minesweeper and based
    at Harwich.
1940: 29 May – 3 June – Was present at the Dunkirk evacuation, and rescued 1,633 men in
    three trips to and from Ramsgate.
1941: Now used as an anti-aircraft gunnery training ship at Port Edgar and in the Solent.
1946: 29 May – Returned to peacetime service, initially as a spare and relief steamer.
1946: mid-July – Returned to the route from Wemyss Bay to Millport and Kilchattan Bay.
1953: 6 June: Made her last sailing and was laid up in the Albert Harbour, Greenock.
1953: 15 September – Arrived at Port Glasgow for scrapping, by which time she was the final
    pre-1914 steamer in service on the Firth of Clyde.

401: *Queen Mary*

Built: 1905
116 tons. Length 130.3 ft
Builders: Napier & Miller Ltd, Yoker
Engine builders: Scott's Ship Building & Engineering Co. Ltd, Greenock. Engine type:
    Compound diagonal; 53rhp
Hull Material: steel; flush-decked
Owners: London County Council
1905: 12 April – Launched.
1905: May – Entered service in the River Thames as *Earl Godwin* from Greenwich to
    Hammersmith.
1907: December – Service ceased.
1909: Sold to the City Steamboat Co, and resumed operation from Greenwich to Hammersmith.

1914: April – Ceased operating. Sold to the Dumbarton & Balloch Joint Line Committee (NBR and CR) for service on Loch Lomond. Renamed *Queen Mary*. Moved to Balloch, but was damaged by fire soon after her arrival on Loch Lomond and never sailed commercially on the loch.

1923: Owners now the London, Midland & Scottish and London and North Eastern Railways.

1928: Sold for scrapping.

402: *Pioneer* (1905)

Built: 1905
241 tons. Length 160 ft
Builders: A. & J. Inglis, Pointhouse
Engine builders: A. & J. Inglis, Pointhouse. Engine type: Compound diagonal; 84rhp
Hull Material: promenade deck to bow, plated in underneath
Owner: David MacBrayne
1905: February – Launched.
1905: April – Entered service from West Loch Tarbert to Port Ellen and Port Askaig, Islay, with calls at Gigha and at Craighouse, Jura, respectively, and also occasional calls at Bruichladdich, Islay.
1905: Owner became David MacBrayne Ltd.
1928: Owner became David MacBrayne (1928) Ltd.
1935: Owners became David MacBrayne Ltd again.
1939-1940: Winter – Operated from Mallaig to Portree.
1941: Used on livestock sailings from Oban, also as the relief Sound of Mull steamer.
1942: Laid up.
1943: Requisitioned by the Admiralty.
1944: March – Used as a Submarine Command HQ Ship at Fairlie.
1945: Purchased by the Admiralty Renamed HMS *Harbinger*.
1946: Paddles and sponsons removed. Used as a floating laboratory at Portland.
1958: Scrapped at Rotterdam.

403: *Princess Patricia*

Built: 1905
127 tons. Length 130 ft
Builders: J. I. Thornycroft, Woolston
Engine builders: Scott's Ship Building & Engineering Co. Ltd, Greenock. Engine type: Compound diagonal; 53rhp
Hull Material: steel; flush-decked
Owners: London County Council
1905: May – Entered service as *Shakespeare* in the River Thames from Greenwich to Hammersmith.
1907: December – Service ceased.
1909: Sold to the City Steamboat Co., and resumed operation from Greenwich to Hammersmith.
1914: August – Ceased operating. Sold to the Dumbarton & Balloch Joint Line Committee (NBR and CR) for service on Loch Lomond. Renamed *Princess Patricia* and moved to Loch Lomond.

1914: Intended for the winter service but saw little use on that. Operated on short excursions from Balloch round the Islands.

1923: Owners now the London, Midland & Scottish and London & North Eastern Railways.

1936: Used in the film *Spy of Napoleon* representing a steamer on Lake Geneva.

1938: Broken up.

404: *Marmion*

Built: 1906
403 tons. Length 210 ft
Builders: A. & J. Inglis, Pointhouse
Engine builders: A. & J. Inglis, Pointhouse. Engine type: Compound 2-cylinder diagonal; 212 hp
Hull Material: deck saloons fore & aft
Owners: North British Railway
1906: 5 May – Launched.
1906: Was in collision with the tug *Telde* near Surrey Commercial Docks.
1906: 18 June – Entered service from Craigendoran to Lochgoilhead and Arrochar.
1915: 26 February – Requisitioned by the Admiralty. Converted to a minesweeper and promenade deck extended to the bow. Renamed HMS *Marmion II*.
1919: April – Returned to her owners.
1920: 1 June – Returned to service, still with her promenade deck extended to the bow. Proved to be very unstable and 5 knots slower than previously. Operated to Lochgoilhead and Arrochar.
1921: Laid up.
1923: Owners absorbed into the London & North Eastern Railway. Promenade deck extension cut away and fore-saloon cut back to well aft of the mast.
1926: Returned to service operating from Craigendoran to Rothesay and the Kyles of Bute.
1932: Reboilered and fitted with a new, slightly wider, funnel.
1939: Early September – Used to evacuate schoolchildren to Auchenlichan.
1939: September – Requisitioned by the Admiralty. Converted to a minesweeper, with bow again built up, and based at Harwich.
1940: May – Was at the Dunkirk evacuation, made three trips and rescued 745 men.
1941: 9 April – Sunk by a German aircraft while at anchor off Harwich. She was raised but found to be Constructive Total Loss.
1941: August – Scrapped at Grays, Essex.

405: *Eagle III*

Built: 1910
432 tons. Length 215.5 ft
Builders: Napier & Miller Ltd, Old Kilpatrick
Engine builders: A. & J. Inglis, Pointhouse. Engine type: 1-cylinder diagonal; 176 hp
Hull Material: deck saloons fore and aft, promenade deck extended to bow
Owners: Buchanan Steamers Ltd
1910: 14 April – Launched.

1910: 2 June – Entered service from Glasgow to Rothesay and an afternoon cruise. Often took on a heavy list with a full passenger load. Was the final single cylinder paddle steamer to be built for Clyde service.

1910: 25 July – Withdrawn from service and returned to her builders, where her hull was rebuilt and her beam increased below the waterline.

1911: Summer – Returned to service.

1915: 1 July – Following the erection of the boom, operated from Glasgow to the Holy Loch and a cruise to the Gareloch, as did she in the early part of the 1916 season.

1916: 2 June – Requisitioned by the Admiralty and converted to a minesweeper based at Grimsby and later at Harwich.

1919: Returned to her owners.

1919: Owners became Williamson-Buchanan Steamers Ltd.

1920: March – Resumed her pre-war service. During reconditioning her bridge had been moved forward of the funnel and a small after-deck shelter added.

1933: Now operated from Glasgow to Rothesay only.

1935: November – Sold to the Caledonian Steam Packet Co. Ltd.

1936: May – Owners became Williamson-Buchanan Steamers (1936) Ltd.

1936: Summer – Operated from Glasgow to Lochgoilhead in this season only.

1939: Evacuated patients from Gartnavel Mental Hospital to Ardrishaig.

1939: October – Requisitioned by the Admiralty. Renamed HMS *Oriole*. Converted to a minesweeper.

1940: 29 May – Beached herself at La Panne to enable troops to cross her to board ships further out.

1940: 30 May to 4 June – Made five trips to the Dunkirk evacuation, one returning to Harwich and four returning to Margate, rescuing 2,587 troops.

1943: Owners now the Caledonian Steam Packet Co. Ltd.

1945: Used to transport supplies to newly-liberated Holland.

1945: Released by the Admiralty and laid up in the Holy Loch. Due to her antiquated single cylinder engine and haystack boiler, she was not reconditioned.

1946: August – Sold to Smith & Houston, Port Glasgow, for scrapping.

406: *Mountaineer* (1910)

Built: 1910
235 tons. Length 180 ft
Builders: A. & J. Inglis, Pointhouse
Engine builders: A. & J. Inglis, Pointhouse. Engine type: Compound 2-cylinder diagonal; 86 rhp
Hull Material: deck saloons fore & aft
Owners: David MacBrayne Ltd.

1910: 10 February – Launched.

1910: Entered services on routes out of Oban, to Fort William, Crinan and Tobermory. Operated in the winter months from Glasgow to Rothesay and, from 1912, Glasgow to Lochgoilhead. Also relieved *Pioneer* on the West Loch Tarbert to Islay service and provided extra sailings there on peak weekends.

1915: Chartered to the North British Railway. Operated from Craigendoran to Garelochhead.

1919: Returned to her owners and her previous services.

1928: Owners became David MacBrayne (1928) Ltd.

1937: Laid up at the end of the summer season.
1938: September – Sold for scrapping at Port Glasgow.

407: *Prince Edward*

Built: 1911
304 tons. Length 175 ft
Builders: A. & J. Inglis, Pointhouse
Engine builders: A. & J. Inglis, Pointhouse. Engine type: compound diagonal; 133 hp
Hull Material: steel; deck saloons
Owners: Dumbarton & Balloch Joint Line Committee (NBR and CR)
1911: 20 March – Launched.
1911: 4 May – Left her builders yard for the River Leven.
1911: 8 May – Stranded at Kirkland, near Bonhill, because of the low water level in the River Leven.
1911: 4 November – Moved upriver to Balloch after water levels had risen, arriving at Balloch on 6 November, where she was slipped.
1912: 1 June – Entered service on Loch Lomond from Balloch to Ardlui.
1923: Joint Committee now owned by the London & North Eastern and London, Midland and Scottish Railways.
1948: Following nationalisation came under the ownership of British Railways.
1955: 29 April – Breaking up commenced at Balloch.

408: *Queen Empress*

Built: 1912
411 tons. Length 210 ft
Builders: Murdoch & Murray, Port Glasgow
Engine builders: Rankin & Blackmore, Greenock. Engine type: Compound 2-cylinder diagonal; 178 hp
Hull Material: deck saloons fore and aft, promenade deck extended to bow & plated in below
Owners: J. Williamson & Co.
1912: 20 April – Launched.
1912: Entered service from Glasgow to Rothesay and to Lochgoilhead.
1914: Operated from Rothesay to Glasgow.
1915: February – Used as a troop transport from Southampton.
1915: 25 October – Requisitioned by the Admiralty. Converted to a minesweeper, and based on the River Tyne.
1917: Was in collision with a destroyer and was rescued by the Caledonian Steam Packet turbine steamer *Duchess of Argyll* , which towed her to Boulogne.
1919: Owners became Williamson-Buchanan Steamers Ltd.
1919: Used as an Ambulance Transport in the White Sea in support of the White Russians.
1919: August 29 – Ran aground on a sandbank in the Dvina River and was pulled off in the nick of time in the face of the advancing Bolshevik armies.
1920: 30 May – Returned to her owners. Now operated on long distance excursions from the Clyde Coast towns, which continued until 1935, and also from Glasgow to Lochgoilhead.

1920: Glasgow Fair fortnight – Operated from Glasgow to Campbeltown and to Ayr.

1920: September – Operated from Greenock (Princes Pier) to Campbeltown after *King Edward* had been withdrawn for the winter. Also did this from 1922 until 1935, except 1928, relieving *Queen Alexandra* from 1927.

1928: September – Chartered to David MacBrayne (1928) Ltd. Operated from Greenock to Ardrishaig.

1931: Now operated from Glasgow to Lochgoilhead and Arrochar.

1935: November – Owners purchased by the London, Midland & Scottish Railway.

1936: 31 March – Owners became Williamson-Buchanan Steamers (1936) Ltd. Operated as a part of the Caledonian Steam Packet fleet, sailing from Wemyss Bay to Rothesay.

1936-1937 – winter: Operated from Greenock (Princes Pier) and Gourock to Rothesay.

1938: Funnel painted in the CSP yellow with a black top.

1939: Moved to the route from Wemyss Bay and Fairlie to Millport and Rothesay.

1939: Early September – Operated from Gourock to Dunoon and Kilmun after the boom had been erected between the Cloch and Dunoon.

1939: October – Requisitioned by the Admiralty. Converted to a minesweeper, became flagship of the 12th Minesweeping Flotilla, based at Harwich.

1940: May – Was not present at the Dunkirk evacuation.

1942: Converted for use as an anti-aircraft ship.

1943: 15 May – Brought down two enemy aircraft.

1943: Ownership transferred to the Caledonian Steam Packet Co. Ltd.

1945: Used to transport supplies to newly-liberated Holland.

1946: Did not return to civilian service after the war and was scrapped at Nieuw Lekkerland in the Netherlands.

409: *Fair Maid*

Built: 1915

432 tons. Length 235 ft

Builders: A. & J. Inglis, Pointhouse

Engine builders: A. & J. Inglis, Pointhouse. Engine type: Compound 2-cylinder diagonal; 304 hp

Hull Material: deck saloons fore and aft, promenade deck extended to bow & plated in below

Owners: North British Railway

1915: 12 July – Purchased by the Admiralty whilst on the stocks and completed as a minesweeper.

1915: 23 December – Launched. She had been intended to replace *Lucy Ashton*.

1916: 6 November – Sunk by a mine in the North Sea.

410: *Jeanie Deans* (1931)

Built: 1931

0 tons. Length 250.5 ft

Builders: Fairfield Shipbuilding & Engineering Ltd. Govan

Engine builders: Fairfield Shipbuilding & Engineering Ltd. Govan. Engine type: Triple Expansion Diagonal; 338 hp

Hull Material: deck saloons fore and aft, promenade deck extended to bow & plated in below

Owners: London & North Eastern Railway

1931: 7 April – Launched.

1931: Entered service from Craigendoran to Lochgoilhead and Arrochar. Had the first set of three-crank triples expansion engines built for a Clyde steamer.

1932: Forward promenade deck shelter/observation lounge added and funnels heightened, the forward one by 9 ft and the aft one by 6 ft., giving her a rather unbalanced appearance for the rest of the decade. Operated on excursions from Craigendoran including to Ayr and round Ailsa Craig on two days a week.

1938: Returned to the Craigendoran to Lochgoilhead and Arrochar service.

1939: 6 September – Evacuated schoolchildren to Tarbert.

1939: September – Requisitioned by the Admiralty – Concrete wheelhouse added and forward observation lounge removed. Based at Irvine, and later at Portsmouth and Milford Haven.

1941: March – Converted for use as an auxiliary anti-aircraft vessel bases on the Thames.

1945: July – Returned to her owners.

1946: 1 June – Returned to service. Promenade deck extended to the stern. Aft deck shelter added. The funnels were now of equal height. Operated from Craigendoran to Rothesay.

1948: With nationalisation, owners became British Railways.

1951: Ownership transferred to the Caledonian Steam Packet Co. Ltd.

1953: Now operated from Craigendoran and Gourock to Rothesay and a cruise Round Bute, and on Saturdays, from Craigendoran and Gourock to Tighnabruaich.

1956-1957 – winter: Converted to oil firing.

1961: Now alternated weekly with *Waverley* operating excursions from Craigendoran including to Arran via the Kyles, Lochgoilhead and Arrochar, and Round the Lochs and Firth of Clyde.

1964: Withdrawn from service at the end of the season and laid up in the Albert Harbour, Greenock.

1965: November – Sold to the Coastal Steam Packet Co. Ltd. Renamed *Queen of the South*. Sailed with red, yellow and black funnels to Tilbury.

1966: Operated from London (Tower Pier) to Southend and Clacton or Herne Bay. Had many sailings cancelled or curtailed for mechanical reasons.

1967: Ran for a second season on the Thames but was no more successful.

1967: December – Sold for scrapping in Belgium at Boom, near Antwerp.

411: *Mercury* (1934)

Built: 1934
621 tons. Length 223.8 ft
Builders: Fairfield Shipbuilding & Engineering Ltd, Govan
Engine builders: Fairfield Shipbuilding & Engineering Ltd, Govan. Engine type: Triple
    Expansion Diagonal; 230 hp
Hull Material: promenade deck saloons fore and aft, promenade deck extended to bow and
    plated in below
Owners: London, Midland & Scottish Railway
Caledonian Steam Packet Co. Ltd. 24 December 1937
1934: 16 January – Launched.
1934: Entered service from Greenock (Princes Pier) and Gourock to Rothesay.
1936: Moved to operate afternoon excursions from Rothesay.
1939: Operated in this season from Gourock to Arran via the Kyles.
1939: 21 September – Requisitioned by the Admiralty and converted to a minesweeper. Based
    on the Clyde and later at Milford Haven.
1940: 24 December – Sank under tow after her stern was blown off while sweeping mines off
    the Irish Coast.

412: *Caledonia* (1934)

Built: 1934
624 tons. Length 227.3 ft
Builders: W. Denny & Bros., Dumbarton
Engine builders: W. Denny & Bros Ltd, Dumbarton. Engine type: Triple Expansion Diagonal;
    193 hp
Hull Material: promenade deck saloons fore and aft, promenade deck extended to bow and
    plated in below
Owners: Caledonian Steam Packet Co. Ltd
1934: 1 February – Launched.
1934: Entered service from Wemyss Bay to Rothesay and to Millport, also used on afternoon
    excursions.
1936: Moved to the route from Gourock to Arran via the Kyles of Bute, alternating with
    sailings and excursions from Rothesay.
1939: 21 September – Requisitioned by the Admiralty and converted to a minesweeper.
    Renamed HMS *Goatfell*. Based on the Clyde, and later at Milford Haven.
1942: Converted for use as an anti-aircraft vessel on the Thames.
1943: Used as an escort vessel between the Tyne and the Humber.
1944: June – Used as a troop transport for the D-Day landing in Normandy.
1944: November – Used as a troop transport to newly-liberated Antwerp.
1945: 22 May – Released by the Admiralty. Returned to her builders for reconditioning.
1946: 20 May – Resumed passenger sailings. Initially ran from Wemyss Bay to Largs and
    Millport.
1946: June – Commenced operation from Gourock and Wemyss Bay to Rothesay.
1954: Moved to the excursion service from Ayr.
1955: Reboilered. New boiler was oil-fired.
1965: Moved to Craigendoran to replace *Jeanie Deans* on excursions from there.
1969: 14 to 23 April – Chartered to David MacBrayne Ltd. for the Gourock to Tarbert service.

1969: 1 to 8 October – Operated from Gourock to Tarbert for the CSP, and then withdrawn from service.

1970: Sold to W. H. Arnott Young & Co. Ltd for breaking up

1971: Sold to Bass Charrington Ltd for static use as floating pub on the Thames at London. Renamed *Old Caledonia*, thanks to the Paddle Steamer Preservation Scoiety (Scottish Branch).

1980: 27 April – Destroyed by fire.

1980vJuly – Broken up at Milton Creek in the River Swale near Sittingbourne, Kent. Her engines were saved and are on display at the Hollycombe Collection, Liphook, Hants occasionally being in operation, using steam from a portable boiler.

413: *Marchioness Of Lorne* (1935)

Built: 1935

449 tons. Length 199.5 ft

Builders: Fairfield Shipbuilding & Engineering Ltd, Govan

Engine builders: Fairfield Shipbuilding & Engineering Ltd, Govan. Engine type: Triple Expansion Diagonal; 140 hp

Hull Material: promenade deck saloons fore and aft, promenade deck extended to bow and plated in below

Owners: Caledonian Steam Packet Co. Ltd

1935: 19 February – Launched.

1935: Entered service from Gourock to Kilmun year-round.

1939-1945: Was the only CSP paddle steamer not to be called up for war service, probably because she was too slow.

1949: Additional calls made in her schedule at Craigendoran.

1953: 25 May – Moved to the Wemyss Bay to Largs and Millport service.

1954: 4 June – Withdrawn from service and laid up.

1955vScrapped at Port Glasgow.

414: *Talisman* (1935)

Built: 1935

450 tons. Length 215 ft

Builders: A. & J. Inglis, Pointhouse

Engine builders: (1) English Electric Co. Ltd, Stafford; (2) British Polar Engines Ltd. Engine type: diesel-electric; 1,530 shp, both engines

Hull Material: promenade deck saloons fore and aft, promenade deck extended to bow and plated in below

Owners: London & North Eastern Railway

1935: 10 April – Launched.

1935: Entered service from Craigendoran to Rothesay and the Kyles of Bute. Was the only Clyde paddle vessel not to have a steam engine.

1939: 24 July – Withdrawn because of cracked entablature casings and laid up in Bowling Harbour.

1939: September – Entablature casings agreed to be replaced by the English Electric Co.

1940: Late May – Engine repairs completed.

1940: 24 June – Requisitioned by the Admiralty and converted to an anti-aircraft vessel.

Renamed HMS *Aristocrat*. Based at Methil and then on the Thames Estuary of Margate.

1942 – spring: Took part in landings near Bridport in preparation for an aborted raid on Dieppe on 7 July, cancelled because of bad weather.

1942: October – Moved to Loch na Keal, Mull, to protect troop transports being assembled there prior to the North Africa invasion, then returned to Sheerness.

1944: 7-11 June – Used as the HQ ship at Arromanches for construction of the Mulberry Harbour, then continued as an anti-aircraft ship off the Normandy beaches.

1944: July – Was struck by a landing craft and returned to Portsmouth for repairs.

1944: 9 September – Was strafed by enemy guns while passing through the Straits of Dover en route from Portsmouth to Sheerness. Taken to Harwich for repairs.

1944: 27 November – Escorted the first convoy up the River Schelde to Antwerp, where she worked until VE Day, 8 May 1945.

1945: May – Worked as a ferry from Chatham to Harwich, carrying naval personnel.

1946: February – Returned to her owners.

1946: Early July – Returned to service operating from Craigendoran to Rothesay.

1948: Taken over by the British Transport Commission on nationalisation of the railways.

1952: Operated from Craigendoran to Lochgoilhead and Arrochar.

1953: July – Laid up.

1954: Re-engined at Stobcross Quay.

1954: June – Moved to the route from Wemyss Bay to Millport and made Cumbrae Circle Cruises.

1966: 17 November – Final day in service, operating from Gourock to Kilmun.

1967: 5 October – Sold to Arnott Young & Co. Ltd for scrapping at Dalmuir.

415: *Jupiter* (1937)

Built: 1937

642 tons. Length 223.6 ft

Builders: Fairfield Shipbuilding & Engineering Ltd, Govan

Engine builders: Fairfield Shipbuilding & Engineering Ltd, Govan. Engine type: Triple Expansion Diagonal; 288 hp

Hull Material: promenade deck saloons fore and aft, promenade deck extended to bow and plated in below

Owners: Caledonian Steam Packet Co. Ltd

1937: 9 April – Launched.

1937: 2 June – Entered service from Gourock and Wemyss Bay to Rothesay and the Kyles of Bute.

1938: Also operated from Gourock to Arran via the Kyles of Bute.

1939: 21 September – Requisitioned by the Admiralty and converted to a minesweeper. Renamed HMS *Scawfell*. Based on the Clyde.

1940: December – Based at Milford Haven.

1941: Converted to an anti-aircraft defence vessel serving convoys from the Tyne and Humber.

1944: June – Used as a troop carrier and AA ship at the D-Day landings in France.

1944: November – Used as a troop transport to Antwerp.

1945: May – Returned to her owners.

1946: February – Returned to Clyde service on her pre-war route.

1952: Operated for this year only from Gourock to Dunoon.

1956: Operated from Glasgow to Lochgoilhead on Sundays only.

1958: Laid up.

1960: Sold to Ulster Agencies Ltd, Belfast, supposedly for excursion and tender duties there, but did not sail for them.

1961: 6 April – Towed to Dublin for scrapping.

416: *Juno* (1937)

Built: 1937

642 tons. Length 223.6 ft

Builders: Fairfield Shipbuilding & Engineering Ltd, Govan

Engine builders: Fairfield Shipbuilding & Engineering Ltd, Govan. Engine type: Triple Expansion Diagonal; 288 hp

Hull Material: promenade deck saloons fore and aft, promenade deck extended to bow and plated in below

Owners: Caledonian Steam Packet Co. Ltd.

1937: 25 May – Launched

1937: 3 July – Entered service from Gourock and Wemyss Bay to Rothesay and the Kyles of Bute.

1939: 21 September – Requisitioned by the Admiralty and converted to a minesweeper. Renamed HMS *Helvellyn* and based on the Clyde.

1940: December – Moved to Milford Haven.

1941: 20 March – Sunk by a bomb in Surrey Commercial Docks, London, whilst fitting out as an anti-aircraft ship

417: *Waverley* (1947)

Built: 1947

693 tons. Length 239.6 ft

Builders: A. & J. Inglis, Pointhouse

Engine builders: Rankin & Blackmore, Greenock. Engine type: Triple Expansion Diagonal; 2,100 bhp

Hull Material: promenade deck saloons fore and aft, promenade deck extended to bow and plated in below

Owners: London & North Eastern Railway

1946: 2 October – Launched.

1947: 16 June – Entered service from Craigendoran and Rothesay to Lochgoilhead and Arrochar. From 1947 to 1953 she was also on the Craigendoran to Rothesay service from early May until the beginning of the summer season.

1948: 1 January – With the nationalisation of the railways, now owned by British Transport Commission, although operated as part of the Caledonian Steam Packet fleet.

1949: 18 February to 29 March – First spell in winter service, relieving *Talisman* for overhaul with sailings from Craigendoran to Gourock and an occasional trip to Rothesay.

1950: 13 January to 1 April – Operated on the winter service from Craigendoran to Rothesay.

1952: Now sailed to Arrochar on Tuesdays, Thursdays and Saturdays, and round Bute on Mondays, Wednesdays and Fridays.

1952: December – Operated the Gourock to Dunoon winter service until 4 March 1953, which she also did from October 1953 to 4 January 1954.

1953: Ownership transferred to the Caledonian Steam Packet Co. Ltd. Sailed to Arrochar on Tuesdays, Wednesdays and Thursdays, to Arran via the Kyles of Bute on Mondays, on a non-landing afternoon cruise to Brodick Bay on Fridays, and on railway connection work between Craigendoran, Gourock, Dunoon and Rothesay on Saturdays. A trip to Tighnabruaich was offered on Sundays.

1954: 4 January – Final day of scheduled winter service, she was replaced by the car ferry *Arran* on the Gourock to Dunoon service at 1220.

1954: Summer – Now did relief sailings on Fridays.

1955: A cruise Round the Lochs and Firth of Clyde cruise replaced the Arrochar sailings on Wednesdays.

1956-1957: Winter – Converted from coal to oil firing.

1958: Up-river cruise from the Clyde resorts to Glasgow (Bridge Wharf) now offered on Fridays. Saturday sailings were now almost entirely between Wemyss Bay and Rothesay.

1958: From now until 1962 replaced *Duchess of Hamilton* on the long-distance excursions to Inveraray and Campbeltown in September.

1961: Alternated rosters week about with *Jeanie Deans*, so that in alternate weeks she had an afternoon cruise from Mondays to Fridays round Bute and a Saturday afternoon sailing to Tighnabruaich. Did so untill 1964.

1963 and 1964: Replaced *Queen Mary II* on the Glasgow to Tighnabruaich cruise in September.

1965: Following the replacement of *Jeanie Deans* by *Caledonia*, did the mix of cruise sailings as before, but with a round Bute cruise on Mondays. Saturday sailings reverted to Craigendoran to Rothesay. She was used on a Sunday cruise to Skipness or round Bute on alternate Sundays. Lochgoilhead pier closed in this year and the call there was substituted by a Loch Goil cruise en route to Arrochar.

1967: Replaced *Talisman* on the Sunday afternoon cruises from Millport and Largs to Rothesay and Tighnabruaich.

1970: With the withdrawal of *Caledonia* after the previous season she was now the sole steamer sailing from Craigendoran. Started a trip to Tarbert and Ardrishaig on Fridays. Following the withdrawal of *Caledonia* she was now the last sea-going paddle steamer in the world.

1971: Now based at Gourock as the Clyde excursion programme contracted. Still sailed on much the same trips, to Arran via the Kyles on Mondays, to Arrochar, on Tuesdays from Rothesay and on Thursdays from Largs, round the Lochs on Wednesdays, this now incorporating an afternoon cruise round Bute, to Tarbert and Ardrishaig on Fridays, and Round Bute on Sundays. For the latter part of the season she sailed with a stump foremast following a collision with Arrochar Pier on 15 July.

1972: Now did a round Bute cruise on Mondays, and additional Round the Lochs sailing on Tuesdays, and no longer called at Ardrishaig on Fridays.

1973: The CSP became part of Caledonian MacBrayne Ltd. Thursday sailing was now Round Bute. Withdrawn from service after the end of the season.

1974: 8 August – Sold to the Paddle Steamer Preservation Society for preservation for a symbolic sum of £1.

1975: 22 May – Funnels repainted in the LNER red, white and black colours. Re-entered service, sailing at from Glasgow (Anderston Quay) weekends and from Ayr in mid-week.

1977: May – First sailings away from the Clyde, when she offered a week's sailings out of Liverpool to Llandudno and other destinations.

1977: 15 July – Grounded on the Gantocks Rocks off Dunoon. Was off service for six weeks for hull repairs.

1978: April to May – First sailings on the Solent and the Thames. These have been offered every season since, more recently in September. Glasgow berth moved from Anderston Quay to Stobcross Quay.

1979: Regular calls at Helensburgh instituted during the Clyde season. First sailings on the Bristol Channel.

1979: 15 September – Made one-off calls at Kilmun and Ardyne on a PSPS charter.

1981: March – New boiler fitted.

1981: April to June – Circumnavigated the British Isles for the first time, offering cruises on the Humber, Tyne and Forth. These were only offered in this and the following year.

1982: First sailings from Oban at the beginning of May, which are now a regular feature of her schedule. Offered a weekend's cruising from Dundee.

1985: 13 April: Sailed from Garlieston to Douglas, Isle of Man.

1985: Made her first cruises from Dublin and other ports in the Republic of Ireland. These were also offered in 1986, but not again since then.

1988: Trips from Kyle of Lochalsh and Portree added to the West Highland sailings.

1989: Sailings made from Tarbert, Harris, and Stornoway, which were also offered in 1990, but not since then.

1990: A sailing was offered from Castlebay, Barra and Lochboisdale, South Uist. These sailings from the Outer Hebrides were not repeated.

1992: 22 September – Made a one-off call at Carradale.

1993: 11 April – Made a one-off call at Otter Ferry.

1994: 22 June – Called at the Admiralty Pier at the former torpedo testing station at Succoth, across Loch Long from Arrochar on a PSPS evening cruise.

1995: 16 April – Made a one-off call at Portencross.

1999: December to July 2000 – Major £3 million rebuild at the yard of George Prior, Great Yarmouth, funded by the Heritage Lottery Fund. Her decks and deckhouses were removed and the central and aft portions of the hull completely stripped and the engines dismantled and rebuilt. A new boiler was fitted and a new emergency exit from the dining salon to the aft deck constructed. The deckhouses were repainted in scumbled wood-effect finish, in a complete return to her LNER colours.

2000: 19 August – First sailing after her rebuild.

2002: 14 October – 11 June 2003 – Second stage of rebuild, where her forward accommodation was rebuilt and the forward deck shelter and foremast replaced.

2003: 29 June – Lochranza pier re-opened. This became a regular call on her Sunday sailings for some years.

2004: Glasgow berth moved to the Science Centre, on the south bank of the river, because of a new bridge being built at Finnieston and a lack of water at Anderston Quay at very low tides due to a lack of dredging in the upper river.

2005: 22 May – Blairmore Pier re-opened. This became a regular call on the Wednesday sailing to Loch Goil.

2006: 14-15 October – Special sailings to commemorate the 60th anniversary of her launch, with a cruise to Loch Long and Loch Goil on Saturday 14 and to Tighnabruaich on Sunday 15, both from Glasgow.

2007: Celebrated sixty years in service.

2012: Celebrated sixty-five years in service.

418: *Maid of the Loch*

Built: 1953
295 tons. Length 555 ft
Builders: A. & J. Inglis, Pointhouse
Engine builders: Rankin & Blackmore, Greenock. Engine type: compound diagonal; 1,060 ihp
Hull Material: full length promenade deck, plated in underneath; deckhouses
Owners: British Transport Commission
1952: Erected at her builders yard, then taken to Balloch in sections and re-erected on the slipway there. Was originally to have been named *Princess Anne*.
1953: 5 March – Launched.
1953: 25 May – Entered service from Balloch to Ardlui.
1957: Ownership transferred to the Caledonian Steam Packet Co. Ltd.
1964: With the closure of Ardlui pier, now operated from Balloch to Inversnaid and a cruise to the Head of the Loch.
1969: Ownership transferred to W. Alexander & Sons (Midland) Ltd.
1971: Balmaha Pier closed.
1975: Tarbert Pier closed.
1980: 24 May – Luss pier re-opened.
1981: Withdrawn from service at the end of the season and laid up at Balloch.
1982: Sold to Ind Coope Alloa Brewery Ltd.
1989: Sold to Sea Management Corporation, Queensland, Australia.
1990: September – Sold to the Francis Hotel Group, Newcastle-upon-Tyne.
1992: Sold to Dumbarton District Council.
1993: Preservation efforts started on the by now derelict steamer.
1996: Sold to the Loch Lomond Steamship Co.
2006: The winch house, steam winding engine and slipway were restored with money from the Heritage Lottery Fund and opened to the Public. *Maid of the Loch* was hauled up the slipway as a demonstration.
2013: Appeal started to return her to service, the major obstacle to this being the need for a new boiler.

419: *Comet replica*

Built: 1962
0 tons. Length 42.5 ft
Builders: G. Thomson, Buckie
Engine builders: Lithgows Ltd, Port Glasgow. Engine type: side-lever jet condenser; 10 hp
Hull Material: wood, flush-decked
Owners: Lithgows Ltd
Inverclyde Council
1962: Built for the *Comet* 150th Anniversary celebrations
1962: 1 September – Made her only trip with passengers, from Greenock to Helensburgh. She was also on public display in Glasgow at Kingston Dock and Bridge Wharf
Mid-1970s: Put on static display at the centre of Port Glasgow.
1991: June – Moved to Helensburgh on a low loader and on display there for a week.
2007: After road realignment, moved to a new location in Port Glasgow, at roundabout near Tesco.
2011: Refurbished by Ferguson's shipyard, although not to operating condition.

Index

Kilmun, 1834 (No. 101) 49
Kilmun, 1851, ex-*Severn* (No. 216) 117
Kingstown (No. 278) 141-142
Koh-I-Noor (No. 211) 115
Kronprinz Friedrich Wilhelm, ex-*Bonnie Doon* (1870) (No. 327) 163
Kylemore (No. 392) 221-222
Kyles (No. 294) 149

La Belgique, ex-*Paris*, later *Glendale* (No. 338) 168
La Corse, ex-*Adela* (No. 344) 171-172
Lady Bridbane (No. 158) 93-94
Lady Clare (No. 373) 210-211
Lady Gertrude (No. 334) 166
Lady Kelburne (No. 163) 95-96
Lady Margaret, ex-*Carrick Castle* (No. 329) 164
Lady of the Isles, ex-*Lord of the Isles* (No. 341) 170
Lady of the Lake (No. 60) 33
Lady Rowena (No. 371) 209-210
Lancelot (No. 322) 160-161
Lapwing (No. 205) 112-113
Largs, 1822 (No. 44) 27
Largs, 1864 (No. 287) 146
Leitao Cunha, ex-*Vesper* (1866) (No. 304) 153
Lennox (No. 290) 147
Levan (No. 310) 155
Leven, 1824 (No. 46) 28
Leven, 1864 (No. 288) 146
Lisboa, later *St Clair of the Isles* (No. 272) 139
Loch Eck (No. 77) 39
Loch Goil, 1840 (No. 155) 92
Loch Long, 1842 (No. 161) 95
Loch Long, 1859 (No. 264) 135
Loch Ness, ex-*Lochgoil* (1853) (No. 235) 124-125
Lochgoil, 1835 (No. 112) 54
Lochgoil, 1853 (No. 235) 124-125
Lochlomond, 1836 (No. 126) 59
Lochlomond, 1845 (No. 181) 103
Lochlomond, 1867 (No. 317) 158
Lochryan (No. 82) 42
Lord Byron, ex-*Clyde* (No. 3) 10
Lord Dundas (No. 87) 44
Lord Nelson (No. 21) 17-18
Lord of the Isles, 1877 (No. 341) 170

Lord of the Isles, 1891 (No. 372) 210
Lord Tregedar, ex-*Carrick Castle* (No. 329) 164
Lorne (No. 330) 164
Lough Foyle, ex-*Lochgoil* (1853) (No. 235) 124-125
Lovedale, ex-*Great Western* (No. 319) 159
Lucy Ashton (No. 363) 204-205
Luna (No. 131) 61

Madge Wildfire (No. 361) 202-203
Maid of Bute (No. 115) 55
Maid of Galloway (No. 127) 60
Maid of Islay, 1815, ex-*Waterloo* (1815) (No. 18) 16
Maid of Islay, 1824, ex-*Maid of Islay No. 2* (No. 53) 30
Maid of Islay No. 1, 1815, ex-*Waterloo* (1815) (No. 18) 16
Maid of Islay No. 2, 1824 (No. 53) 30
Maid of Leven (No. 149) 69
Maid of Lorn (No. 209) 114
Maid of Morvern (No. 67) 36
Maid of the Loch (No. 418) 239
Mail, 1856 (No. 250) 130
Mail, 1860 (No. 270) 138
Manchester (No. 95) 47
Mangkor Almansoer, ex-*St Clair of the Isles* (No. 272) 139
Marchioness of Breadalbane, 1847 (No. 199) 110-111
Marchioness of Breadlabane, 1890 (No. 367) 207
Marchioness of Bute (No. 368) 207-208
Marchioness of Lorne, 1891 (No. 370) 208-209
Marchioness of Lorne, 1935 (No. 413) 234
Margaret (No. 25) 19
Margery (No. 10) 12-13
Marion (No. 24) 19
Marjory, alternative name for *Margery* (No. 10) 12-13
Marmion (No. 404) 228
Marquis of Bute, 1818 (No. 30) 21
Marquis of Bute, 1868 (No. 324) 161-162
Marquis of Lorne, ex-*Victory* (No. 283) 143-144
Marquis of Stafford (No. 206) 113
Mars, 1845 (No. 179) 102
Mars, 1902 (No. 399) 225-226

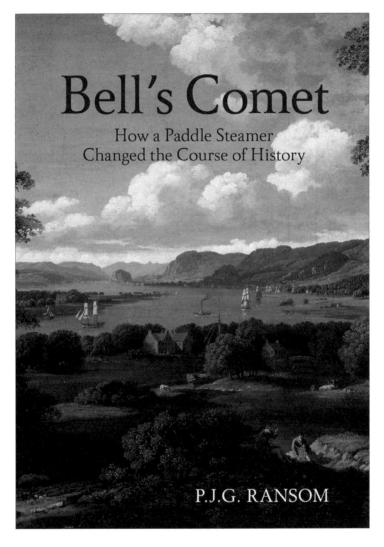

ALSO AVAILABLE FROM AMBERLEY PUBLISHING

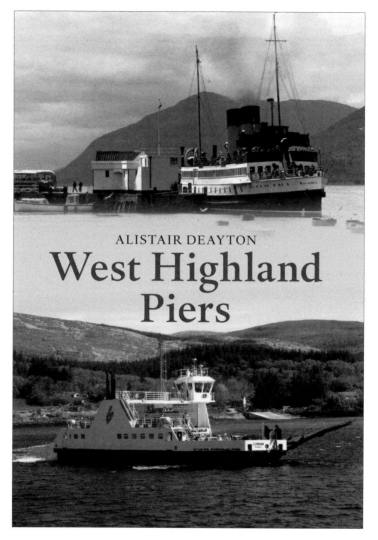

West Highland Piers
Alistair Deayton

This fascinating selection of photographs traces some of the many
ways in which the West Highland piers have changed and developed
over the last century.

978 1 4456 0097 0
96 pages, full colour

Available from all good bookshops or order direct
from our website www.amberleybooks.com

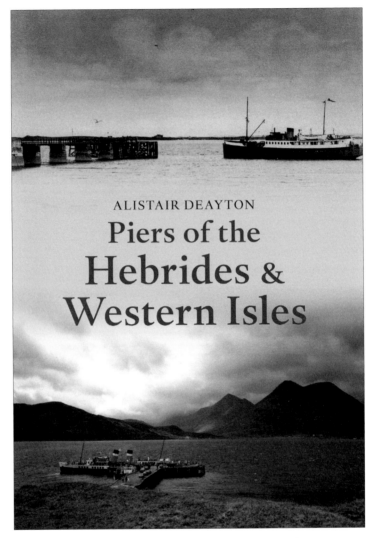